THE HISTORY
OF THE
HOUSEWIFE
1650–1950

THE ENGLISH
HOVSE-WIFE,

Containing the inward and outward
Vertues which ought to be in a
complcate Woman.

As her skill in Physick, Surgery, Cookery,
Extraction of Oyles, Banquetting ltuffe, Ordering of
great Feasts, Preserving of all sorts of Wines, Conceited Secrets, Distilations, Perfumes, ordering of Wooll, Hempe, Flax,
making Cloth, and Dying : the knowledge of Dayries, Office of
Malting, of Oates, their excellent uses in a Family, of
Brewing, Baking, and all other things belonging
to an Houshold.

A Worke generally approved, and now the fifth time much
augmented, purged and made most profitable and neceſſary for
all men, and the generall good of this Kingdome.

By G. M.

LONDON,
Printed by *Anne Griffin* for *Iohn Harrison*, at the Golden
Vnicorne in Pater-noſter-row. 1637.

Title page to *The English House-wife* by Gervase Markham, detailing the skills demanded of the housewife. The fifth
edition of 1637. (Trustees of the National Library of Scotland)

THE HISTORY
OF THE
HOUSEWIFE
1650–1950

Una A. Robertson

SUTTON PUBLISHING

First published in the United Kingdom in 1997 by
Sutton Publishing Limited · Phoenix Mill
Thrupp · Stroud · Gloucestershire · GL5 2BU

This edition first published in 1999

British Library Cataloguing in Publication Data
A catalogue record for this book is available from the British Library

ISBN 0 7509 2017 3

Endpapers: A crowd waiting their turn for water. Wooden stoups and
the girrs for carrying them are seen. From J. Colston, *Edinburgh &
District Water Supply*, 1890. (Trustees of the National Library of
Scotland)

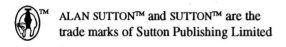 ALAN SUTTON™ and SUTTON™ are the
trade marks of Sutton Publishing Limited

Typeset in 11/14 pt Garamond.
Typesetting and origination by
Sutton Publishing Limited.
Printed in Great Britain
by Butler & Tanner, Frome, Somerset.

Contents

Contents

List of Illustrations

Preface

In the broadest of terms the housewife was concerned with the comfort, health and well-being of every member of her household. Throughout England, Wales and Scotland there were wide variations in the standards achieved, as well as the measures taken to realize those aims but, by and large, the responsibilities of the housewife in one locality were remarkably similar to those of her counterparts at the other end of the country. Her workplace was in or around the home. Her duties included preparing food, cleaning the dwelling, supplying and laundering clothing, fetching fuel and water, provisioning the household, supporting her husband in his enterprises and keeping a watchful eye over the welfare of servants, children and neighbours, quite apart from any occupations undertaken for her own personal interest. These created a veritable patchwork of activities that fully engaged the housewife's attention.

By its very nature much of the work done within a house is ephemeral – the cooked food is eaten, the polished floor is muddied, laundered clothes are used again and furnishings become shabby, in a never-ending sequence of tasks that has to be done, redone and done again. It is therefore surprising that, in spite of so many transitory elements, there is more than enough evidence to draw up a convincing picture of the housewife's daily life during the period of 1650 to 1950.

These three hundred years cover a time of immense change in Britain's history and the housewife working within the home was certainly not immune to what was happening outside it. Such influences might emanate from innumerable sources but, in due course, they filtered down into the home and affected the housewife in her everyday life. However, the rate of change was not constant, either geographically or socially, and this has been one of the major problems in a study of this kind – how to do justice to all housewives at all times, wherever they lived, whatever their economic standing and whichever era they graced. The evidence is plentiful and pertains to every strata of society and locality of Britain. To include it all, each time, would have made the study unwieldy; yet to mention a housewife in one part of the country is to exclude her many sisters and their domestic practices elsewhere. Indeed, is it feasible to equate the life of the housewife in a self-sufficient farmstead in a Welsh valley with that of the housewife in a spacious town house in London or Edinburgh, the cramped terrace of an industrial community or the aristocratic residence on a country estate? Some housewives continued to lead lives almost medieval in their hardship right into the twentieth century, while others were able to take advantage of new developments rather sooner. Therefore, with so many permutations to choose from it is only possible to offer a generalized picture, while including a few examples where local practices differed widely from those prevalent elsewhere.

It is almost inevitable that those housewives with fewer of the world's goods will receive less attention than their wealthier counterparts. Once it has been said that there is plenty of evidence to show housing conditions for 'the poor' were frequently intolerable, that many of these households were devoid of all but the barest necessities and that their diet was meagre with a heavy reliance on a few staple commodities then what can be said about them, while certainly not lacking in interest, has to be somewhat circumscribed by the very nature of the lifestyle portrayed. On the other hand, the lives of those in easier circumstances provide greater detail. As these housewives possessed more in the way of worldly goods, so they made lists of what they had and what they had used. There are inventories of furniture, of china, of silver; accounts relating to transactions of every description; records of meals eaten and wines drunk; memoranda of servants' wages; their letters can be read, the books they read can still be read as, indeed, can the books that some of them wrote. These were the housewives who could take advantage of the many printed works, written with the specific objective of assisting them in the accomplishment of their duties.

If the world outside the home changed greatly and those same changes affected the housewife within the home, it is equally true to say that the housewife's own attitude to her role changed across the years as did the way in which her role was perceived by others. For generations the housewife's contribution to the household was seen as essential to its welfare. She was the central figure, the pivot, around which domestic life revolved and her daughters were brought up in the expectation that they would become wives and mothers in their turn rather than work for wages outside the home.

For some time now these certainties have been whittled away, so much so that, in the 1970s when 'women's liberation' was much in the news, it was common to hear the somewhat apologetic response, 'What do I do? Oh, I'm only a housewife.' Why that 'only'? Why was it that being a housewife, a full-time housewife, was suddenly considered to be a job of lesser worth than someone in paid employment outside the home? With an insight into what the housewife's workload used to comprise, combined with the realization of how her work has gradually changed, an understanding of this seemingly dramatic change in attitude can be gained.

Generations of housewives have come and gone and many of the tasks that were once part of their daily routine have been eradicated. The tasks that do remain have been considerably eased with the development of user-friendly materials of every description and equipment designed to obviate much of the physical labour related to running a home. Yet the fact remains that a house and those living within its walls still have the same needs as in previous generations. Someone must be responsible for the comfort, health and well-being of its members and, historically, that has been the duty of the housewife. The altered perception of the role is a phenomenon of the later twentieth century and what the current generation make of it will be a study for the historians of the future.

Acknowledgements

Permission to reproduce extracts from published works has kindly been given by the following: Cambridge University Press for the extracts from F.A.F. de la Rochefoucauld-Liancourt, *A Frenchman in England in 1784* [1933]; Macmillan Publishers, for the extracts from D.M. Stuart, *The English Abigail* [1946]; Navy Records Society for the extract from D. Bonner-Smith (ed), *Capt Boteler's Recollections* [1942]; Oxford University Press for extracts from F. Thompson, *Lark Rise to Candleford* [1945]; Routledge & Keegan Paul for the extract from J.J. Hecht, *The Domestic Servant in Eighteenth-Century England* [1980]; Scottish Beekepers'Association for the extract from The Revd J. Beveridge, *A Veteran Beemaster looks back* [1941]; A.P. Watt Ltd. on behalf of Rosemary Beresford, J.C. Beresford, B.W. Beresford and Ruth Longman for the extracts from: J. Beresford (ed.), *Diary of a Country Parson* [5 vols, Humphrey Milford, OUP, 1924–31]; Yale University and the Edinburgh University Press for the extract from F.A. Pottle (ed.), *Boswell's London Journal 1762–3* [1950].

I wish to thank the following for permission to reproduce illustrations from material in their possession: The Trustees of the National Library of Scotland; The National Gallery of Scotland; The Earl of Southesk and the Royal Commission on the Ancient & Historical Monuments of Scotland; Hopetoun Papers Trust, South Queensferry.

For permission to make use of my own photographs, taken on their premises, I am indebted to the following organizations: Auchindrain Museum, Inveraray; Beamish, North of England Open Air Museum; City of York Museums Service, York Castle Museum; Falkirk Museums (Callendar House); Gwent Rural Life Museum, Usk; The Highland Council (Highland Folk Museum, Kingussie); Ironbridge Gorge Museum Trust, Telford; Leeds Museum & Galleries (Temple Newsam House); Llancaiach Fawr Manor, Treharris; Museum of Welsh Life, Cardiff; Plas Newydd, Llangollen (Courtesy of Denbighshire County Council); Weald & Downland Open Air Museum, Singleton.

CHAPTER ONE

Who are the Housewives?

Mrs Beeton was under no illusion as to what the job of housewife entailed: 'As with the Commander of an Army, or the leader of any enterprise, so is it with the mistress of a house. Her spirit will be seen through the whole establishment; and just in proportion as she performs her duties intelligently and thoroughly, so will her domestics follow in her path. Of all those acquirements, which may particularly belong to the feminine character, there are none that take a higher rank, in our estimation, than such as enter into a knowledge of household duties; for on these are perpetually dependent the happiness, comfort and well-being of a family.'[1]

Many others, before and after, have also attempted to define the role of the housewife. Many centuries ago the author of the Old Testament's book of Proverbs declared: 'She looketh well to the ways of her household; and eateth not the bread of idleness. Her children arise up and call her blessed; her husband also, and he praiseth her.'[2]

Those same 'ways of her household' were spelt out in greater detail by Gervase Markham, the seventeenth-century author of a book on domestic management. The housewife's skills specifically encompassed healing the sick, cookery and the finer confectionery work, organizing great feasts, the management of wines and the production of cures, cosmetics and perfumes. Nor was she confined to indoors, being expected to act over the spinning of wool, linen and hemp and the subsequent making and dyeing of cloth. She was also to manage her dairy and understand the importance of oats to a family, alongside 'Brewing, Baking, and all other things belonging to an Houshold'.[3]

If housewives came in every shape and size so did their homes. Terraced housing, in all its permutations, can be found throughout Britain. Economical in the use of ground space, the basic design allowed considerable flexibility in the internal arrangements.

Modern day definitions are briefer, albeit less evocative. The housewife is depicted as the mistress and manager of a house, a definition which can also be covered by the term 'housekeeper', although this has acquired the more commonly accepted meaning of a female employee paid to do such work. The term 'wife' tacked on to 'house' suggests an element of marriage – though not necessarily the presence of children – but this gives the impression that the housewife is a somewhat transitory being, who becomes disenfranchised when widowed, for example, or which denies the title altogether to a spinster.

Across the years many housewives are encountered going about their everyday business, in every geographical location and social strata.

Some of the evidence comes from their own hands via account books and domestic memoranda, collections of recipes gathered together from friends and family, letters, poetry, biographies of husbands or fathers, reminiscences of times past or journeys made and so on and so forth – too numerous for each to be mentioned individually. Scotland's Lady Grisell Baillie, of Mellerstain, near Kelso, is now better known through her book of domestic accounts than for her childhood heroism in saving her father's life; it is significant to note that as she lay dying she asked that those lines from the book of Proverbs be read aloud to her.[4] Mrs Purefroy of Shalstone, near Buckingham lives vividly in the voluminous correspondence she and her son engaged in over many years in pursuit of the goods and services required for themselves and their household.[5] Biographical ventures, such as those written by Lady Fanshawe or her contemporary, Margaret, Duchess of Newcastle, reveal something of their authors at the same time, while many women, housewives and mothers among them, wrote poetry and used domestic imagery to express their feelings.[6]

Through his eyes, Samuel Pepys' young wife, who was only fifteen years old when they married, can be followed in her efforts at housekeeping in Restoration London, whereas, a hundred years later, it is domestic management in a Norfolk parish that comes to life in another diary – even though the Rev. James Woodforde is hardly a housewife within the meaning of the term.[7] Taking over where he left off, reminiscences of a genuine housewife and a distinctive way of life were recorded by Elizabeth Grant of Rothiemurchus, whose family home was in the Scottish Highlands.[8] Reminiscences of a different flavour, incorporating an awareness of change, of times past, are another form of evidence. These range in extent from memoirs of a personal nature to the writings of an authority such as Gertrude Jekyll, who felt it necessary to gather together memories of the domestic life in her own corner of Surrey before all the old ways were swept away by the pace of change. In turn, these selfsame 'modern' ways are now deemed to be of historical import and worthy of being recorded for posterity.[9]

Somewhere between the historical and the fictional lies Mistress Margaret Dods, a character from Sir Walter Scott's novel *St Ronans Well*, who purportedly 'kept a small old-fashioned inn where excellent small dinners were served' and compiled a cookery book; the fictional character was based on a real life prototype in the Borders town of Innerleithen.[10] Similar examples of almost genuine domesticity abound, disguised as fiction, in novels such as Mrs Gaskell's *Cranford* and Flora Thompson's *Lark Rise to Candleford* where material has been recycled from the authors' own memories. The genteel housekeeping and social niceties in the small town of 'Cranford' are portrayed delicately, with understanding and humour. The story of 'Lark Rise', an agricultural hamlet dominated by poverty where housewives struggled to bring up their families, contains many domestic details caught at the moment before such ways vanished for ever and the hamlet dwellings act as a foil to the modest comforts found at Candleford Green. A Scottish example covering an earlier period is John Galt's *Annals of the Parish,* told from the point of view of the local parish minister.[11]

Another body of evidence is circumstantial in nature and is derived from someone else's observations, such as the official and semi-official investigations into the social and domestic habits of 'the poor' which provide a wealth of information about innumerable households which would otherwise have gone unnoticed.[12] On a different level are the works of the diarist and the traveller, native born or foreigner, with motives as varied as their origins. Hundreds of housewives are glimpsed only in passing – good, bad or indifferent, gracious or feckless, richer or poorer – recorded for posterity in a somewhat arbitrary fashion because someone happened to be on the spot at that particular moment.

Celia Fiennes travelled extensively through England during the latter years of the seventeenth century, commenting enthusiastically on all manner of people, places and events met with on her way; she touched on Wales too, as well as Scotland, thought rather poorly of both and stayed only briefly.[13]

In fact Scotland, regarded in its day as a *terra incognita,* seems to have acted as a magnet for a positive cavalcade of visitors. Samuel Johnson and James Boswell are probably the best known; both kept a

A traditional Highland 'blackhouse' built with low walls, rounded corners and roped-down thatch to withstand the wind. The central portion is taken up by the kitchen, with the 'ben' or best room at one end and a byre for the animals at the other. (Highland Folk Museum)

This two-storeyed Welsh farm house, Y Garreg Fawr, was home to a wealthy farmer when it was built in 1544. (By courtesy of the Museum of Welsh Life)

record as they travelled from Edinburgh to the Western Islands and included matters of domestic interest.[14] In the nineteenth century Dorothy Wordsworth's journal of a tour made in Scotland with her brother, for whom she kept house, frequently commented favourably or otherwise on dwellings and their inhabitants, while a few years afterwards the volumes of Elizabeth Isabella Spence followed a similar format.[15]

Wales attracted a parallel crop of observers, wishing to explain the seemingly foreign to an audience reluctant or unable to leave home. There is no doubt that once the two 'Ladies of Llangollen' had settled in the town in 1778 they became the focal point for innumerable visitors, all keen to establish the facts about this celebrated household and its occupants' way of life.[16] Other authors confined themselves to matters of topography, or agriculture, or to the northern counties of the principality, or a journey by railway along the southern coast, or a walking tour 'with a knapsack' – undertaken by 'Four Schoolmistresses' sustained in their efforts by the receipt of daily parcels containing clean clothes and chocolate bars, sent from home to post offices *en route*.[17] Yet in spite of so much published material it was possible for one author to state, even in 1894: 'The remote districts of Wales are unknown to them' (i.e. to the traveller and the tourist) and that her objective was 'To awaken English interest in the land and life of the Cymru.'[18]

To explain the Welsh, or for that matter the Scots, to the English was one thing but many foreigners came to Britain and also recorded their experiences. From France in 1725 came Cesar de Saussure, who was not altogether complimentary in his findings, and his countryman F.A.F. de la Rochefoucauld who followed him some half a century later.[19] In the years between came the Swede, Pehr Kalm, who was scandalized by the way English women had freed themselves of many traditional duties – at the expense of their menfolk. He cited the fact that they rarely took the trouble to bake or to brew, had no need to spin or weave, and let the menfolk tend the cattle as well as do the milking: 'In short, when one enters a house, and has seen the women cooking, washing floors, plates and dishes, darning a stocking, or sewing a chemise, washing and starching linen cloths, he has, in fact, seen all their household economy and all that they do the whole of God's long day.'[20] In his opinion English women would not be well-suited to Sweden where, it was assumed, the wife would be the other half of an active partnership – in the manner visualized by Thomas Tusser in the sixteenth century:

> Good husband without, it is needful there bee,
> Good huswife within, is as needfull as hee.

It was, perhaps, unfortunate that Kalm did not visit Wales as there, throughout most of the nineteenth century, the Welsh housewife was winning praise for continuing to carry out her multifarious domestic duties in the manner of her forebears.[21]

A further source of evidence is idealistic or educational in concept, dedicated to teaching the housewife about her domestic duties. This could take the form of a manual instructing her in one particular aspect, such as cookery, the work of servants, the preparation of herbal remedies or social etiquette for example, or take a more generalized approach. The housewife who had tried out every recipe in the cookbook or read her way through the close-packed pages of some domestic encyclopedia would, indeed, come close to the ideal.

Servants had long been subjected to improving pamphlets outlining their duties which, if nothing else, begs the question as to the levels of literacy among female servants. In 1743 Eliza Haywood, the novelist, was just one of many who addressed herself to the subject, seeing that 'servants should be in general so bad'. Introduced by the words 'Dear Girls', the rules for personal behaviour and for

Seventeenth-century Sussex cottage built out of flint and brick. (The Weald & Downland Open Air Museum, Singleton)

the obedience and loyalty owed to the employer are spelt out in detail and a high moral tone is evident throughout.[22] By the nineteenth century it was not only the servants who were being exhorted in this manner but also, somewhat surprisingly, the housewife – to the extent that succeeding authors promote not only the same themes but often do so in phrases that begin to sound remarkably familiar. One such manual from 1807 states: 'There was a time when ladies knew nothing *beyond* their own family concerns: but in the present day there are many who know nothing *about* them. Each of these extremes should be avoided.' In her opinion the rudiments of domestic knowledge should be taught to every young girl, irrespective of her social status, 'before she entered into the delusive scenes of pleasure, presented by the theatre and other dissipations'. Carrying the observations on to married life, the author declares in ringing tones that a life of employment is the source of unnumbered pleasures: to nurse and instruct the young, to preside over the household and regulate the income allotted to its maintenance, as well as 'to make home the sweet refuge of a husband fatigued by intercourse with a jarring world: to be his enlightened companion and the chosen friend of his heart: these, these, are woman's duties! . . . Can anyone urge that the female mind is contracted by domestic employ?'[23] When the far-reaching essentials of good housekeeping, enumerated at length thereafter, are taken into account the answer has to be 'probably not'. So many works like these were produced at about this time, highlighting the magnitude of the housewife's calling and 'the sacred obligations', together with the personal fulfilment and spiritual contentment to be gained from a total commitment to domestic life, that it becomes necessary to ask what had happened to trigger such a significant change of tone?

The nineteenth-century housewife was a very different being to her seventeenth-century counterpart. Outside the home the world had changed dramatically over the years for innumerable reasons, all interlinked. The whole of society had been affected by these changes, with the reverberations being felt in the kitchen and the servants' hall no less than in the dining room, parlour or gardens outside.

Until the seventeenth century, household servants were male, apart from the occasional waiting-woman, nursemaid, washerwoman, dairymaid and henwife. The housewife worked closely with her servants, regarded them as members of an extended family and supervised their work herself; at this point the housekeeper was a low-ranking servant who looked after a bachelor or widower. It was customary for the entire household, comprising family, guests and servants, to dine together in the same room – the great hall if the residence was of that calibre, otherwise the hall, hall-house, house-place, fire-house or kitchen depending on the locality and era. By the nineteenth century such customs rarely survived; society had become organized into a class system, with a gap between each level. Domestic servants were considered a race apart and separated from 'the family' by the celebrated green baize door, while the day-to-day management of many households was in the hands of a paid housekeeper. How had such a radical change come about?

During the upheavals of the seventeenth century (economic, political and religious, among others) reasons of economy saw menservants of a lower calibre, who therefore earned lower wages, replacing those previously employed. Many households also took to employing women instead for jobs such as cooking and cleaning, as their wages were traditionally about half those given to men.

There followed a period of considerable social mobility when people could move up the social scale quite easily, although money was required to maintain the new position – money and the things that money could buy, such as servants. The newly risen found it appropriate to disassociate themselves from the class they had just left and in such circumstances the housewife would not wish to work too closely with her domestic staff; in addition, it was considered demeaning to her husband's position to do so. More servants were needed as a result of rising standards of living along with higher expectations in standards of cleanliness and comfort. As female staff increased in numbers it was considered necessary, as well as fashionable, to employ someone to supervise their day-to-day work, which is where the paid housekeeper, the substitute housewife, entered the picture. Daughters caught their mothers' disdain for domestic pursuits, to such an extent that there was a widespread feeling that the younger generation was totally ignorant of household management.

The trends continued. The housekeeper took over from the housewife, who was thereby freed from her domestic duties. Thanks to (initially modest) improvements in the design of coaches and the condition of roads, those who wished and could afford to were able to leave home more easily and enjoy the delights of London or Edinburgh or a spa such as Tunbridge Wells, Harrogate or Moffat. They no longer had time for their former occupations of spinning, salting down a pig for the winter or making confections in the still-room; such pursuits came to be thought very old fashioned indeed and were gladly given over to the housekeeper.

The erstwhile housewife's pleasure in the social round could be further justified if the family included unmarried daughters, as it served to introduce them to a wider circle of acquaintances and better their chance of marriage; to remain unmarried was a disaster and kept the girl tied to her family for ever. Education was geared to increasing their attractiveness to the opposite sex, so that accomplishments such as dancing and needlework were considered of greater importance than more academic disciplines, another divide between the generations. A young man might be scared off by the thought of a clever wife and, as marriage was the expected career, what would a girl need with 'book learning' anyway?

By the time Queen Victoria was on the throne it was inconceivable for a woman of the middle classes or upwards to do her own housework, yet the attitudes of the day prohibited her from working

Kinnaird Castle, Brechin, Angus. Enlarged and remodelled in the French Baronial style between 1854–62, the south wing contains the remains of the original fifteenth-century tower house. (Copyright: Royal Commission on the Ancient & Historical Monuments of Scotland)

outside the home. It was degrading for a married woman to take paid employment as it reflected badly on the husband, implying that his income was insufficient. Yet the innumerable changes brought about outside the home in the spheres of agriculture, industry, transport and commerce meant that it was no longer necessary for a housewife to spin her own wool, make her own beer or gather her own fuel as these could be provided more economically by others, thereby leaving her with far fewer household chores and with time on her hands. To redress this imbalance a plethora of works advised the young woman how to use her time wisely to improve herself as to character, education, accomplishments, religious observance, charitable practices and similar interests, and to counsel her in the management of household, servants, hospitality and children. Total commitment to her domestic obligations would endear her to everyone around her, so she was led to believe, and ensure comfort and happiness in every direction.[24]

Many housewives conformed happily to the pattern and immersed themselves in domestic employment, Mrs Grant of Rothiemurchus being one of them. Having outlined the complexities of living in the Scottish Highlands in the early nineteenth century where the household was largely dependent on what the estate could produce, her daughter added: 'The regular routine of business, where so much was done at home, was really a perpetual amusement. I used to wonder when travellers asked my mother if she did not find her life dull.'[25] However, this viewpoint was far from acceptable to everyone. Even in the seventeenth century there were women who preferred to exercise their talents in other directions, Margaret, Duchess of Newcastle, for example. She was far more exercised over philosophical speculation and the writing of plays than her domestic duties so, on being chided by her neighbours, she considered some household activites she might engage in, such as spinning, making silk flowers and preserving fruit. Her gentlewoman laughed at her notion and dissuaded her by saying it would be cheaper to buy such things already made, as her Grace was so out of practice she would spoil far more than she produced. The Duchess left domestic pursuits to others and happily returned to her writings.[26]

The women with other interests and the strength of character to carry them through were fortunate. Two hundred years later Florence Nightingale, better known for her nursing reforms in the Crimea, was vehement on the subject of the total passivity and stultifying boredom faced by middle-class women, who were increasingly restricted in what they were or were not allowed to do.[27]

The debate over women's place in society and women's rights has been a controversial issue for many years and will continue to be so in the future. In the meantime, this book will not be following that particular route but takes as its theme the history of the housewife, examining the patchwork of activities carried on within the home and the changes that have occurred there across the years.

After all, as Hannah Robertson said over two hundred years ago: 'A woman has it not in her power to make herself a beauty or a wit; that is the gift of Heaven; but every woman has it in her power to be a good housewife.'[28]

CHAPTER TWO

Fuels and Fireplaces

'There being no bell in the parlour, I had occasion to go several times and ask for what we wanted in the kitchen . . . About seven or eight travellers, probably drovers, with as many dogs, were sitting in a complete circle round a large peat-fire in the middle of the floor, each with a mess of porridge, in a wooden vessel, upon his knee; a pot, suspended from one of the black beams, was boiling on the fire; two or three women pursuing their household business on the outside of the circle, children playing on the floor. There was nothing uncomfortable in this confusion; happy, busy, or vacant faces, all looked pleasant.'[1]

Although this particular instance occurred in Scotland in 1803, scenes of this sort would have been familiar throughout much of Britain at that time and, indeed, for another one hundred years or so thereafter. A fire was central to the household. Without fire the housewife was deprived of the means of heating, lighting, cooking, preserving and drying, while it also acted as a gathering place for the occupants and offered a measure of security against the terrors of the night. For many households it was the one and the same fire that served for all these purposes and others besides. Even when the dwelling consisted of a single room, shared between the inhabitants and their livestock, it was common to find a fireplace and such a scene was often described: 'It had two Beds at the Upper-end, a Goat and two Pigs at the Lower-end, and a Fireplace in the Middle' wrote an early traveller to Wales, but his words were equally applicable to almost every region of Britain.[2]

A cottage fireplace was generally of the simplest construction with only a semicircle of stones to keep the fuel in place or some clay tiles up-ended in a chalk floor to denote the hearth. These fires needed little in the way of additional equipment, maybe a poker or fire dogs to encourage it to burn, while the cooking pot might rest over the

A simple hearth consisting of clay tiles inserted in the chalk floor. (The Weald & Downland Open Air Museum, Singleton)

fire, be placed among the embers or hang from a convenient beam. The fuel burnt would depend on what was available locally, for it was not until the coming of the canals and, later, the railways, that it was convenient to transport coal over considerable distances. Until then a wide variety of materials were burnt on or in the domestic hearth.

How often does that familiar phrase 'By hook or by crook' come to mind? The words have changed their meaning somewhere along the way and instead of the current sense of 'by one means or another' the phrase is said to have originated with the right of workers in certain areas to remove dead woods with the aid of a (labourer's) hook or a (shepherd's) crook. The wood might not be cut but it could be taken out with these tools, a measure designed to ensure that the fuel went to those who had 'earned' it rather than to any passing vagrant.

Everyone who could was expected to contribute to the collecting of firewood. Back in Tudor times Thomas Tusser had declared:

> Make servant at night lug in wood or a log,
> let none come in emptie* but slut and thy dog[3]

Even at the start of the twentieth century women in Surrey could still be seen 'bringing home on their backs faggots of dead wood, or sacks of fir-cones, picked up in the fir-woods a mile away or more' with some being bent almost double under their loads and accompanied by tiny children clinging to their skirts.[4] Speaking of past days on the Wiltshire Downs one woman recalled how, after gathering her wood, she used to tie it into a firm barrel-shaped bundle so that she could roll it the 2 miles home 'without so much groaning and sweating'.[5]

The burning of wood was widespread, as long as supplies lasted, but certain areas ran out of timber sooner than others due to the ever-increasing demands made upon them. The story is often repeated that supplies in Fife were totally exhausted early in the sixteenth century by the building of King James IV's warship *The Great Michael*.[6] Across the Forth the housewives of Edinburgh certainly became accustomed to burning coal in their grates early on but, equally, coal was readily available from nearby sources and transport was no problem. By the beginning of the nineteenth century the woodlands and commons of England and Wales were estimated to have shrunk to between 15 and 21 per cent of the land cover and it was far from evenly distributed.[7] In the north of England fuel was still cheap and the agricultural labourer ate a more varied diet as a result. By contrast, many of their southern compatriots were driven by the shortage of fuel to live on an unvarying weekday diet of bread and cheese. The bread had always to be bought and any meat on the Sunday was taken to the local bakers to be cooked although, it was argued, the fire required to boil the southerners' tea-kettle twice a

* i.e. empty-handed

14

day could well, with proper management, have cooked a nourishing soup instead.[8] Thirty years later when Cobbett travelled the country the situation seemed unchanged.[9]

Dwindling areas of woodland, common and wasteland were one problem but even greater hardship was caused when access to them was denied by landowners bent on enclosing their lands, whether for agriculture or for sport. Where wood was unobtainable materials such as heather, furze, gorse, seaweed, straw, stubble, thistles, rushes and pine cones were cut or gathered at appropriate times of the year, carried home and set aside to dry until required.

Another readily available fuel was cow or horse dung, which only needed collecting and drying by way of preparation. It was far more widely used than is generally realized, burns easily and has over half the calorific value of coal. In 1698 while Celia Fiennes was travelling the country, she recorded that it was much in evidence near Peterborough: 'I saw upon ye walls of ye ordinary peoples houses and walls of their out houses, ye Cow dung plaister'd up to drie in Cakes wch they use for fireing.' She commented that the country folk thereabouts used little else, although in her opinion it was 'a very offensive fewell'.[10] It was widely used in Wales[11] as well as in other regions and one hundred years later the hope was expressed that the introduction of canal-borne coal to the area around Louth, Lincolnshire, 'will induce the inhabitants to desist from their ancient practice, not yet entirely disused, of using the dung of their cattle for fuel'.[12]

Peat was widely available in many regions and was therefore much used as a domestic fuel. Gathering it was a task that called for teamwork. One man would cut the peat, using a special tool to slice out two blocks at a time, while another man working ahead of him prepared the bank for cutting. A third would stack the blocks, about 24 inches long and 6 inches square, into a barrow which was then wheeled away and emptied on to the ground. It would need two to four days of working together in this way to dig the annual supply of peat for a single-hearth household.[13] Over the next few weeks women and children would ensure the peats dried sufficiently in the sun and the wind, by spreading them out, turning them, heaping about six of them into a stack, then into larger stacks. The men would build them into yet larger stacks before the peats were carried home, either with the aid of a horse or in creels on the women's backs. Once home, the peats were piled up somewhere convenient and covered over against the worst of the weather.

A wooden barrow for carrying peats. (Auchindrain, Inveraray)

Peat fires created relatively little work for the housewife and were easy to manage. Dorothy Wordsworth noted, at one place they stayed, how easily their hostess had 'heaped up some dry peats and heather, and, blowing on it with her breath, in a short time raised a blaze that scorched us into comfortable feelings'. How very different from 'the little public-house . . . or rather a hut' they entered later on, where the fire was slow to get going because the woman had 'no fuel but green wood, and no bellows but her breath'.[14] For those unaccustomed to peat fires there were two disadvantages, particularly in dwellings lacking a proper chimney. The peat-smoke was apt to swirl around at head height which rendered sitting on anything other than a low stool unpleasant; the other was described simply, but eloquently, by Celia Fiennes:' . . . it makes one smell as if smoked Like Bacon'.[15]

The great advantage of all these fuels was that they would burn on a simple hearth or directly on the ground with only minimal equipment. There was no need for a chimney and many such dwellings had none, the smoke from the fire eventually finding its own way out through the door, the window or through the thatching of turf or heather. There was no need, either, to raise these fuels off the floor in a comparatively costly iron grate, as was necessary for coal. However, they could be burned in a raised basket if so wished, as Dr Johnson observed on Skye: 'The only fuel of the Islands is peat.

Their wood is all consumed, and coal they have not yet found . . . The common method of making peat fires, is by heaping it on the hearth; but it burns well in grates, and in the best houses is so used.'[16]

Coal, contrary to general belief, had been the predominant fuel in certain areas of Britain since medieval times and possibly much longer, so that where it was available locally, such as in North Wales, it was coal that was burnt. Thomas Pennant argued that the ancient Britons there were manufacturing brass with it even before the Romans arrived.[17] Welsh coal supplied Dublin and the east coast of Ireland in the seventeenth century, as well as southern Cornwall, and London's 'sea-coals' were so called because they were brought by sea from Newcastle-upon-Tyne. Elsewhere, the use of coal depended on water-borne transport as it was uneconomic to carry it more than a few miles by packhorse or equivalent means.

Different types of coal were mined, each with its own properties. Celia Fiennes described vividly the operations involved in both bringing up the coal and preventing the mines from flooding. She was very taken with 'channell [i.e. cannel] coal' which she came across at Newcastle-under-Lyme and again at Wigan: 'Here it is that the fine Channell Coales are in perfection – burns as light as a Candle – set the Coales together wth some fire and it shall give a snap and burn up light' and she made a joke about 'taking coals to Newcastle'.[18] Pennant, one hundred years later, echoed her opinion, while describing North Wales: 'Beds of canal are met with: inferior indeed in elegance to those of *Lancashire*, but greatly coveted by the lime burners. Sometimes is also found the *Peacock* coal . . . remarkable for the beauty of its surface, glossed over with the changeable brilliancy of the colours of that beautiful bird.'[19]

The change-over to coal increased dramatically with the building of canals during the second half of the eighteenth century, and over half the waterways built during that period were specifically intended to carry coals. However, it was the railways that sparked an even greater increase and production soared, from some 64.5 million tons in 1854 to almost 147 million tons by 1880.[20]

For the housewife coal was a mixed blessing and, even though it was available, it might be shunned in favour of something simpler.

Coal is harder to light as it needs to be coaxed into life with some form of kindling and the assistance of a pair of bellows, or similar. If not burning cleanly it produces much fume-laden and dirty smoke, which leaves a hard-to-remove deposit over everything, while any

A grate raised off the floor was essential for the burning of coal. This one is built into the fireplace and has hobs on either side of the basket, Plas Newydd, Llangollen. (By courtesy of Denbighshire County Council)

coal dust or ash shed upon the floor needs to be dealt with immediately or the mess spreads even further afield. Ash from wood or peats, on the other hand, settles lightly on furniture and floors and little effort is needed to remove it. When coal is burnt more equipment is needed and this must be bought. It is reluctant to ignite if placed on the ground and was, therefore, generally burnt in either a free-standing raised basket-grate or else confined within the chimney by built-in iron bars. Because coal's calorific value is greater than either peat or wood it was necessary to protect the brickwork behind the fire with an iron plate or fire back, some of which were cast with the most elaborate designs. A set of fire irons comprising poker, shovel and tongs became a necessity to keep the fire going, as was a fender to stop sparks showering on to the floor and a non-combustible area of brick or tiles in front of it.

Also needed is an up-draught, hence the siting of the grate beneath a chimney, but although chimneys of brick and stone had been built into or added on to buildings for many centuries the principles governing their use were not always fully understood. Many manuals were written and much time was spent explaining the principles governing the production of heat, the most effective methods of warming or ventilating rooms and the prevention of smoking chimneys.

Foreigners were always amazed by the British preference for an open fire and their resistance to the idea of a closed stove, no matter how much time and effort was spent on preaching the benefits of such appliances. A Swedish visitor to London noted in amazement that the temperature of his host's drawing room rarely rose above 10°C and was often rather less, whereas when he had visited Norway anything under 15° 'we thought . . . was tolerably cold and chilly'. Sweden found 15°C 'very moderately warm, but 20° Celsius is too hot for most people'.[21] It was Benjamin Franklin who pointed out that most of the heat from an ordinary open fire went straight up the flue and he advocated the installation of one of his own 'Pennsylvania grates', designed to warm the entire room, not just the area immediately in front of it as English fires did, leaving the rest of the room – and its occupants – unheated. Towards the end of the century his fellow American, Benjamin Thompson (alias Count Rumford) carried on the crusade, expounding on the theories of heating and the best ways of getting the most from one's fuel. Considering that a fire gives out most of its heat by radiation, he declared, the fireplace should be made of a substance such as brick or firestone, but definitely not of iron as was the custom; the grate should be made shallow, with sloping sides, so that the fuel heated as much of the surface area as possible. He also pointed out the importance of narrowing the throat of the flue, which not only increased the air flow but prevented smoke being blown downwards.

James Woodforde, the Norfolk parson, dutifully read his 'Rumford' in due course in an attempt to cure his smoking chimneys once and for all. In 1781 he had noted his study chimney place had been altered for the fourth time 'but am still afraid of it'. Two years later all looked well when he wrote 'My Study Grate pleases me much, no smoking', but his pleasure proved to be short-lived and thereafter there were many instances when he was driven from his study to the parlour or else found the parlour unusable 'the Wind being mostly Westerly'.

Determined to get to the bottom of the problem, Woodforde studied Rumford on the subject in 1796, but one evening in 1798 he was not only driven from study to parlour but was obliged to keep open the doors of both cellar and study while closing every other door. As late as 1801 he was writing: 'Our . . . Study smoaked amazingly'; however, there was one benefit to be found in all this for when a swarm of bees settled on the top of this particular chimney, it was easy to smoke them out.[22]

Throughout the nineteenth century the problems of inadequately installed fireplaces and improperly burning coal bedevilled towns of any size. Even in 1748 Kalm had noted the harmful effects in London where tin and silver discoloured, statues blackened and snow took on a grimy hue. 'To a foreigner,' he wrote, '. . . this coal-smoke was very annoying, for it affected the chest excessively, especially at night.'[23] By 1865 numerous patents for smokeless fuels had been processed and in 1882 the Smoke Abatement Exhibition tested a number of appliances, most of which proved disappointing. London's smogs* were literally killers, causing many thousands of deaths until the causes were eradicated by legislation and persistent effort. Edinburgh, in its day, was known as 'Auld Reekie' for much the same reason. It is said that an old gentleman across the water in Fife 'was in the habit . . . of regulating the time of evening worship by the appearance of the smoke of Edinburgh . . . increasing in density in consequence of the good folk of the city preparing their supper'.[24]

The increased use of coal brought in its wake another major problem. Flues needed regular sweeping to clear the deposits of soot which, if left, might catch alight or drop down into the room, thus causing extra work for the housewife. Many cleaned their own flues, either by putting up a lighted paper at frequent intervals or by pulling up a rope from the top with something abrasive such as a branch of holly tied to it. Others, though, depended on the chimney sweep. Early chimneys were built on a generous scale with wide flues and were relatively simple to clean as men could climb through them to dislodge deposits from protruding ledges or interconnecting passageways. With the increasing use of coal, flues were constructed to greatly reduced measurements – and it was at this point that children were made to climb up the chimneys instead of the men. The outcry against the employment of 'climbing boys' began halfway through the eighteenth century. Legislation was enacted in 1778, but both this and subsequent acts in 1840 and 1864 proved ineffective in spite of the enormous publicity generated by the portrayal of chimney sweeps in works such as *Oliver Twist* (1837–8) and *The Water*

---

* smoke-laden fogs

Babies (1863). In 1864 a Royal Commission was set up, but it was not until 1875 and the introduction of a licencing system for sweeps that Lord Shaftesbury's efforts were finally rewarded and the evil of climbing boys was abolished. In Scotland, where tenements were prevalent, it was customary for two sweeps to operate in tandem as one had to be on the roof to identify the correct chimney.

Relief of another kind was in sight by this stage. Alternative fuels were coming into use which would eventually obviate the need for an open fire altogether and the consequent need for chimney sweeping, even though, initially, these substances were apt to create more, rather than less, work for the housewife.

Oils from assorted sources, whether animal, vegetable or mineral in origin, had been used for lighting for many centuries, but when a new substance was discovered by distilling oily coal at low temperatures, it was used for more than just lighting. In Nova Scotia Abraham Gesner called his invention kerosene, meaning 'wax-oil', but in Britain James Young named his version paraffin and patented the process. In 1850 Young's Paraffin Oil Company was established in Bathgate, West Lothian to refine the substance from the area's coal-bearing shale. When seemingly unlimited deposits of petroleum were discovered in both Ontario and Pennsylvania at the end of the decade, kerosene became both readily available and very cheap. Almost overnight it was fuelling lamps and cookers as well as heaters for domestic purposes. Ornate cast-iron columns or 'chimneys' surrounded the tall glass cylinder which contained the air to be heated and tinted glass inserts proved popular; alternatively, designs could be open-fronted with a reflector behind, generally of copper. Some designs incorporated a flat cooking surface on top or a towel rail at the side.

At much the same time gas was beginning to find a place in the home. As early as the seventeenth century natural gas was exciting comment and attracting the passing tourist, as witnessed by Celia Fiennes who wrote that, on leaving 'Wiggons [i.e. Wigan] . . . another pretty Market town built of stone and brick' she had made a detour to see 'the Burning well wch burns like brandy'. Here, 'Y^e man wch shewed it me . . . set ye water in ye well on fire and it burn'd blewish just like spirits and Continued a good while.'[25] Combustible gases from assorted substances had been attracting the attention of scientists since the sixteenth century and in the eighteenth century many experimented with coal gas. However, it was not until the century was near its end that any serious thought was given to making practical use of the potential to light and to heat. William

Murdoch is generally credited with being the first in the field when he used coal gas to light his own home and offices at Redruth, Cornwall in 1792. But, although gas rapidly became popular as an illuminant in streets, public buildings, mills, business premises and so on, the smells and the heat given off rendered it unsuitable for domestic use. Once these defects had been cured it became increasingly popular and was then promoted as a means of cooking and heating.

The gas fire became a practicable proposition when, following Count Rumford's tenets regarding open fires and radiant heat, the gas flame was played upon a surface such as tufted asbestos or fireclay bricks thereby greatly augmenting the amount of heat given off. Fashions in the design and materials of the surrounds came and went, and a log-fire effect first went on sale in the 1920s.

To run a gas fire, of course, it had to be connected up to a source of gas; most towns by this time were well supplied with a network of pipelines supplying the street lamps, but these did not extend into rural areas. The new oils fulfilled the needs of country dwellers well into the twentieth century, but the producers of both oil and gas had to contend with fuel from yet another source – electricity.

The term itself had been coined as long ago as 1600 and its properties had attracted endless attention from scientists, with names like Sir Humphry Davy and Michael Faraday being prominent, but electricity was slow to find a place within the home. As with gas, so with electricity: installation of a supply system was costly and, as householders tended to be reluctant to change their ways, electricity remained an expensive alternative to existing fuels and it was not until the 1930s that it was adopted to any great extent. Its first appearance was as a means of lighting but it was quickly promoted for cooking, ironing and heating, with radiators following the designs of comparable appliances.

Once installed, both gas and electricity would eventually take the question of heating out of the hands of the housewife. Turn a tap, light the gas and that was that. Electricity was even simpler.

It remains to consider one further aspect, which played a considerable role in distancing the housewife from the whole question of fuels and fireplaces, and that concerns the subject of central heating.

The Romans, it is well known, circulated hot air beneath their floors to warm their houses, but that particular method had fallen out of use. Although not dignified by the term 'central heating', simple methods of increasing warmth in the home were certainly practised. Arthur Young observed when in Ireland that the peat smoke in the 'cabbins' was tolerated as a means of warmth; he also remarked that the family lay on straw 'equally partook of by cows, calves and pigs, though the luxury of sties is coming in in Ireland, which excludes the poor pigs from the warmth of the bodies of their master and mistress'.[26] In dwellings graced by a chimney a fire warmed the walls nearby as well as any space above, while a chimney built in the centre of a house gave warmth to the rooms either side. Poorer folk liked gas lighting because it gave a measure of warmth along with the light, while the despised and neglected closed-stove gave off heat the full length of its stovepipe connection to the chimney.

Central heating itself was slow to catch on in Britain, though rapidly accepted in the United States. Various methods were tried, either using the fire to heat the air directly or to circulate steam through a system of pipes. In the 1820s numerous examples of both had been installed, mostly in factories or warehouses, but also in a London theatre, Lowther Castle in Westmorland and Sir Walter Scott's mansion, Abbotsford. Space heating by hot water was a somewhat later development and tended, meantime, to be reserved for hothouses or orangeries. While low-pressure hot-water systems were slow to be accepted, by the 1830s high-pressure systems had been installed in the British Museum, the London Patent Office, Stratfield Saye (the Duke of Wellington's country residence) and an Edinburgh bookbinding business, among others. During the century the whole subject of heating became intertwined with those of ventilation and fresh air and central heating made little headway in the average household until well into the present century.

Why were people so reluctant to change to cleaner and more efficient methods of heating their homes, which could lead to a considerable lessening of several time-consuming chores? In the first place, servants were readily available and could carry coal and clean grates; there was the cost of installing any new system with its necessary appliances and so on; gas was considerably more expensive than solid fuels and electricity more expensive again. There was also the basic factor that the British enjoyed seeing flames flickering in an open fireplace and it was immaterial whether it was an efficient means of heating a room or not. So much was this the case that, even in 1920, one expert declared: 'The great majority of houses in this country are equipped for warming purposes with nothing but open fires for burning solid fuel.'[27]

CHAPTER THREE

Lighting the Home

Lighting is almost the most difficult subject of all to discuss. It requires an enormous leap of the imagination to understand just how little artificial light was available in the past compared with the plentiful supplies of today, when light is instantly accessible without any effort on the part of the housewife. The only exertion nowadays might involve hauling out the household ladder or standing on a chair to replace a light bulb or, even more occasionally, to dust down the light-fitting. Compare this to what her predecessors had to do before they achieved any light at all. Those unwilling or unable to purchase ready-made candles from a chandler or other merchant had to collect together the substances required to make them; they needed the equipment in which to make them as well as somewhere to store them until required; there was also the matter of providing the wherewithal to ignite them, something with which to trim the wick as it burnt and of supplying a holder of some sort in which to stand the candle in order to avoid being splashed by melting grease and to free the hands for other work. Even in those houses now 'restored' or 'put back how they might have been' the requirements of modern day health and safety regulations demand a far higher level of illumination than was ever present when the house was in full working order.

It could be argued that, during the earlier part of the period, when it came to lighting the most important item was the tinder box as it was the means generally used in the home to generate a new source of fire. For a damp climate such as ours the alternative, such as wood friction – the 'boy scout' method of rubbing two sticks together to generate heat and eventually fire – was not very reliable. The tinder box itself was a lidded container which could be of wood though was more often of some type of metal. Inside was stored a steel, a flint and a candle end or splinter of wood dipped in something combustible, together with the 'tinder', generally a rag, dried and charred in advance; housewives availed themselves of other materials such as the puffball fungus (also used at one time by beekeepers for smoking the bees before looking into a hive), old goose-down and so on. Striking the flint against the steel produced sparks which would drop on to the tinder in the opened container, thereby setting the charred rag smouldering, and from this a light could be obtained. That was the theory. In practice, however, damp tinder, cold hands, uncooperative flint or steel, all compounded by darkness, contrived to lengthen the process considerably.

James Boswell, biographer of Dr Samuel Johnson, left a graphic description of what could happen. He was writing late into the night, his fire had gone out and at 2 a.m. he accidentally extinguished his candle. In total darkness, he said, he crept downstairs to the kitchen to look for the tinder box: 'But this tinder box I could not see, nor knew where to find. I was now filled with gloomy ideas of the terrors of the night. I was also apprehensive that my landlord, who always kept a pair of loaded pistols by him, might fire at me as a thief. I went up to my room, sat quietly till I heard the watchman calling "Past three o'clock". I then called to him to knock on the door of the house where I lodged and got my candle relumed without danger.'[1]

Over the next two hundred years the housewife witnessed many changes in the process of generating fire although it is debatable how quickly such developments penetrated into the domestic arena. On the one hand the housewife would surely have welcomed anything that made life easier for herself and her servants; on the other, some of the 'new, improved' versions were more trouble than they were worth, as well as being positively dangerous in unskilled hands.

The tinder box itself was improved, with the steel and the flint being shaped and given a handle to ensure easier manipulation. A tinder pistol was developed which, imitating the action of the flintlock pistol, set off a tiny charge of gunpowder to ignite the flame that ignited the tinder in the barrel. Subsequently, the gunpowder was replaced by a mechanism operating a steel and flint to make the spark, and other developments followed thereafter.

Many experiments were carried out to try and find other, easier and more reliable means of obtaining fire. By the end of the eighteenth century these centred on the interaction of one chemical with another and, as some were highly combustible, devices of this nature were hazardous in the extreme. The more popular kits were introduced from France in about 1810 and were known as 'instantaneous light boxes' but other versions were produced, including the 'Promethean match' of 1828. By this date John Walker's 'friction lights' were already on sale in Stockton-on-Tees. He took short flat sticks of wood and dipped one end into a paste made from a mixture of chlorate of potash, sulphide of antimony, gum arabic and water. To achieve ignition the treated end was placed inside a fold of sandpaper and withdrawn smartly. A tin of 100 sold for a shilling, which would have represented a significant proportion of a working man's weekly wage at the time. As John Walker did not patent his invention others developed the idea further, one adding sulphur, another yellow phosphorus, a third camphor, or a new type of stem was devised for specific purposes, and they were sold under names such as the Lucifer, the Chlorate match, the Congreve or the Vesta. Containers for them were often of metal, to guard against unintentional ignition, and it was thanks to a Swede, Johan Lindstrom, who devised the first 'safety match' in 1855, that such untoward events were considerably curtailed.

Once the tinder box or something more up to date had been operated successfully what forms of illumination were available to the housewife? It has to be remembered that all but the most meagre forms of lighting were taxed from 1709 to 1831; the higher the quality, the higher the tax.[2] This even applied to homemade items and was instrumental in retarding the use of artificial lighting in the home. Because of this women were accustomed to doing certain domestic jobs outdoors, whenever practicable, such as spinning and laundrywork. It is also the reason why people made full use of daylight hours.

Artificial lighting came primarily from variations of the candle and the lamp and many dwellings continued to be lit in this way into the twentieth century, although other, somewhat localized, means of lighting also existed. In certain areas of Yorkshire, Scotland and Ulster quantities of resinous fir and oak wood were dug from the moors and when dried, split into smaller pieces and set alight, proved to be a good source of light as well as of heat. Osgood Mackenzie, recalling how the Highland 'black houses' were lit, wrote:' . . . a big heap of carefully prepared bog-fir splinters full of resin [was] all ready in a corner, and a small boy or girl did nothing else but keep these burning during the evening, so that the women could see to card and spin and the men to make their herring nets by hand'.[3] Celia Fiennes, as has already been noted, was impressed by 'channell coal' and observed that 'The poorer sort works by it and so it serves for heate and light', and it was certainly still being used this way in the mid-nineteenth century.[4]

These were relatively simple compared to the lengths to which the islanders of St Kilda went to obtain their lighting. They relied on the oil ejected from the beak of the fulmar, a sea bird that abounded in those parts; but first they had, somehow, to surprise or capture the birds and force them to vomit the oil into a container. Some of their practices were hair-raising in the extreme.

Lamps provided the simplest form of lighting, and went by different names in different regions – pan lamps or cressets, crassets in the Channel Islands, cruisies in Scotland and so on. The fuels for them were liquid, so a lamp consisted of a container and a wick to take the flame. The container could be of iron or earthernware, or even a large shell or hollowed stone, while the wick might be a peeled rush or a twist of linen rag. The fuel itself depended on local availability – fish, whale or shark oil, animal fats or vegetable oil. They tended to be somewhat malodorous in the burning, frequently dripped and the wicks needed constant attention.

Directions for making a simple lamp suitable for cottage folk were given by Esther Hewlett in 1827: 'Fill a common teacup with any kind of melted grease that is free from salt', she wrote and then described how to twist a small piece of paper so as to form a wick which was to be placed in the centre of the teacup once the fat had solidified. 'This lamp will burn ten hours, without any attention; and hence is very useful for night burning; but if wanted to work by, some grease must be occasionally supplied, so as to keep it to the top of the cup.' She says such a lamp is very easily prepared 'and is by many persons preferred to rush candles'.[5]

A candle was not dissimilar to a lamp, except that its wick was held inside a solidified fatty substance. This was either tallow or wax, the former being basically mutton fat while the latter was produced by honey bees. For outdoor work the candle was put into a lantern of brass or tin with numerous perforations or panels of flattened horn. A thinner version of a candle was a taper, while the thinnest version of all was the rushlight or the rush candle. This was often made and used by country folk but they were also to be found lighting servants' quarters and lesser bedrooms in inns and the houses of the gentry. Dr Johnson described them as 'A small blinking taper, made by stripping a rush, and dipping it in tallow.'[6] They avoided the tax payable on other forms of illumination and continued to be used well through the nineteenth century, as they involved minimal expenditure, except in time and patience. Their wicks, too, unlike the wicks of candles, needed little attention as the rushlight was held on a slant by the holder and the burnt wick dropped overboard by itself.

They were made in the following manner:

The proper species of rush for this purpose seems to be the *juncus conglomeratus* or common soft rush, which is to be found in most moist pastures, by the sides of streams, and under hedges. These rushes are in best condition in the height of summer; but may be gathered, so as to serve the purpose well, quite on to autumn. It would be needless to add that the largest and longest are best. Decayed labourers, women, and children, make it their business to procure and prepare them. As soon as they are cut they must be flung into water, and kept there; for otherwise they will dry and shrink, and the peel will not run. At first a person would find it no easy matter to divest a rush of its peel or rind, so as to leave one regular, narrow, even rib from top to bottom that may support the pith. . . . When these *junci* are thus far prepared, they must lie out on the grass to be bleached, and take the dew for some nights, and afterwards be dried in the sun.

After that, the rushes had to be dipped into hot fat or grease and, we are told: 'The careful wife of an industrious Hampshire labourer obtains all her fat for nothing; for she saves the scummings of her bacon-pot for this use.' This was common in other regions too. It took six pounds of grease to coat one pound of rushes and anyone with beeswax at their disposal was advised to mix a little in with the grease to improve the consistency. There might be as many as 1,600 rushes to the pound, each one measuring up to 28 inches in length, and each would burn for almost an hour with a good clear light while some burnt for even longer.[7]

Candles were made either by repeatedly dipping the wick, of twisted cotton or linen, into melted fat or beeswax until the required thickness was achieved, or by moulding them. For this latter method wicks were fastened centrally into elongated cone-shaped metal moulds and the melted grease was poured in; after it had cooled and solidified the candles could be withdrawn. Beeswax made a vastly superior product which burnt with a better light and attractive scent and, according to an eminent beekeeper, 'It maketh the most

One method of making candles was by dipping the wicks into a trough of melted wax or tallow and repeating the process until the required thickness had been reached. (By courtesy of City of York Museums Services)

excellent light, fit for the uses of the most excellent; for cleernesse, sweetnesse, neatnesse, to be preferred before all other'[8] but, equally, they were more expensive to make and carried a heavier tax.

Once the candles had been made, and housewives were advised that this was best done in colder weather, they had to be stored: 'They are the better for keeping eight or ten months, and will not injure for two years, if properly placed in the cool' said one manual,[9] as this continued the process of drying off and hardening the fats, thus making them more economical to use. For longer-term storage blanket kists or chests often had a built-in lidded compartment in which to place the candles, while for more immediate use candles were stored in containers of wood or tin hanging on the wall away from the depredations of rats or mice.

The housewife had not only to provide the sources of light but also to supply various accessories. What held the candle upright is a specialist subject in its own right. To some extent their holders are still familiar even now, or at least the more decorative pieces are.

Candles with reflector behind to increase the amount of light, Callendar House, Falkirk. (By courtesy of Falkirk Museums)

Candlesticks came in many forms and followed the fashionable shapes of the day. Those made of metals such as silver, pewter, brass or iron are frequently to be met with, as are those of china (in the widest sense of the word) and glass. Less familiar, perhaps, because they were discarded earlier, are those bedroom candlesticks with a handle and a cone-shaped extinguisher attached to it; also the sconces for holding candles against the wall or in front of a mirror. Some taper holders resembled small candlesticks while others provided a greater measure of support. Rushlights, though, had a specialized form of holder comprising a solid base of wood or metal which held a spike with a clip, so that the rushlight was held firmly yet was readily adjustable as it burnt.

Holder for rushlights. (By courtesy of the Museum of Welsh Life)

Another necessity was a pair of 'snuffers', which looked like scissors with a small box on one blade. Because the wick was not completely consumed by the flame it needed to be 'snuffed' (i.e. clipped) from time to time, otherwise it drooped over the edge of the candle and formed a channel for the melting wax. This was over and above the everyday problems associated with draughts from an opened door or too much laughter around the dinner table! One reference speaks of the 'complete epaulettes of wax-spots on our shoulders,' which befell the unwary when standing under a chandelier at a ball[10] and, judging from the way domestic manuals so readily gave advice on the removal of grease stains from clothing or from the furnishings, many candles must have dripped and guttered unchecked: *'To take Grease from papered Walls or Paper.* Apply dry hot flannel to the spot, then rub it over with hot spirit of turpentine. Repeat this till the grease is removed. If turpentine would injure the colours in the paper, lay several folds of blotting-paper on the spot, and apply a hot piece of iron over that, till the grease is absorbed by the blotting-paper.'[11] The development of the plaited cotton wick in the 1820s rendered the trimming of wicks unnecessary so that the verb 'to snuff' came to mean 'to extinguish' and the name was transferred to the object with which this was done – a small metal cone on the end of a handle which was held over the flame to extinguish it without it smouldering thereafter.

It seems strange to us that candle-ends should have any part to play in the domestic economy, let alone be seen as one of the 'perks' (i.e. perquisites) of a servant's job and, as such, form part of the wages. Menservants, where employed, were in charge of lighting in the public rooms and allowed whatever was left of the previous evening's candles.

For one servant in the opening years of the eighteenth century this perk proved the proverbial goldmine. He left his native Oxfordshire to search for work in London, took lodgings with a shopkeeper in St James's Market close to the site of what is now Piccadilly Circus, and became a footman in Queen Anne's household. Part of his job entailed the daily replenishing of the royal candlesticks and, as it was accepted practice that the candles were replaced whether they had been used or not, there was a plentiful supply to sell on to whoever wanted them. When the young man retired on his profits he joined forces with his landlord to set up a grocery shop in Jermyn Street. The connection with the Queen's household was kept up and where royalty placed their grocery orders the fashionable world followed suit. The partners also set up a livery stable to provide accommodation for the horses and carriages of those living nearby in houses without stabling of their own and to shelter the many dray horses involved in transporting goods into and out of London.

The business has flourished on the same site for almost three hundred years. Their names? The young man was Fortnum; his landlord was Mason.

Lesser mortals, such as the average scullion, had to make do with the grease taken off the candlesticks in their daily cleaning. Hannah Glasse, better known as the author of a famous cookery book than for her *Servant's Directory,* advised: 'The Advantage will be great both to your Mistress and self, if she allow you the Grease; . . . for certainly the Grease that comes off the Candlesticks . . . amounts to Money in the Year'. How this could be achieved was described at length. A pan kept for the purpose should be filled with water and metal candlesticks immersed in it once the water was boiling; they should then be taken out one at a time, dried and polished with an appropriate polish. China holders were only to be dipped in the hot water, while steel ones had the tallow melted off them. Once the cleaning water had cooled, the grease that set on the surface could be skimmed off and set aside. Every so often these residues were to be melted down, clarified and strained when they would be 'fit for the Tallow-chandler' although if further clarified, refined and kept well-covered it 'will keep twenty Years in a cold place, and will make as fine Puff-paste as Butter'.[12] This is no different from the thinking of some of the nineteenth-century Arctic expeditions that reputedly specified supplies of tallow candles so that in an emergency they could double as a source of food.

Even in the 1920s candle-ends formed part of the domestic economy, if no longer part of the servants' wages, and housewives were being advised how to make use of them: 'They form excellent fire-lighters' said one directory 'and when melted and mixed with turpentine may be employed as a floor polish. Again, home-made night lights have been manufactured from melted candle-ends into which a cotton wick is introduced; these articles, however, may be bought so cheaply, that the result achieved with the home-made variety hardly justifies the trouble involved.'[13]

An oil-burning lamp with clear glass globe and chimney, carved wooden pillar and base. It is 32 inches high overall.

The changes that took place in both the technology and the fuels used to light the home led to a gradual erosion of the housewife's responsibility in such matters, as she no longer needed to gather together or prepare the materials for herself.

New types of candle were introduced. In the 1830s the wax from the sperm whale's head was found to burn with a steadier light and was less liable to 'guttering'; in the 1850s it was stearine candles, from chemically purified animal or vegetable fats, but these in turn were superseded by paraffin candles, a by-product of the emerging petroleum industry.

Lamp fuels also changed, with the increasing use of colza oil derived from rape seed, whale oils and, by the 1860s, of kerosene or paraffin. The lamps themselves changed, too, from the simple container and ad hoc wicks to something altogether more efficient. The Argand table lamp was the creation of a Frenchman who had left France on account of the political situation and patented his invention in Britain in 1784. He devised the idea of an open circular wick, which enabled a greater amount of air to be drawn through as it burnt, thereby improving the quality of the light given off while the tall glass chimney, which was supposedly an accidental discovery, increased the flow of air from below. Thereafter lamps were developed with two or more burners fed from the same reservoir, along with hanging lamps with a ring-shaped reservoir which allowed light through from above and obliterated the shadow cast by the original form of reservoir.

These lamps, and their many successors, required constant care and daily cleaning if they were to burn well. Contemporary domestic manuals gave copious, detailed instructions on how this should be accomplished and these instructions were certainly being repeated into the 1920s.[14]

However, an alternative source of light was coming into use during the nineteenth century although its acceptance into the home was slow. Coal gas had been used to light various large buildings from 1792 onwards, while a section of London's Pall Mall was illuminated in 1807. In 1812, after several abortive attempts, the Gas Light & Coke Co. was the first company set up to provide gas lighting to selected areas of London, and after ten years some 215 miles of the city's streets were being lit by gas. Edinburgh had its Gas Light Company in 1817 and over fifty towns had gas supplies within the next six years.

By 1840 gas lighting was moving indoors and being used in the hallways and living rooms of the well to do and fashions for these fittings were apt to follow the styles of the day for other lighting devices. Just as candles burnt in 'chandeliers' so gas lights burnt in 'gasoliers' and some magnificent examples were supplied to the Prince Regent's Pavilion in Brighton. Later, following the same reasoning, there were 'electroliers'.

It was the 1870s before gas lighting in the home became widespread. In 1889 the introduction of the 'penny-in-the-slot' meter made lighting by gas a more affordable proposition in poorer homes. Over the years numerous improvements were made to the

Gas lighting within the home became increasingly common after 1840. The heat given off was considerable but, in poorer homes, this was seen as a bonus. (Ironbridge Gorge Museum Trust)

burners, making them both more efficient and cheaper to run. In 1887 Carl von Welsbach invented the incandescent gas mantle that sat over the gas jet, which greatly increased the amount of light given out; it took him rather longer to develop the inverted mantle which sat beneath the flame, doubled the amount of light and removed the shadow thrown by the gas pipe and the cock.

By this time gas lighting was being overtaken by another form of lighting that was clean, noiseless, efficient and safe – electricity. As it became more popular, gas companies switched to promoting themselves as suppliers of heaters and cookers.

Carbon arc lamps had been around since the 1860s but they were unsuited to home use. Numerous attempts had been made to provide something more manageable but without much success until, in 1878, both Joseph Swan in England and Thomas Edison in the USA independently produced a successful electric incandescent filament lamp. The two agreed to set aside differences as to who had the prior claim to be called 'the inventor' and joined forces to become The Edison and Swan United Electric Company. In the meantime Joseph Swan's friend, Sir William Armstrong, installed the new style of lighting in Cragside, Northumberland in December 1880, which has strong claims to be the first house in the world to be lit in this way, although Hatfield House in Hertfordshire was only marginally behind.

Howls of protest greeted the new form of lighting: 'The horrified protests of ballroom dames and damsels . . . the wild complaints that no one who was not made up as for the stage could possibly show herself in the glare of such a cruel searchlight without alienating the affections of every man who loved her; the obstinate refusal of many of London's great ones to so much as recognise the existence of electric light, which they condemned as a vulgar, low, blatant commercial form of illumination and one which nothing would ever induce them to allow in *their* houses.' For them 'the good old candles . . . and the dear old colza-oil lamps' were quite sufficient and far preferable but, of course, they did not have the daily chores connected with them.[15]

The filament lamp was not only brighter but also safer than a light burning with a naked flame. Equally, it was more costly and so did not become successful and popular overnight. On this subject the housewife was told in 1920: 'Gas from coal is still the most common form of artificial light, though it is prophesied that electricity is the illuminant of the future and, indeed, it is even now superseding all other lighting mediums.' However, it was not always trouble free, as the authors pointed out: 'Should an accident occur or the light fail, the services of a qualified electrician must be solicited, since amateurs not infrequently add to the trouble, when endeavouring to remedy it.'[16]

CHAPTER FOUR

Water and Drainage

T here can be few visitors to a medieval castle who have not, at some time or another, succumbed to the temptation of throwing a pebble into the well to check the depth, and Celia Fiennes is not one of their number. Describing Carisbrooke Castle on the Isle of Wight with its deep well, she divulged: 'A stone thrown down sounds a long tyme ere you hear it splash into yᵉ water.'[1] Such wells tend to be prominently situated within a castle's precinct, have a low stone wall around them and, nowadays, a heavy cast-iron grating across the top for safety reasons. It takes a great deal of imagination to realize that this hole in the ground was the main source of water for all the needs of the castle's inhabitants, along with their horses, livestock and so on, although in some instances additional amounts might be gained by channelling rainwater from the roof into a cistern.

But not everyone had a well on their doorstep, nor a sufficiently substantial roof-span. Many households had to find their water as and where they could, from whatever source was available, be it stream, pond, spring or river – regardless of who or what might also be using the same source and for what purpose.[2]

Although the following account of housewives fetching water in the Oxfordshire hamlet of 'Lark Rise' relates to the 1880s, it must have been all too familiar to many women across the centuries:

> Only three out of the thirty cottages had their own water supply. The less fortunate tenants obtained their water from a well on a vacant plot on the outskirts of the hamlet, from which the cottage had disappeared. There was no public well or pump. They just had to get their water where and how they could; the landlords did not undertake to supply water.

The well at Caerphilly Castle
with the East Inner Gatehouse
behind it.

Against the wall of every well-kept cottage stood a tarred or
green-painted water butt to catch and store the rain water from
the roof. This saved many journeys to the well with buckets, as it
could be used for cleaning and washing clothes and for watering
small, precious things in the garden. . . .When the water butts
failed, the women went to the well in all weathers, drawing up
the buckets with a windlass and carting them home suspended
from their shoulders by a yoke.[3]

In dry summers when the hamlet wells failed, the women had to
walk half a mile to the pump at a farm.

This situation was far from unique. The Hampshire parish of Selbourne had two sources of water, one of which frequently failed although the inhabitants were fortunate that the other was reliable even in drought conditions.[4] In neighbouring Wiltshire a number of downland villages had copious supplies once the autumn and winter rains had fallen but, come the spring, the underground reservoirs dried up and the women had to return to the laborious work of drawing water from the well.[5] During much the same period, it was recalled of a Surrey village: 'Then, too, many cottages had not so much as a sink where work with water could be done; many had no water save in wet weather; there was not one cottage in which it could be drawn from a tap, but it all had to be drawn from a well or a tank. . . . In times of drought water had often to be carried long distances in pails, and it may be imagined how the housework would go in such circumstances.'[6]

Collecting water from a stream. From the 1905 edition of M.R. Mitford's *Our Village*, illustrated by H. Thomson.

How water was carried home and what the container was called varied according to locality. Not everyone used a yoke. In Wales the women balanced a pitcher of water upon their heads, carried a child or a loaf in their wrapper* and knitted as they walked along.[7] The staved wooden vessels balanced this way in parts of Scotland and the north of England were called 'skeels'; they narrowed towards the top and had one longer stave to act as the handle. Water was also taken home in a hand-held 'stoup', which was a wooden bucket or pail banded with iron and again narrowing at the top; according to one authority they often came in pairs and were a gift from the groomsman to the bride. Women carrying more than one stoup might make use of a 'girr', which resembled a wooden hoop; she walked inside it with the stoups attached to it one on either side to balance the load and prevent it splashing.[8] In some areas two girls might share the load of a much larger tub, hanging from a pole carried between them on their shoulders.

It takes a real effort to imagine just how burdensome and time-consuming a task the fetching and carrying of water for the household's everyday needs could be and what a handicap the lack of water was to the conscientious housewife striving to fulfil her domestic duties. Each Imperial gallon of water weighs 10 lbs.[9] So, if it can be estimated that a woman carried 2 gallons in each hand, to which must be added the weight of the two wooden buckets, banded in iron, and that the source of water was however many yards or metres distant, it does not take much of a mathematician

* a long piece of woollen cloth wrapped around the waist

A girl carries two stoups of water with the aid of a girr which prevents splashing. From J. Colston, *Edinburgh & District Water Supply*, 1890. (Trustees of the National Library of Scotland)

to calculate the loads carried by the housewife and the exertion involved in pursuit of her chores. A comparison of the burden can be made, purely for reference, with the 1996 international airline baggage allowance of 44 lbs or 22 kilos.

What was the water needed for? The preparation of foods, cooking, scouring of dishes and utensils, scrubbing of floors; then, depending on the household, maybe for the brewing of beer and other homemade drinks or for dyeing home-spun wools; there was also washing, either of a personal nature or of the family's clothes and the household linens. However, for some chores demanding copious amounts of water it was easier to take the job to the water rather than the other way about, hence communal places for laundering set up beside a river or other source of water.

It is salutary to consider that some medieval dwellings were better equipped in matters relating to the provision of water and drainage than were to be seen again until the late eighteenth or early nineteenth century. It has to be said that, even though the potential existed, relatively few benefited from such facilities.

Religious establishments, such as those of the Cistercians, were carefully located close to a good supply of running water which was usually brought from a source at a higher level and channelled into the site via a conduit made of stone or wood. It generally supplied water to several points, such as the kitchens, the bakehouse and brewhouse, and the infirmary, and it was also piped to the *lavatorium*, the trough or basin in which the monks washed their hands prior to mealtimes. The communal life meant that many monks were doing the same thing at the same time, so supplies of water needed to be sufficient for the numbers involved. Equally, a drainage system was provided to remove the water after use, while the *rere-dorter* or *necessarium*, with one or more rows of seats, divided by partitions, was generally situated over the main drain through which a constant flow of water ran.

The domestic form of the *necessarium* was the garde-robe and many are still evident in medieval buildings. They took the form of small rooms built into the thickness of the walls which nearly always had a small window, an alcove for a candle and a pierced wooden seat set over a vertical chute. This chute could either drop down to ground level within the walls or merely be corbelled out for a short distance and stop at a considerable height above the ground; some were cleaned by means of rainwater collected from the roof. The garde-robe might discharge into a midden, a moat, on to the sea shore or merely empty itself at the foot of the castle walls. Some historians consider that this was the underlying reason for the peripatetic nature of medieval households. Once the smells became overpowering the household packed up its belongings and moved on

A pump with stone trough beneath. (The Weald & Downland Open Air Museum, Singleton)

to the next residence. The alternative to the built-in plumbing of the garde-robe was the 'close-stool', which was basically a seat over a container 'enclosed' within a box or stool; the container had to be taken out and the contents emptied into a midden or dumped out in the street, a system that was independent of any supply of water whatsoever.

Such residences might also be supplied with gravity-fed water from nearby sources but this was not possible for many strongholds, built on hill tops for defensive purposes, which were dependent on wells or any rainwater that could be collected.

Raising water from any depth was laborious but mechanical assistance was generally available, although it is unlikely that the average housewife concerned herself unduly with the technology underlying her own operation. Wells, whether public or private, could be worked with the aid of a winch or windlass or with manually operated pumps. Larger establishments could make use of similar mechanisms to draw up water which would then be stored in a roof-top cistern or in a specially built water tower and subsequently distributed to various points by means of conduits. The donkey wheel was another possibility, operating on the treadmill system, and Celia Fiennes' well at Carisbrooke was one such: 'They draw up ye bucket by a great Wheele in wch they put a horse or ass,' she observed.[10] Even more ambitious was the shifting of large amounts of water by techniques developed for the draining of mines where wheels could raise water 100 feet. Supplies from the Thames were being pumped to parts of the City by these means from 1581 and the system was extended in the 1650s. In 1675 a celebrated experiment took place at Windsor Castle when water, dyed red with a barrel of wine, was pumped from the Thames not only to the top of the castle but for a further 60 feet into the air, a total height of some 250 feet, at the rate of 60 barrels an hour. Some years later John Evelyn was at Windsor and noted various innovations since his previous visit, among which, he said: '. . . nor less observable and famous is the throwing so huge a quantity of excellent water to the enormous height of the Castle, for the use of the whole house, by an extraordinary invention of Sir Samuel Morland'.[11]

The years that followed witnessed many developments in the way in which water was moved from one place to another but whether this was motivated primarily by the necessity of supplying a sufficiency of water for people's everyday wants or by the prevailing fashions in horticulture, which demanded elaborate water works, remains debatable. Near Romsey, the ever-observant Celia Fiennes noted: 'There is a water house that by a Wheele Casts up the Water out of ye River just by, and fills ye pipes to Serve all ye house and to fill ye bason designed in the middle of the Garden wth a Spout in the middle.'[12] She was intrigued by water and the way it could be moved around at will and noted numerous examples as she travelled around the country at the end of the seventeenth century.

It was not long before the first effective steam-powered pumps were in operation and supplying unimaginable quantities of water not only to the houses of the aristocracy but to their gardens and their stables too. In spite of such an exciting advance relatively few private households installed such costly systems. For the well to do, labour was cheap and readily available while the majority of the population had never known any other state of affairs and lacked both the wherewithal and expertise to make any changes. Many country estates continued in the old style, with cisterns being gravity-fed from a nearby source.

Although not found universally in private houses, up-to-date technology might be brought into use to supply urban areas. As villages grew into towns and towns grew into cities, with some developing almost overnight, many outpaced their water supplies and other methods had to be employed to augment traditional sources.

If the hamlet of 'Lark Rise' typified the situation of the rural housewife then a city such as London or Edinburgh was representative of the town dweller, though many variations for better or worse coexisted throughout Britain. London's supplies were a veritable patchwork of means and methods – mostly inadequate. There were wells, conduits to bring in water from a distance, water carriers and water carts; from 1582 onwards waterwheels utilized the flow of water under London Bridge to pump water into the City while further west a horse-powered 'engine' supplied the area around Cheapside and St Paul's Cathedral. Over the years there were assorted water companies, some funded by the City, others a matter of private speculation, with insufficiently demarcated boundaries which caused endless hassle, recriminations, flouting of regulations and uncoordinated pipe-laying and repairs.

Likewise, London's drainage was deemed to be primitive, haphazard and a chronic danger to health with the rivers acting as open sewers until well into the nineteenth century. Edinburgh was no better and many a visitor commented on the city's stench due to the primitive method of sewage disposal:

Edinburgh is certainly a fine City,' said one who was there in the 1740s, 'and I believe can boast of the highest Houses in Europe; notwithstanding it has its Faults, for the City being very close built, and the Want of common Shores [i.e. drains] to carry off, occasions the Town to be very nasty, and about Seven o'Clock in the Morning it stinks intollerably, before the Excrements are swept away from the Doors, which they throw out of the Windows in the Night; for after Ten o'Clock, it is Fortune favours you, if a Chamber Pot with Excrements, &c. is not thrown on your Head; if you are walking in the Streets, it is then diverting to Strangers, to hear all Passers by cry out with a loud Voice, sufficient to reach the Tops of the Houses . . . hoad yare Hand i.e. Hold your Hand, and means do not throw till I am past . . .[13]

When water was piped into houses it eradicated the trade of the water carrier. From A.H. Dunlop, *Anent Old Edinburgh*, 1890.

Water supplies in Edinburgh's Old Town were even more precarious than those in London owing to its position on a high ridge surrounded by flat ground and supplies coming from the Nor' Loch at its foot and the South Loch nearby* were polluted by sewage, butcher's offal from the slaughter houses and other waste products. However, the numerous breweries had no problem tapping into a prolific underground source and for centuries the city was famous for the quality of its ales.[14] The citizens obtained their water from draw wells, with a chain and bucket, though some pumps did exist as they were 'repaired' in 1631. Proposals for improving the water supply had already been made by that date but it was over forty years before a scheme was implemented to bring in supplies from 3½ miles away. The water was fed into a sizeable cistern near the Castle, from whence it was gravity-fed through pipes of lead, later of elm wood and, later again, of iron, to various cisterns or wells through the town. Supplies were intermittent and queues tended to collect, waiting their turn; a noisy, quarrelsome crowd who, while they waited, filled the time 'with as much scandal as could be talked, or with as much inspiration as the use of tobacco or snuff could instill into them,'[15] while quarrels frequently broke out between the servant girls and the 'caddies' who were the professional water carriers.

'They were a very curious tribe consisting of both men and women,' wrote Lord Cockburn of these caddies, 'but the former were perhaps the more numerous. Their business was to carry water into houses; and therefore their days were passed in climbing up lofty stairs, in order to get into flats. The water was borne in little casks, . . . [which] when filled, were slung upon

---

* now, respectively, Princes Street Gardens and The Meadows

their backs, suspended by a leather strap, which was held in front by the hand. . . . Their backs . . . were protected by thick layers of hard black leather, on which the barrels lay; and the leather had a slight curl up at its lower edge, which, acting as a lip, threw the droppings, by which they could always be tracked, off to the sides. . . . They very seldom required to be called; for every house had its favourite "Water Caddie" who knew the habits and wants of the family, and the capacity of the single cistern, which he kept always replenishing at his own discretion, at the fee . . . of a penny for each barrel.'[16]

Not until supplies of water were regular and plentiful did householders consider it worthwhile to pay for it to be piped into their houses but, once that happened, the occupation of water caddie ceased to exist within a matter of years.

By the time Lord Cockburn was writing (*c.* 1821–30) there was growing concern about the state of the poor; the connection between health and living conditions and between health and unadulterated foods was being made; the desirability of a sufficiency of clean water for everybody with the parallel necessity for efficient sewage removal and rubbish collection was being recognized; and there was a fear of epidemic diseases such as cholera and tuberculosis. Much the same was happening throughout the country and it was due to the campaigning vigour of the great 'sanitary reformers' that much-needed legislation was forced through against stiff opposition. Improvements to the water supplies, seen as integral to the scheme, which did so much to lighten the domestic workload for the housewife, actually came about incidentally, in the interests of what is now termed public health.

Once a regular supply of water was brought into a house enormous changes occurred in women's lives. Their lives became very much easier and domestic chores simpler and easier to plan, although such changes did not happen overnight. There was another part to the story as, once water was piped into a house, there was a need for an equivalent method of taking used water away. Although wealthier households might be supplied with drains leading into the town's sewers there were many problems initially, owing to such causes as faulty building techniques, inadequate ventilation and a lack of understanding of what could or should not be put down a drain. In the meantime, the poorer areas had to wait longer for their drains to be installed and faced even greater problems, especially where several households shared one facility.

The earth or ash closet, privy or 'netty' was frequently found as the alternative to the water closet, especially in areas without main drains, and they were very much a fact of life throughout the 1920s and '30s. The larger ones might have several holes and there was generally a smaller hole for the children to use.

The invention of the water closet with a mechanism using water as a cleansing agent is generally attributed to Sir John Harington, godson of Queen Elizabeth I, and some were certainly in use by the time Celia Fiennes was travelling the country. In the castle yard at Windsor 'is a Little box* the queen has bought of Lord Godolphin . . .', and she noted while walking through the royal apartments: 'W^th^in the dressing roome is a Closet on one hand, the other side is a Closet y^t^ leads to a little place wth a seate of Easement of Marble wth sluces of water to wash all down'. This was used by Prince George of Denmark and a comparable arrangement was provided for the Queen's apartments on the floor above.[17] However, until Joseph Bramah's improvements to the valve mechanism, patented in 1778, such facilities were not widely used. The alternative was the earth (or ash) closet in a small building in a discreet corner of the garden, shrouded by shrubs, or across the back yard if there was no garden. Somewhat resembling the medieval garde-robe with a little window and a ledge on which to set a candle, there was generally more than one hole, with a smaller sized one for children. If drainage was laid on it would lead straight into a nearby midden; otherwise the container would need to be emptied. These earth closets were often

* i.e. a comparatively small house

retained for the use of the servants after water closets had been installed in the house, but many were still being used in the 1920s and '30s in dwellings lacking a supply of piped water.[18]

Once there was a sufficiency of water to run a water closet, or two, there was sufficient to make it worthwhile installing a formal bathroom with plumbed-in bath, shower and wash-hand basin. In time the bathroom came to replace the bedroom washstand with its matching basin, ewer, soap and sponge dishes, along with the comforts of a hip bath taken in front of the open fire, a system totally dependent on someone's physical labour.

Statistics show that when a supply of water was provided, people certainly knew how to make use of it: 'By 1878 it was 15 gallons per head per day in Norwich and Liverpool, 18 in Sheffield, 25 in Manchester, 26 in London, 34 in Edinburgh and 50 in Glasgow.' The differences in amounts were accounted for by such diverse reasons as leakage from the supply pipes, whether trade usage was included or not and the fact that water closets in Glasgow were more numerous in proportion to the population than in most other towns.[19] Quantities have increased considerably since that date; Edinburgh, for example, had almost doubled its level of consumption by 1973. Translated into quantities carried in 2-gallon buckets for a family consisting of husband, wife and several children, it soon becomes apparent how difficult it was for poorer folk to live up to the standards expected by the authors of the domestic manuals.

Generally speaking, the housewife no longer has to concern herself unduly with the provision of water unless in exceptional circumstances. The census of 1951 was the first to include questions regarding water and sanitation and it was estimated that by that time water was being piped into 80 per cent of private households in Britain. Water has been taken out of the sphere of domestic concern, in the same way that heating and lighting are now largely the responsibility of professionals outside the home.

CHAPTER FIVE

The Workforce

Today's ideas regarding servants are governed by nineteenth-century experiences as well as by the residual vestiges of domestic service that survived two world wars with their ensuing social and economic upheavals. However, this ignores the radical changes which occurred before the Victorian era, when the nature of servants, the work they carried out and how they were perceived were continuously evolving, in a linked chain of cause and effect. Such concepts and attitudes reflected the changes in society itself as surely as the houses the servants worked in, the furniture they polished and the foods they prepared.

Since domestic service is thought of today in purely Victorian terms, the oft-quoted Mrs Beeton serves as a convenient starting point. Her weighty tome first appeared in 1861, the year of Prince Albert's death, and although she is principally regarded as the compiler of a cookery book she has much to say on the subject of servants, the duties of the housewife and the day-to-day running of the home. Indeed, the book's title is not 'Mrs Beeton', as it is almost universally called, but *The Book of Household Management*. The imagery of its opening page, which compares the mistress of the household to an army commander, evokes the scene; the housewife held overall responsibility within the household and supervised every aspect of domestic management. Over two hundred years before the 'inward & outward Vertues which ought to be in a compleate Woman' had been spelt out in detail.[1] So demanding was the job and so multi-faceted the activities that it was illogical to expect one woman to achieve it all single handed. There would not have been sufficient hours in the day; in addition, many housewives were also mothers, contending with numerous pregnancies and the aftermath of childbirth, so from time to time they must have been physically unable to carry out their domestic duties, quite apart from the times

	When not found in Livery.	When found in Livery.
The House Steward	From £40 to £80	—
The Valet	„ 25 to 50	From £20 to £30
The Butler	„ 25 to 50	—
The Cook	„ 20 to 40	—
The Gardener	„ 20 to 40	—
The Footman	„ 20 to 40	„ 15 to 25
The Under Butler	„ 15 to 30	„ 15 to 25
The Coachman	—	„ 20 to 35
The Groom	„ 15 to 30	„ 12 to 20
The Under Footman	—	„ 12 to 20
The Page or Footboy	„ 8 to 18	„ 6 to 14
The Stableboy	„ 6 to 12	—

	When no extra allowance is made for Tea, Sugar, and Beer.	When an extra allowance is made for Tea, Sugar, and Beer.
The Housekeeper	From £20 to £45	From £18 to £40
The Lady's-maid	„ 12 to 25	„ 10 to 20
The Head Nurse	„ 15 to 30	„ 13 to 26
The Cook	„ 14 to 30	„ 12 to 26
The Upper Housemaid	„ 12 to 20	„ 10 to 17
The Upper Laundry-maid	„ 12 to 18	„ 10 to 15
The Maid-of-all-work	„ 9 to 14	„ 7½ to 11
The Under Housemaid	„ 8 to 12	„ 6½ to 10
The Still-room Maid	„ 9 to 14	„ 8 to 12
The Nursemaid	„ 8 to 12	„ 5 to 10
The Under Laundry-maid	„ 9 to 14	„ 8 to 12
The Kitchen-maid	„ 9 to 14	„ 8 to 12
The Scullery-maid	„ 5 to 9	„ 4 to 8

These quotations of wages are those usually given in or near the metropolis; but, of course, there are many circumstances connected with locality, and also having reference to the long service on the one hand, or the inexperience on the other, of domestics, which may render the wages still higher or lower than those named above. All the domestics mentioned in the above table would enter into the establishment of a wealthy nobleman. The number of servants, of course, would become smaller in proportion to the lesser size of the establishment; and we may here enumerate a scale of servants suited to various incomes, commencing with—

About £1,000 a year—A cook, upper housemaid, nursemaid, under housemaid, and a man servant.

About £750 a year—A cook, housemaid, nursemaid, and footboy.

About £500 a year—A cook, housemaid, and nursemaid.

About £300 a year—A maid-of-all-work and nursemaid.

About £200 or £150 a year—A maid-of-all-work (and girl occasionally).

Guidelines as to servants and their wages, as suggested by Mrs Beeton in *The Book of Household Management* [n.d. but 140th thousand].

when they were incapacitated by ill-health. Extra help in the home was seen as the norm, but the amount of help and the calibre of that help depended on the money available.

Mrs Beeton provided guidelines and several theoretical incomes are given, the lowest being from £150 to £200 per year. On such a sum 'a maid-of-all-work (and girl occasionally)' might be kept.[2] The list ascends through the different levels to £1,000 per year, sufficient for the employment of four female servants and one male – a cook, upper housemaid, nursemaid, under housemaid and a manservant. Above that income, employment levels are not specified although approximate wages are given for the full complement of domestic servants that 'would enter into the establishment of a wealthy nobleman'.

Almost forty years earlier Samuel and Sarah Adams' 'Fifty years Servants in different Families'[3] had produced similar guidelines but of a wider range, along with much moralistic advice to both mistress and servant. The starting point for an employer's income was then £100 per year, 'or guineas', on which a 'Widow or other unmarried Lady may keep a Young Maid Servant, at a low salary; say from 5 to 10 Guineas a year', whereas with an income between '£150–180 a Gentleman and Lady without Children, may afford to keep a better Servant-Maid, at about 10 to 12 Guineas'.[4] Arrangements on these smaller sums are subtly depicted in the novel *Cranford*. Before the collapse of The Town & Country Bank lost Miss Matty £149 13s 4d of her yearly income and left her with a meagre £13, she employed the faithful Martha, described as a servant-of-all-work, whereas old Mrs Forrester whose income 'did not nearly amount to £100' was helped by a charity-school maiden.[5]

The Adams' outline increasing levels of income until they come to the employment of a full panoply of eleven female and thirteen menservants, which they considered desirable, or necessary, on an annual income of £4–5,000: 'A Housekeeper, Cook, Lady's-Maid, Nurse, two House-Maids, Laundry-Maid, Still-Room Maid, Nursery-Maid, Kitchen-Maid and Scullion, with Butler, Valet, House-Steward, Coachman, two Grooms, one Assistant Ditto, two Footmen, three Gardeners, and a Labourer.'[6] The list contains a mixture of what were termed personal servants and domestic servants. The former category included the lady's-maid, the nurse and the valet, who were generally appointed personally by the master or mistress of the household, whereas the others might be hired or fired by the steward or the housekeeper, depending on which department they came into.

The domestic hierarchy could be likened to a series of interlocking triangles, the number and size relating to the household's income, with each triangle being broad at the base and narrow at the apex. Heading each would be a servant with responsibility and supervisory powers over the lesser servants, but one would have over-all responsibility. There must always have been a certain amount of flexibility as to the precise number and style of servants employed. A household without children would not need a nanny, nursery maids, governess or a nursery footman to carry food and fuel up to the childrens' quarters; a household without carriage or horses would need neither coachman nor groom.

Jane Jeffreys, laundrymaid at Kinnaird Castle, near Brechin, Angus in 1898. In the foreground is the laundry stove for heating irons; behind it lies a pile of wood. (Copyright: Royal Commission on the Ancient & Historical Monuments of Scotland)

The female ranking was quite straightforward, both in the nineteenth century and earlier. At its apex was a housekeeper who acted as a substitute housewife. She had first appeared on the scene as someone who cared for a bachelor or tended the sick and the job had gradually increased in importance as the notion developed that managing a household was somehow demeaning. She supervised the other female domestics and, if the most senior servant in a household, would also be responsible for a manservant where present, pay the domestic accounts and employ staff; she generally stayed in one house, rarely moving around with the family. Part of her work was carried out in the still-room, preparing jams, pickles and preserves as well as items required for dessert, and in this she would be assisted by a still-room maid or two.

To clean the rooms there were housemaids, who came in various designations: 'first', 'second', 'third', even 'fourth' and 'fifth', each with well-defined tasks, in the most substantial houses; 'upper' or 'under' in more modest homes; 'maid-of-all-work' at the bottom of the scale. Previously they were 'chambermaids'. On a slightly different footing, because they worked outside the house, were laundrymaids, with similar rankings, and the dairymaid who supplied the house with milk, cream, buttermilk, wheys and syllabubs. She also made butter and cheeses, both for immediate use and for winter keeping, and sometimes baked the family's bread as well as making ready the poultry for the kitchen.[7] Over much of the country it was her duty to milk the cows, whose care was in the

Mrs Green, cook at Kinnaird Castle, near Brechin, Angus in 1898. Such a large establishment would surely have employed more than one member of staff in the kitchen. (Copyright: Royal Commission on the Ancient & Historical Monuments of Scotland)

hands of a cowman, but a Swedish visitor was amazed at what he saw outside London: 'I confess that I at first rubbed my eyes several times to make them clear, because I could not believe I saw aright.' Just what had he seen? 'The farmers' houses full of young women, while the men, . . . went out both morning and evening to where the cattle were, milk-pail in hand, sat down to milk, and afterwards carried the milk home'.[8]

Cook reigned in the kitchen, assisted by one or more kitchen maids, while the scullery maid did the most menial tasks. Because male cooks were more prestigious than women and considerably more costly to employ, they were not often found in private households. In 1825 it was estimated that they were kept only in a maximum of 400 wealthy households and in about 40 or 50 London hotels.[9] The grandest households might still employ a clerk to the kitchen, who supervised all deliveries to the kitchen and recorded when and how they were used thereafter. This individual would be superior to the cook. There might also be a baker, to produce bread and rolls of differing grades, a pastrycook or confectioner, and a slaughterer, to deal with home-reared livestock.

The third domestic department comprised the menservants. By Mrs Beeton's day the senior position was that of the butler, who was taking over the position formerly held by the house steward. Originally, the butler had been a rather lowly individual in charge of the *bouteilles* which were kept in a *bouteillerie* – hence buttery – but the job had expanded, absorbing the duties of other individuals, until the Victorian version held a most responsible position. Not only did he supervise the menservants' work, direct operations in the dining room, see to the cellar and keep the silverware polished as well as secure, but he also employed staff and payed domestic accounts. His position was similar to that of the housekeeper's, but took precedence over her's where both were employed.

Footmen assisted the butler in many of his duties but had others as well. Whereas housemaids were expected to be invisible while doing their work, footmen were there to be highly visible and, in order to reflect the household's prestige and position in society, wore livery both indoors and while on the family's business out of doors. Theirs was another job that had risen in status, as they had started by being a type of groom, running alongside a coach to help it out of the mire when it went off the road. When household economies became necessary they were brought indoors, so to speak, to replace the more highly paid domestic 'yeomen', who had previously waited at table and done similar jobs. A hall porter, steward's room boy and one or two odd-job men might also be added to the list.

Outdoors, the stable staff were often regarded as part of the domestic hierarchy, because of their contacts with the household. The most senior was generally the coachman, although sometimes it might be the stud groom, with postilions, grooms, stable helpers, huntsmen, kennelmen and so on down the line. Gardeners, on the other hand, were generally counted as outdoor or estate workers, in spite of being the means by which the house was provided with a suitable setting and kept supplied with fruit, flowers and vegetables.

The domestic accounts of the 2nd Earl of Hopetoun (d. 1781) reveal that, in organizing his staff along these lines, he was ahead of his time and it was noted by his contemporaries: 'The most striking feature in the conduct of this great man, was the admirable order established in his domestic affairs, his household being so well regulated, that although hardly any nobleman in *Britain* lived in greater state, or kept a more numerous retinue, nothing could ever be wasted or misapplied.'[10]

Servants' wages appear miniscule, even when allowance is made for the changing value of money. Wages were only part of the costs to the employer. As most servants 'lived in' there were the expenses of feeding and housing them; there was a daily ration of beer and, later on, a similar arrangement for tea and sugar or for money in lieu; articles of clothing were provided for certain jobs, such as aprons for a cook or livery for footmen and coachman; 'washing found' meant that the servant's laundry was included in the household wash; and then there was on-the-job training, whether by the mistress or fellow servants passing on their knowledge. Over and above such elements were certain recognized 'perquisites' that ultimately came from the pocket of the employers and were a cause of real concern, as it was felt many servants took advantage of the system. Some of the better known involved the tips, or 'vails' as they were called, extracted from any visitor who dined or stayed in the house, and the entitlement of the cook to surplus dripping or used tea leaves, the lady's maid to cast-off clothing, while the butler was allowed the old bottles and playing cards. There were many others.[11]

The servant hierarchy mimicked that of the world outside, with any status being zealously maintained. Within the household, a servant's ranking was differentiated by factors such as work, clothing, wages, the food provided and the place in which it was eaten, and the potential for perks or other largess. Visiting servants were accorded the courtesy of their employer's rank, with the footmen of a duke having greater prestige than those of a viscount. In the same way an employer's social standing reflected on to his servants – until it came to the lowly scullery maid: 'As for the honour it matters little whether it be with a duke or an earl'.[12]

How much did the housewife have to do with all this? 'After breakfast is over,' Mrs Beeton advises, 'it will be well for the mistress to make a round of the kitchen and other offices, to see that all are in order, and that the morning's work has been properly performed by the various domestics. The orders for the day should then be given, and any questions which the domestics desire to ask, respecting their several departments, should be answered, and any special articles they may require, handed to them from the store closet.' In small print beneath is the rider: 'In those establishments where there is a housekeeper, it will not be so necessary for the mistress, personally, to perform the above-named duties.'[13] Possibly not; but it was common for the two to have a daily meeting, if only for the housewife to give instructions for the day's events, such as the number of visitors expected and to approve the menus sent up from the kitchens. Domestic accounts were presented each week for checking. This was in marked contrast to the housewife of an earlier age who, it was said, having ordered the day's duties in the morning and instructed her numerous daughters in a variety of arts, elegant and domestic, would go round her whole domain 'from hop garth to hen yard, from linen closet to lardour' prying, tasting and admonishing until the family and the servants were summoned to dine 'at xi of ye clocke'.[14]

MEMORADUMS AND DERECTIONS to Servants and ruels layd down by my Mother both fer their diet and work. Copyd and colected together 1752, made by her Decr. 1743, and the derections given to the severl Servants.

TO THE BUTLER

1. You must rise airly in the morning which will make your whole business and houshold accounts easie.

2. Two bells are to be rung fer every meal; for break- At the stated fast half an hour after 8 and at 9; for diner half an hour hours. after 1 and at 2; for super half an hour after 8 and at 9. At the first bell for super lay the bible and cushions for prayers.

3. Have bread toasted, butterd tost or whatever is orderd for breakfast all set ready by the second bell.

4. Consider your business and have a little forethought that you may never be in a hurry or have anything to seek, to which nothing will contribut more than having a fixt and regular places for seting every thing in your custody in order, and never fail seting every thing in its own place, which will prevent much trouble and con-fution, and soon make every thing easie, when you know where to go derectly for what you want.

5. See that the back doors of the Porch be shut as soon as the last bell rings for diner and super. *N.B.*

6. That all the servants that are to wate at table be ready *in the room before we come.*

7. That you may never have occation to run out of the room for what is wanted have always at the sideboard what follows or any thing ells you can foresee there can be occation for

Bread	Water	peper	vinigar
Ail	wines	mustard	shalot
smal Beer	sugar	oyle	sallad

Instructions to the butler, drawn up in 1743. From *The Household Book of Lady Grisell Baillie*, R. Scott Moncrieff (ed.), 1911.

Many examples of notable housewives are to be found across the centuries but no discussion on servants should omit Lady Grisell Baillie (1665–1746) whose account book holds a wealth of information. She was much concerned with the prudent running of every household department and, after her death, her daughter headed a bundle of papers 'Memoradums and Derections to Servants and ruels layd down by my Mother both fer their diet and work. Copyd and colected together 1752, made by her Decr. 1743, and the derections given to the severl Servants.' The housekeeper was instructed: 'To get up airly is most necessary to see that all the maids and other servants be about their proper business', but Lady Grisell was just as concerned that the butler should be efficiently prepared for carrying out his duties in the dining room.[15]

Although the housekeeper and butler had well-defined duties, the lesser servants were not so specialized at this date, with an apparent flexibility as to who did what. Lady Grisell expected her laundrymaids, when not engaged in actual laundering, to sit and spin and the housekeeper was instructed to see that they did so 'when they have not other necessary business, such as Hay and Harvest and the Barn which the dairy maid goes to when she has a moments time for it, and always to the miln with any melder [i.e. a batch of oats]. the dairy maid, house maid and kitchin maid always to spine when they are not otherways necessarily imployd which they will often pretend to be if they are not diligently lookt after and keep to it.'[16]

In much the same way one of Lady Grisell's contemporaries, in listing the duties expected of a potential maid servant, could write:

Mrs ffenimore.

I had notice that your Daughter desired to come & live with mee. She must milk 3 or 4 cows & understand how to manage that Dairy, & know how to boyll & roast ffowlls & butcher's meatt. Wee wash once a month, she & the washerwoman wash all but the small linnen, & next day she & the washerwoman wash the Buck [i.e. the heavier items]. She helps the other maid wash the rooms when they are done, she makes the Garrett beds & cleans them, & cleans ye great stairs & scours all the Irons & scours the Pewter in use, & wee have an woman to help when 't is all done. There is a very good time to do all this provided she is a [?good] servant, & when she has done her worke she sits down to spin.[17]

It was only latterly that domestic work became specialized. Indeed, it had for long been considered admirable, if not verging on essential, that servants should be able to take one another's place in order that 'they may be sometimes hearers of a good sermon'.[18]

Not only was the eighteenth-century servant a multi-purpose helper but there was far less segregation between family and servants – what might be termed the 'upstairs-downstairs' syndrome – and their position was decidedly better than in later periods. Samuel Pepys' *Diary* reveals instances when the entire household participated in assorted outings,whether going by river to Gravesend or walking to the Half-Way House, where they picked cowslips; and when one of their servants married the wedding feast was held in Seething Lane and the newly married couple spent the wedding night 'in our blue chamber'.[19] Others, too, when referring to their family meant their whole household, not merely their relations.[20] Equally, though, disadvantages attended such familiarities: 'Coming homeward again,' writes Samuel Pepys, 'saw my door and hatch open, left so by Luce, our cookmayde, which so vexed me, that I did give her a kick in our entry, and offered a blow at her, and was seen doing so by Sir W. Pen's footboy, which did vex me to the heart, because I know he will be telling their family of it.'[21]

The concept of all the members of the household being one large family derived ultimately from the days when the feudal lord gathered his household together to dine in the great hall, a semi-communal existence that was followed for centuries. Such ways lingered longest in rural areas and were still evident last century, as recalled by an old Derbyshire farmer: 'The master of the house and his servants had dinner in one and the same room – the kitchen – a large apartment. The master and his family sat at a table near the fire, and the servants at a long table on the opposite side of the room. First the master carved for his family and himself, and then the joint was passed on to the servants' table. The head man presided over the servants' table, and always sat at the end of it, and at the opposite end sat a woman. The men sat next to the chair in order of seniority, and were very particular about keeping their proper places.'[22] The fictitious Laura of 'Lark Rise' found the old ways were still being followed in the 1880s when she went to work at the Candleford Green Post Office; the post-mistress, Laura herself, the foreman blacksmith, the three journeymen and Zillah the maid all ate in the same room but with distinct gradations in the seating arrangements.[23] This was all very different to the situation of a former kitchen maid, who was recalling her eighteen months' service in a 'big house' during the 1930s: 'Which room were the Family using then as their Dining Room?' she was asked; but she was unable to say, never having been 'Upstairs' in all that time. In fact, she had only once met her employer – on the occasion when that august individual entered the kitchen to complain in person about the lack of gravy in the dogs' dinners.

Such a dramatic departure from long-established practices requires some explanation.

Throughout the nineteenth century employers complained of servants being unwilling to work, demanding increased wages, or having ideas above their station, and the question was frequently asked: what has happened to the 'good servants' of yesteryear? In fact, every age had been asking the same question: 'The servant of the present day is not, in character or qualifications, the same being as the servant of fifty years ago' said one commentator in 1864, and he argued that the explanation lay not only in the numerical increase and power of the middle classes, allied to greater openings for female labour, but also in the attractions of cheap rail travel and mass emigration.[24]

Many of this expanded middle class had only recently achieved their status and servants were a means of reinforcing it. To ensure that the somewhat narrow divide between them was never breached, increasingly harsh restrictions were imposed on their domestic staff.

The changes had started long before. As 'society' evolved, so did its members. Those draughty, medieval great halls, full of men-at-arms and serving men of every degree (for female servants were a rare species) were all very well, but gradually a desire for greater comfort, warmth and privacy arose. Smaller rooms for the lord and his family spelt exclusion for the lesser servants, who stayed put in the great hall, as well as a decrease in ceremonial and so on. By the sixteenth century the feudal nature of society was ceasing to have its customary significance. Households were reduced in size, the scale of the retinues curtailed, their functions rendered obsolete; the very nature of those prepared to serve in another's household had changed too and, whereas in former times well-born, well-educated men were happy to attend upon the local lord, such men were now busy with their own estates and concerns. To replace them came those of lesser calibre requiring, in turn, fewer servants of their own. Economic considerations meant fewer were taken on, jobs were amalgamated and cheaper alternatives looked for, either a lower grade of manservant or else women, whose pay was roughly half that of a man's. To continue employing men within the house conferred an element of prestige which was all the more marked after 1777 when a tax on menservants was introduced.[25] Soon after it was noted that 'while there are certain English noblemen who have thirty or forty menservants, the cooking and the house-work that is not seen are generally done by women, and menservants are employed only for such duties as are performed in the presence of guests'.[26]

Running parallel to all this there evolved the concept that female domestics were a humble species of humanity, somewhere near the bottom of the social heap, a perception that tarnished their work as well. This was despite the fact that between 1700 and 1900 estimates suggested anything from 10 to 15 per cent of the country's workforce was engaged in domestic service at any one time. By extension, it came to be considered demeaning for a housewife to manage her own household; and almost as many complaints focused on young women being ignorant of the rudiments of domestic management as queried the disappearance of the 'good servants' of the past. In spite of the enormous numbers engaged in domestic service it became apparent late in the nineteenth century that girls were no longer willing to become servants. Traditional methods of finding new staff no longer sufficed; 'mop fairs', when those looking for work went to the local fair and stood in lines holding an article denoting their trade, no longer attracted the crowds. The Mrs Purefroys of this world were accustomed to asking friends and tradesmen for recommendations: 'I want a footman to work in the garden, lay the Cloath, wait at Table, & go to cart with Thomas when hee is ordered, or do any other Business hee is ordered to do, and not too large sized a man that hee may not be too great a load for an horse when hee rides,' she demanded of one, and again: 'The Cookmaid I hired this last Michas [i.e. Michaelmas] is gone from mee by reason she has had a bastard, I entreat you will look out for a cookmaid for mee.'[27] The daughters of farmers or workers on the estate, along with the little 'charity-school maidens' and the daughters of hamlets such as 'Lark Rise', who had entered service at the age of twelve or thirteen, were now reluctant to respond to advertisements placed in the press by individual householders or by registry offices such as that started in Manchester by Mrs Raffald, author of *The Experienced English House-keeper*. 'Service' had acquired a bad name and there were other openings for women. As early as 1864 a dreadful possibility had been mooted. Edinburgh's population was then estimated at around 168,000 with some 14,000 female domestic servants, mostly drawn from the Highlands and south-west Scotland: 'Shut up these various sources,' it was argued, 'and the families of Edinburgh must serve themselves. Perhaps it may eventually come to this'.[28] Indeed it might!

Between 1861 and 1891 the decline in domestic service was noticeable and it accelerated thereafter, although larger establishments continued to employ their customary staff until the Second World War. Housewives without servants were on the receiving end of much good advice, telling them how they should cope with the new situation and although some mourned the passing of the old order others found it surprisingly easy and relaxing once they had made the adjustment. Silverware could no longer be kept out on display permanently, but was wrapped up until required; meals were simplified; time-consuming jobs such as blackleading or starching were either omitted altogether or considerably reduced; kitchens were brought closer to dining rooms or else revamped to become places in which the family could eat; while the servant's wing with its endless domestic offices was the first part of a house to be converted to other purposes or demolished altogether.

CHAPTER SIX

Cleaning: Methods and Mixtures

'It is the privilege of women of the superior order to be provided for, served, and protected by others; and any labour, therefore, which they undertake is chiefly voluntary.'[1] Many a housewife over the years, outside that superior order, might well have smiled grimly on reading such a statement and asked herself whether housework *per se* really qualified as a voluntary pursuit. Whatever her feelings, the house had to be kept clean and tidy and it fell to her lot to see that the work was done to the best of her ability or to supervise the work of her helpers. In the background, and following many centuries of tradition, lay that oft-misquoted adage which can hardly be omitted from any chapter relating to the subject: 'Cleanliness is, indeed, next to Godliness'.[2] While generations of housewives rose to the challenge how many others were cowed by the weight of such moralistic precepts? Over and above this potent combination was the viewpoint, equally prevalent in the nineteenth century, that an ill-ordered household reflected badly on its master so that hospitality also became inextricably intertwined with cleanliness and moral virtue, an equation that is still met with today. Expecting visitors? Must get the house cleaned!

It is, perhaps, stating the obvious to point out that the amount of housework done would depend on the household's living conditions. The family in a spacious, terraced town house would carry out very different cleaning routines to the family in a Highland but-and-ben with two rooms, earth floors and a byre for their animals under the same roof. A fire of peats on an earth floor needs little cleaning and certainly no polishing, compared to the Georgian grate made of steel with brass insets and a brick, marble or tile surround.

How much time was actually spent on cleaning is difficult to calculate and, with so many variables involved, would differ from one dwelling to the next. All the domestic manuals give credence to the belief that housework is a never-ending task which lasts from dawn to dusk six days a week; it has to be remembered, though, that such works portray the ideal rather than the reality. It is easier, therefore, to assess what observers recorded in spite of the dangers of generalization. There must have been many exceptions.

It is generally someone from outside the community who notes variations from the norm, as locals are unlikely to see anything strange in their own customs. Fortunately, there were many who travelled in a country, or region, not their own and some who happily included observations of a domestic nature as well as agricultural, commercial or other points of interest. 'The amount of water English people employ is inconceivable,' said one, 'especially for the cleaning of their houses. Though they are not slaves to cleanliness, like the Dutch, still they are very remarkable for this virtue'[3]; 'English women generally,' said another, 'have the character of keeping floors, steps, and such things very clean. They are not particularly pleased if anyone comes in with dirty shoes, and soils their clean floors, but he ought first to rub his shoes and feet very clean, if he would be at peace with them in other things'[4]; while a third considered the amazing cleanliness was the reason why there were more servants in England than in France: 'Every Saturday, for instance, it is customary to wash the whole house from attic to basement, outside and in.'[5]

Out of England, though, and it was English standards that acted as the yardstick, a propensity that had been observed by a Frenchman: 'I do not think there is a people more prejudiced in its own favour than the British people, . . . They look on foreigners in general with contempt, and think nothing is as well done elsewhere as in their own country.'[6]

For much of the time Scotland was regarded as being an exceedingly foreign country but some did make the journey north, for various reasons; once safely home, their impressions were published and circulated to a wider audience. Edward Burt in the 1750s observed how the Scots servants used their feet to do all sorts of washing jobs: 'When they wash a room,' he said, 'which the English lodgers require to be sometimes done, they likewise do it with their feet.' They would stand on a damp cloth and shuffle it round the floor and then, to dry the floor, wring out the cloth and shuffle it round again. He ordered a mop to be made to demonstrate it to the girls, but they were unimpressed. He admitted the Scots used their feet for other chores, such as washing vegetables or grinding off the beards and husks of barley as well as for washing clothes – a practice which outraged some because of the manner in which the girls lifted up their petticoats and showed their bare legs.[7]

Dorothy Wordsworth was another who was apt to comment on domestic details while she toured round the Highlands. Once she praised a woman who 'had an excellent fire and her cottage, though very small, looked comfortable and cleanly'; however, she added cautiously 'but remember I saw it only by firelight'. On a different occasion, she exclaimed: 'How light the labour of such a house as this! Little sweeping, no washing of floors . . .' but her words expressed disgust at the dirtiness surrounding her.[8]

In Edinburgh, the capital, it was not so much the cleanliness of the dwellings that visitors noticed but the smell that dominated the city. This was generated by the inhabitants' close-stools, which were emptied into the streets every evening to the cry of 'Gardy loo!', the localized variant of 'Gardez l'eau!' James Boswell, walking up the High Street arm-in-arm with Dr Johnson after the latter's arrival in the city on 14 August 1773 wrote, somewhat euphemistically: 'It was a dusky night; I could not prevent his being assailed by the evening effluvia of Edinburgh.' Dr Johnson, meanwhile, grumbled in his ear: 'I smell you in the dark!'[9]

Dublin was no better: 'Walking in the streets there . . . from the dirt and wretchedness of the canaille, is a most uneasy and disgusting exercise'. Meanwhile, on domestic matters it was noted: 'All the lower ranks in this city have no idea of English cleanliness, either in apartments, persons or cookery.'[10]

In one memoir a single sentence damned the entire population of Wales for being 'much addicted to the sin of *Nastiness*, wallowing in Filthiness like so many Swine; so that the whole Province seems but a general Sty'.[11] To set against that another account concludes: 'I have been delighted with the scenery; and better still, I have been delighted with the inhabitants. A more warm-hearted, patriotic, hospitable, intelligent race cannot be found. We have met with nothing but good treatment, and have not seen an uncivil Welshman',[12] which conjures up an altogether different picture.

For those who aspired to a clean house there were assorted tools and equipment to help them through their work, but as many of these items, or their updated descendants made of plastic or polyester, are still around today they need little in the way of explanation.

A traditional besom made from local materials. (Auchindrain, Inveraray)

Brooms, besoms and brushes often feature in old household accounts. The simplest would be a bundle of twigs, or heather roots, tied to some sort of a handle and this type was widespread. Something slightly different was known to Gilbert White: 'It may not be improper to mention a pretty implement of housewifery that we have seen nowhere else; that is, little neat besoms which our foresters make from the stalks of the *polytricum commune* or *great golden maidenhair*.'[13] Brushes made by professional brush-makers had the bristles, whether of animal or vegetable fibres, inserted and fixed into a wooden base. Subsequently there evolved specialized brushes for different purposes – whether short and stubby for scrubbing floors or curved and softly bristled for dusting staircase banisters. An alternative was the trimmed goose-wing, recommended for dusting shelves or awkward corners and for brushing clothes. The mop must surely have evolved from the idea of pushing a cloth across the floor with the aid of a stick and it would have been a simple development to nail strips of cloth to a handle of convenient length. Other necessities were pails, tubs and similar containers for carrying water, coal, ashes, laundry and so on. Dusting and polishing furniture, silverware and other items called for assorted rubbers, leathers, cloths – of silk, wool, flannel or linen – and rags.

Although similar equipment is still used today, the nature and purpose of the many once familiar cleaning agents and polishes met with in the same sources are now largely forgotten, even though substances such as camstone, rottenstone, Spanish whiting and sand were certainly in use until after the First World War. Other items like Fuller's earth, blacklead, sweet oil, ox-gall, camphor, linseed oil, sifted wood ash and borax, to name but a few, were once the stock-in-trade of every competent housewife.

Sand was much in demand, both as a scouring agent and as a finish to stone, brick or wood floors. After scrubbing with sand and water, floors might be finished with an all-over carpet of sand, which absorbed grease, mud and other problems brought in on people's feet, or the sand might be strewn in decorative patterns. In some areas sawdust served the same purpose, a practice continued by butchers and publicans for many years. Fine sand also scoured metal cooking pots or polished brass or pewter. It could be employed in scrubbing kitchen tables and shelves but housewives were warned against it, 'sand being disagreable because of laying things on them'.[14]

Emery was another scouring agent, harder than sand, that was imported in lumps from the Isle of Naxos, then ground in a stamping mill. Used with water or oil, depending on the particular need, it came either as powder, as emery paper or as emery cloth. A local variant much used in Cornwall was powdered granite. Glass paper was powdered glass adhering to strong paper and was sharper again.

'Fine yellow fand' upon the floor
Is good for either rich or poor.

Sand was much used for scouring purposes in the home and was sold from door to door by itinerant traders. From *The Book of the Old Edinburgh Club*, vol. 2 (1909).

Other products were dual-purpose, cleaning and polishing simultaneously. Whitening (or whiting) was chalk freed of any sand, so as to render it scratch free; pipe-clay was very similar. In Scotland it was called camstone, caum or cawm and the use of a blue 'caum' was peculiar to the Angus area.[15] Hearthstone and firestone were similar again, the names being dependent on locality. It was used to whiten hearths, doorsteps and so on and was equally handy for cleaning windows or for polishing silver, although Lady Grisell Baillie forbade her butler to use it. Her plate, she ordered, must only be cleaned by 'a little soap suds to wash it, or spirit of wine [i.e. alcohol] if it has got any spots'.[16] There was a form called 'Spanish whiting', but 'Paris whiting' was considered best of all.

Rottenstone was a type of silicious limestone, found mainly in Derbyshire and North Wales, although a version imported from the Continent was called 'tripoli'. It was a valuable aid in polishing metals, glass and even hard stone, but in Scotland it acted as a scouring agent and was known as 'rottstone'.

Brick dust or 'common brick' was soft, red brick reduced to powder. It scoured and polished metals and, when mixed with linseed oil, would also clean table tops; for cleaning fire-irons or fenders the (English) housemaid was instructed to burnish with rottenstone or white brick since 'red Brick makes sad Work'.[17] This white brick or 'bath-brick' was a preparation of silicious silt that came from near Bridgwater in brick-shaped blocks. It was widely employed to clean steel-bladed knives and suchlike, as well as tin or brass; latterly, though, its use on brass was discouraged as it was thought to tarnish quickly.

When it comes to the actual cleaning routine to be followed or the mixtures advocated for stain removal or polishing there is no lack of evidence from the many printed works offering advice to any housewife uncertain of domestic procedures or diffident about organizing her servants. Throughout the period being discussed authors such as Hannah Woolley, Hannah Glasse, the Adams' and Mrs Beeton, along with domestic encyclopedias such as *Webster's* and *Cassell's*[18] provided their readers with copious instructions as to how every task should be approached.

Hannah Glasse is better known for her cookery book than for her book on domestic servants in which the work of the different female members of staff 'are fully and distinctly explained'. This was printed in 1760 and thus can be taken as representative of a certain level of domestic practice of that era. The torrent of instructions addressed to 'my little young House-maid' must have severely confused that individual, had she been able to read them.[19]

In cleaning a room it made sense that the fireplace should be dealt with first. Ashes and cinders had to be removed and everything within the hearth – including fire-bars, fenders and fire-irons – had to be cleaned, polished, burnished or otherwise finished according to its composition, the grate reassembled and the fire re-laid.

After the door locks had been polished with rottenstone or white brick, attention focused on the floor. Carpets were either swept or brushed, but it was not until the nineteenth century that tea leaves became sufficiently abundant to be strewn across them, which would 'not only lay all dust, but give a slightly fragrant smell to the room'.[20]

A housemaid's box well
stocked with brushes and
polishes for the domestic
chores. (By courtesy of
Beamish, North of England
Open Air Museum)

Smaller carpets were taken out of doors and beaten; larger ones were
dealt with *in situ*. Alternatively, they could be turned face to the floor
so that the dust would fall out as they were walked over and this was
the technique specified by Susanna Whatman when writing to her
housekeeper in Kent, while she herself was away from home.[21]

The carpet was then rolled right back, but before the boards were
swept they were to be strewn with damp sand to 'lick up all the Dust.
. . . Nothing looks so sluttish as leaving Dirt in Holes and Corners',
stresses Mrs Glasse. If scrubbing proved necessary, cold water was
preferable as hot water soaked in more 'and causes the Damps to hold
longer', while scouring with sand was better than soap as it showed
up the grain of the wood. There was another method somewhere
between the two, explained thus: 'Take Tanzy, Mint, and Balm; first
sweep the Room, then strew the Herbs on the Floor, and with a long
hard Brush rub them well all over the Boards, till you have scrubb'd
the Floor clean. When the Boards are quite dry, sweep off the Greens,
and with a dry Rubbing-brush, dry-rub them well and they will . . .

never want any other washing, and gives a sweet Smell to the Room.' Floors covered with oil cloth were to be dry-rubbed daily, as wet washing spoilt them, and once a year they were to be cleaned with milk which, when dry, could be polished. Marble floors in halls were washed with soap and water, though sand and water was better. For stone stairs, wet sand should be placed on the top step and swept down with the dust and certainly 'never rub them with Fire-stone, as some do, it makes sad work with Petticoats'.[22]

To clean windows two people were advised to work together, one inside and one out. The windows would be dusted, wiped with a damp cloth and then with a dry one; whiting could be applied with a damp cloth, then rubbed dry but was not really necessary. For a finer gloss rottenstone was advised, which was also useful on mirrors.

Dusting required assorted cloths and leathers but to remove the dust from stucco work or picture frames a pair of large bellows with long handles, made for the purpose, was recommended. After dusting came polishing, once any stains or marks on the furniture had been given the appropriate remedial treatment. Again, many 'receipts' (i.e. recipes) could be made up, depending on what wood was involved, but a mixture based on beeswax not only polished the furniture but had a delicious smell too. It was very simple to make. Clarified beeswax, with enough turpentine to moisten it, was put into a jar and placed on a warm corner of the stove; once softened and well stirred it was ready for use.[23]

The cleaning of bedrooms followed a similar pattern although making a bed cost the maid much time and effort. An extra chore was pouring the dirty water from basins and ewers into a slop pail and emptying the chamber pots, in which a little clean water was always to be left to prevent any residual smell.

The eighteenth-century housewife faced a serious difficulty. Under the heading 'To keep clear from Bugs' Mrs Glasse states: 'If your Rooms are very bad and they have got into the Walls, its hard to get them out', though several ways are suggested for the determined housewife to try, including 'Another Receipt where the Bedstead only swarms'. The problem was so widespread that houses advertised for sale as being 'free of bugs' fetched a premium, although in a town such a desirable condition might be difficult to maintain. Someone with first-hand experience was Mrs Glasse's contemporary, Parson Woodforde who, while *en route* for Somerset, stayed at the Bell Savage Inn on Ludgate Hill, London. Despite being bitten during the night he did not wake, he noted, but on arrival at his destination: 'I was terribly swelled in the face and hands by the Buggs.' A subsequent visit to the Bell Savage was even more unpleasant. The first night the bed bugs pestered him; the second they gave him no rest, so 4 a.m. found him walking around the City until breakfast time. The night after that he did not undress but sat in a chair with his feet up on the bed 'and slept very well considering' and he repeated the method on the fourth and final night 'and slept tolerably well'.[24] However, one hundred years before, when Samuel Pepys, his wife and servants were confronted by a similar situation, they had reacted somewhat differently: 'Up, finding our beds good, but lousy; which made us merry.'[25]

When it came to the cleaning of kitchen and basement offices there is a curious silence from the manuals, apart from noting that such work fell to the lowest ranking servant. It was left to a later generation to detail the routine.[26] Early rising was essential. The kitchen fire was to be laid and lit; water put to heat; kitchen tables, dressers and shelves scoured and larders scrubbed out; then the girl tackled the kitchen, housekeeper's room, hall and adjacent passages, steps at both the front door and the rear, and the butler's pantry; 'in doing which the scullion (if there be one kept) takes the dirtiest and most laborious part'. By then the family's and the servants' breakfasts had to be prepared and the remainder of the day was spent at the cook's beck and call.

Each generation in turn stressed the importance of cleanliness. All the pots and pans, whether of pewter, tin or copper, had to be cleaned after use, 'any Crock or Nastiness' being washed off first with sand and water; burnt pans were to be soaked and scraped only with a fingernail; every item was to be well dried in front of the fire before being put away or evil consequences might follow. This was graphically illustrated by Hannah Glasse with the tale of an entire family wiped out by verdigris forming in an unwashed pan. In view, therefore, of her strong feelings both as to cleanliness as well as to the employment of French cooks, she would have reacted strongly (had she still been alive at the time) to the aspersions cast upon the English kitchen by none other than a Frenchman. However, one such visitor had noted how spectacularly clean English houses were and that 'All furniture, especially all kitchen utensils, are kept with the greatest cleanliness'.[27] One of his compatriots had a different story to tell. Initially, he too had been astonished at the cleanliness he saw all around him but, on pursuing his investigations, he concluded: 'I was led to see quite clearly that it was only external; everything that you are supposed to see partakes of this most desirable quality, but the English continue to neglect it in what you are not supposed to see. To give a single instance, I need only mention the kitchen . . . the worst thing that could befall you would be to go into the kitchen before dinner – the dirt is indescribable.'[28] Such an incident was not an isolated occurrence. A kitchen maid of the 1930s recalled how one of her first jobs was to clear out a meat safe neglected by her predecessor, who was merely 'serving out her notice', and from it she removed no less than two whole pails of maggots and other unsavouries.

The above domestic practices pertain to a certain level of society in the mid-eighteenth century. What is striking, though, is the similarity of so many of the instructions printed in so many domestic manuals over the next one hundred and fifty years. Even after the First World War housewives were still being told how to make up polishes such as blacklead, metal paste, onion water for gilt frames and mixtures suitable for washing pewter or removing grease stains from wooden floors, in words that echoed so many earlier works, although it was just occasionally hinted that manufactured products might be purchased.

Although the housewife of the 1920s and beyond might still be using tools and cleansing agents familiar to generations of her predecessors some changes had occurred, although fewer than might have been expected given the laborious and repetitive nature of the job. Laundrywork had seen numerous developments (see Chapter 7) and there can be no doubt that the introduction of both water and drainage into an ever-increasing percentage of homes did go some way to easing the burden of housework.

As far as equipment went the phrase 'labour-saving' did not mean quite what it means today as, prior to the advent of an electric motor small enough for domestic use, the words almost always involved somebody's labour to work the technology on offer. The job of knife cleaning was a good example of this. Before the introduction of stainless steel, steel-bladed knives were tedious things to keep clean. Because they rusted if put into water they had to be kept separate from other washing-up and instructions for cleaning them were lengthy.[29] In due course Mrs Beeton could claim: 'Knives are now generally cleaned by means of Kent's or Master's machine, which gives very little trouble, and is very effective.'[30] The rotary knife cleaner was a large, drum-like container with a sturdy handle to turn. After cleaning the blades, the knives were pushed into slots across the top; a special abrasive powder such as Oakey's Britannia Knife Polish was added; the sturdy handle was turned to operate alternating felt pads and bristles and four – even six – knives were polished simultaneously! After that, a good polish, a quick wipe over and, once they were replaced in a knife-box or basket, the job was done.

In its day, this piece of labour-saving equipment was at the forefront of domestic technology. Such a claim may seem unlikely, but it is salutary to reflect how each generation laughs at the advances of the one before, thinking them no advance whatsoever.

The domestic carpet sweeper as we know it today was an American development that was made available to the world in 1876, although inefficient variations on the theme had been in use for much of the century. The story goes that Mr M.R. Bissell of Grand Rapids, Michigan, kept a china shop and as he suffered from an allergic reaction to the packaging used he decided to do something about it. In his design the tufts of bristles are placed in a spiral, there is a friction drive from the four wheels that render the sweeper mobile, and a lever-operated dust box; it was also adjustable to cope with different thicknesses of carpet. Within a few years The Bissell Carpet Sweeper Co. was housed in a purpose-built factory and other manufacturers were producing models on similar lines.

Running parallel to Mr Bissell's endeavours were many experiments utilizing a pump to blow or suck the dust out of carpets, but the machines tended to be unwieldy and only suitable for commercial premises. The first practical, effective model for domestic use was devised by Hubert Booth, who witnessed a demonstration to clean railway carriages at St Pancras Station, London and was singularly unimpressed by a machine which blew the dust from one end of the carriage to a container placed at the far end. On going home he put a handkerchief over the arm of a chair and sucked; a ring of dirt appeared. Suction, therefore, was his chosen method and in 1901 he was granted a patent, but at this stage his machine was equally unwieldy. It was a huge affair, painted bright red and, although operated by a petrol-driven piston engine, it arrived at its destination courtesy of the original form of horse-power. Flexible hoses were inserted into the house via the windows, whereupon a team of operators set to work and it was said that the initial cleaning reduced the weight of the carpets by 50 per cent. Many models were produced by other manufacturers but there was a basic problem – either the large motors fitted to them rendered the vacuum cleaner unwieldy or the smaller hand-operated versions needed two people to work them. Tubular models such as the 'Star' or the 'Good Housekeeping', designed to be worked by one person, were awkward to use as one hand had to press the nozzle on to the carpet while the other pumped the handle.

The revolution came about in 1907 when J. Murray Spangler of Ohio attached a small electric motor to a conveniently sized vacuum.

Technological progress: a housewife vacuums her carpets, 1937. (By courtesy of The Hulton Getty Picture Collection Limited)

He sold the rights to a firm of saddlers, who were looking for new outlets to offset declining trade in the face of motorized transport, and the following year the firm W.H. Hoover produced the first electrically powered upright vacuum cleaner with exterior dustbag. It was a success right from the start, so much so that for many years, the name of the firm has been used in the English language as a verb and as a generic term for all such articles. It is by chance we say 'to hoover' when we might have said 'to spangle'.

The development of electrically operated devices suitable for the home assisted the housewife greatly, once a supply of electricity was available to her, and certainly did much to lessen the amount of physical labour involved in running a home. However, to all intents and purposes, the application of electricity to the actual cleaning processes was limited to the vacuum cleaner and the floor polisher. Helpful as these items were, and are, many areas of housework yet remain to be done by hand, unaided by the benefits of electricity.

CHAPTER SEVEN

Laundrywork

'It is commonly believed that our ancestors were lacking in cleanliness, rarely taking the trouble to wash either themselves or their clothing. While there is an element of truth in such a statement the criteria cannot be applied across the whole of society. That some people were not as clean as they might have been was likely to be related to the lack of water supplies, the high price of soaps, the nature of many fabrics and the amount of physical labour involved in the laundry processes. Equally, in those houses able to have a separate wash house, furnished with specialized tubs, coppers, and drying racks, the chore was greatly simplified, although at this level of sophistication there was likely to be far more washing done – and done to a higher standard. Accounts from wealthier households rarely fail to include purchases of assorted soaps and starch or repairs to laundry equipment, while including payments to their own laundrymaids or to washerwomen if items were 'sent out to wash'. Those lower down the social scale often did their washing out of doors and continued to do so even in the coldest weather, which argues a certain determination.

Where water was piped into the kitchen or scullery wash day was less onerous than where all the necessary water had to be collected and carried home before the job could even start, and on this score it is salutary to consider that, even as late as 1951, around 20 per cent of the population of England and Wales still lacked a piped water supply for their own exclusive use.[1] Instead of carrying home many loads of water it was often easier to reverse the process and to carry out the job either in the river itself or in tubs on the river bank. Sometimes a shelter was erected with a paved area beneath and a built-in copper for heating the water. At one time such wash houses must have been a familiar sight and something similar can still sometimes be seen in rural France.

Burt, as already noted, had observed Scots women using their feet for certain jobs around the house; he found it even stranger that they insisted on doing their washing in the river and, what was to be deplored, 'as people pass by, they divert themselves by talking very freely to them'. He frequently saw women, 'with their coats tucked up, stamping, in tubs, upon linen by way of washing; and this not only in summer, but in the hardest frosty weather, when their legs and feet are almost literally as red as blood with the cold; and often two of these wenches stamp in one tub, supporting themselves by their arms thrown over each other's shoulders'.[2] This practice continued well into the nineteenth century when it was noted that 'it renders the linen beautifully soft and white, with little expense of soap'.[3] Irish women, too, had a similar habit: 'By washing their cloaths no where but in rivers and streams, the cold, especially as they roast their legs in their cabbins till they are fire-spotted, must swell them to a wonderful size and horrid black and blue colour always met with both in young and old. They stand in rivers and beat the linen against the great stones found there with a beetle.'[4]

This was the simplest washing method of all – putting articles into the water and beating them with a type of wooden mallet or pounding the items against a convenient rock. No soap or cleansing agent was involved. The Scots' method was a variation on this with the washing being trampled in wooden tubs as well as in the river. After being pounded the articles were wrung out and spread out to dry upon the grass or on nearby bushes where sun and air could aid the bleaching process.

Another method involved washing the articles in water to which a cleansing agent other than soap had been added. This was termed 'bucking' and Lady Grisell Baillie was in favour of her bed and table linen being 'bouckt' whenever the weather permitted, whereas Mrs Purefroy described her laundry routine as being 'One day Soap & another day yᵉ Buck'.[5] However, Hannah Glasse summed up the variation in methods by saying: 'Different Countries and different Places have all a different Manner or Way of preparing for the great Wash. In some Places they buck their Clothes, which I do not understand, neither is it needful in *London* . . . . No doubt on it, the clearer the Water is and the sweeter the Air the better the Clothes will look', although she excluded Hampstead from this general rule on account of its water.[6]

Articles for bucking were placed in a barrel or deep tub, a wooden tray with a perforated base went across the top and water with added potash, cow dung or stale urine was poured in. This drained through the washing and, ideally, ran out of a spigot into a bowl and was poured back into the tray, the process being repeated several times. The alkalis present in the lye reacted on the grease and dirt in the fabrics thereby economizing on the soap or obviating its use altogether. The urine, a cheap source of ammonia, was collected in tubs or troughs and was known by different names in different areas – chamberlye, lant in Lancashire, weeting or old waish in Yorkshire, while the Scots knew it as wash or wesche and gathered it in wooden 'wash-tubs' or earthernware 'maister-cans'.

Potash was obtained by burning vegetable matter. Wood-ashes were plentiful where wood was the local fuel, otherwise bracken or brake was burnt to produce 'ash balls', as Celia Fiennes had noted around Cannock Wood in Staffordshire.[7] The ash was moistened, then pressed into balls some 3 or 4 inches in diameter, and vast numbers were sold for use in London. In Ireland it was called 'weed ash' since the vegetable matter included dried potato stalks and leaves, thistles, docks and other such plants.[8] Latterly potash was imported in bulk from North America where, with land being cleared for agriculture, timber was burnt as an encumbrance.

A refined type of potash was known as pearl-ash, after its blue-white colour. Hannah Glasse recommended hanging a bagful in the water while boiling clothes to whiten them,[9] whereas by the 1820s the Adams' were suggesting that it saved on soap.[10] By that date soda was an alternative economy measure, as a little added to the water softened it. Soda, as a mineral, could be mined and at one time it had been procured by burning enormous quantities of kelp, a type of seaweed, and Spanish barilla. A cheaper way of mass producing it from salt was devised by Nicolas Leblanc, a Frenchman, which enabled further developments to take place within the soap industry so that by the 1840s pearl-ash was almost superseded.[11]

Washing with soap differed from the other methods in requiring hot water to be efficacious, an added cause of expense and effort and hence a deterrent to its use; soaps were also heavily taxed at fluctuating rates between 1712 and 1853. The duty, introduced as a means of helping to pay for the War of Spanish Succession, was initially set at the rate of one penny per pound weight for British-made soap and two pence for imported, and commissioners were introduced at the same time to 'manage the tax' according to an elaborate set of regulations. As a result, considerable amounts of soap were made illicitly as well as being smuggled into the West Country and North Wales from Ireland where it carried no duty. By 1793, at the start of another period of war, the tax yielded £373,090 a year in England and £30,441 in Scotland.

By the end of the wars in 1815 the sum raised was well on the way to being double that amount and by 1827 it was £1,200,000. There was growing pressure to remove the tax altogether as, it was argued, the poor were being deprived of an article necessary for their cleanliness, comfort and health and after a period of reduced duties Gladstone repealed the tax altogether in 1853.[12]

Soaps fell into two basic types, 'hard' or 'soft', with further variations within these categories. The former was made with animal fats or oil mixed with soda, a mineral alkali; the latter was 'of similar oily matters and potash, a vegetable alkali' and this type had been known since ancient times. The Adams' considered that 'the use of soft soap, saves nearly half in washing'.[13] The north of England preferred 'ball soap' made from lees of ashes mixed with tallow.

Just because the articles were clean did not mean the washing process was complete: 'blueing' and 'starching' were further options.

The final rinsing water could be tinted with 'powder blue' or 'stone blue' derived from coarse smalt, which was glass coloured blue by zaffre or oxide of cobalt. This counteracted the yellowish tone imparted by the starch and it also neutralized the yellow-brown tints of ill-coloured linen. Starching was done after the articles had dried. Starch, whereby stiffness was added to a fabric or to part of a garment, had been introduced from The Netherlands in Elizabethan times and was quickly taken up by fashionable folk. It is easy to see why, when studying the portraits of the day. Until the Commonwealth put paid to such frivolities the making of these 'great and monstrous ruffes . . . whereof some be a quarter of a yarde deep' and the laundering of them thereafter was a considerable business: 'Then, least they should fall down, they are smeared and starched in the Devils Liquore I meane Starch' said one who disapproved. The heavily starched frills and collars were held in place and set by heated 'poking sticks'. The English weather was not kind to this fashion because, when it rained, 'They goe flip flap in the winde, like rags flying abroad, and lye upon their shoulders like the dishcloute of a slut'.[14] Incidentally, without this particular fashion London might not have had its Piccadilly. One explanation for its origin suggests it came about from the nickname given to a house built there by a tailor who had amassed a fortune from the sale of 'piccadils' or 'pikadells', the name given to both the framework supporting a starched ruff or collar and to a type of wide high collar.

Starch for laundry use could be derived from potatoes; or from rice, which found favour because the fabric did not stick to the iron in the ironing process; or from horse chestnuts, for which a patent was granted in 1796; or from various plants found in the wild, such as cuckoo-pint roots; but it was mostly wheat-based starch that was used. Later in the nineteenth century it was this same substance that was the 'powder' that covered footmen's hair in the interests of uniformity.

In former times wash day, like baking day, was a time when all the domestic energies were devoted to that one pursuit although in the case of washing the process extended over the rest of the week as well. Samuel Pepys' references to 'the pickle of wash day' and 'the house foul with the washing' gives an idea of what was involved, especially in a town house with limited drying space.[15]

Starching garments was a necessary part of laundrywork. An advertisement from F.B. Jack, *Art of Laundry-work*, 3rd edition, 1898.

It was customary to accumulate dirty clothing, bed and table linen for several weeks and have the occasional mammoth wash rather than to do smaller loads more regularly. To wash frequently was considered demeaning as it denoted a paucity of supplies. By the mid-nineteenth century a monthly washing was customary although it was suggested every fortnight would be better. When Laura went to work at the Candleford Green Post Office in the 1880s the household followed the old middle-class practice of one huge wash every six weeks and a professional washerwoman was employed for two days, arriving at 6 a.m. on the Monday morning. As the girl had insufficient clothing to last that long she sent everything home each week for her mother to wash.[16]

There are several examples from the eighteenth century. Parson Woodforde noted: 'We wash every five Wks. . . . Washing and Ironing generally take us four Days' and two extra washerwomen came in on the Monday and Tuesday. Mrs Purefroy on the other hand stated: 'Wee wash once a month' and, as already indicated, the actual washing process was a two-day affair divided between 'soap' and 'ye Buck'.[17] Lady Grisell Baillie's household in the 1740s was unusual in working a three-week rota. Even though her spelling might be flexible, her domestic routine was fixed: 'One week the body linnin is washt, the second week table and bed linnin and always bouckt when the weather will alow of it, the third week the landry maids must be kept closs at spining.' She urged her housekeeper to 'weight out to them exactly the soap, and often go to the wash house to see it is not wasted but made the proper use of . . . often see that they waste not fire either in the wash house or Landry and that the Landry be keept clean.'[18]

A drying rack, which pulled out from the wall, was heated by the nearby fire. Six shirts supposedly dried in an hour. (By courtesy of Leeds Museum & Galleries, Temple Newsam House)

In these houses a distinction was made between the wash house, where the actual washing process was carried out, and the laundry used for drying and pressing; other households, as at Erddig, near Wrexham, might call them the wet and dry laundries. There might also be a divide between what the laundrymaids washed and the finer items which were dealt with by the lady's maid, where present. A well-designed washing place would have paved or tiled floors, built-in coppers with grates underneath, a row of troughs or tubs, piped water, drainage and adequate ventilation to draw off all the steam and it was here that the baskets of dirty washing were sorted. Spots and stains would be given special treatment, items set to soak, coppers and tubs filled and fires laid in readiness. Sometimes this was done on Saturday so the clothes could soak over Sunday but other households started the process on the Monday. Early rising was a prerequisite. Pepys recorded how his wife had sat up until 2 a.m. in order to 'call the wench up to wash'. Another time they were both vexed when 'our bell did not wake them sooner' but, Samuel resolved, 'I will get a bigger bell'.[19]

After soaking items were washed individually, then transferred into clean water and washed through again. Plain linens and cottons were put to boil in the coppers in order to give them a good colour and remove the soap; if boiled any sooner in the process the dirt would be fixed in, never to be removed thereafter. Everything was then rinsed several times and blued or given other, specialized finishes, after which the items were wrung out and put to dry, either on an outdoor drying green provided with lines slung between upright posts or on an area of grass, in which case the articles had to be watched lest they blew away in the wind or were stolen. During inclement weather drying was done indoors in the laundry, with items being draped over wooden clothes horses or on racks drawn up to the ceiling. There might even be the luxury of a 'drying closet', heated by the laundry fire, with wheeled wooden racks that pulled in and out along grooves in the floor. Each rack could take six shirts or the equivalent and items supposedly dried in an hour. In the meantime townsfolk had to dry clothes as best they could; poorer households stretched ropes across the street while Scottish tenements had 'pullishees', a framework with ropes and a pulley protruding from below the window.

Smoothing wrinkles out of fabrics was an age-old practice. The idea of a press for household or heavy items came from the Romans. Bed and table linen was dried, pulled straight, folded and put into a press between adjustable boards and pressure was applied by means of a wooden turnscrew. In due course these presses became substantial pieces of furniture, often incorporating drawers in which the pressed linen could be stored.

In humbler homes shaped, polished stones known as slickstones or slykestones were used, as were mangling bats. The latter comprised a flat piece of wood some 24 inches long and 4 inches wide with a carved handle at one end. The damp item was wrapped around a wooden roller, placed on a flat surface and rolled backwards and forwards with the aid of the bat until the fabric was smooth. Such mangle bats were widespread across northern Europe and in Norway they were often given as a love-token from a lover to his lass, with the horse-shaped handle being considered a fertility symbol. While

A box mangle made by Joseph Farrer, Halifax. Items for ironing were wrapped round the rollers and, when the handle was turned, the weighted box moved over them. (By courtesy of Leeds Museum & Galleries, Temple Newsam House)

in Scotland Dorothy Wordsworth witnessed 'one most indecent practice' in Melrose churchyard: 'Several women brought their linen to the flat table-tombstones, and, having spread it upon them, began to batter as hard as they could with a wooden roller, a substitute for a mangle' but the reason for her disapproval is unclear especially when she described the churchyard as being 'exceedingly slovenly and dirty'.[20] Around Dumfries, women managed without any iron or mangle at all. Just as they trampled their linen to wash it, so they spread a blanket on the ground, placed the dried articles upon it and tramped them smooth with their bare feet.[21]

By the eighteenth century the box mangle was appearing in wealthier homes. This took the form of a large wooden box, about 6 feet long by 3 feet wide by 2 feet deep, filled with heavy stones, the whole supported within a strong wooden frame. The box rested upon several removable wooden rollers around which the linen was wrapped and the articles were smoothed by rolling the box backwards and forwards. Movement was achieved by turning a crank handle and a tipping or lifting device was incorporated to allow the rollers to be inserted and removed in reasonable safety. A good sheen could be given to articles by interleaving them with plain brown Holland mangling cloths which were never washed. By the 1850s the cast-iron upright mangle had evolved which was more compact and less laborious to manipulate. By turning the handle on a large wheel two wooden rollers were operated; a turnscrew at the top adjusted the pressure of the rollers and the folded articles were passed between them.

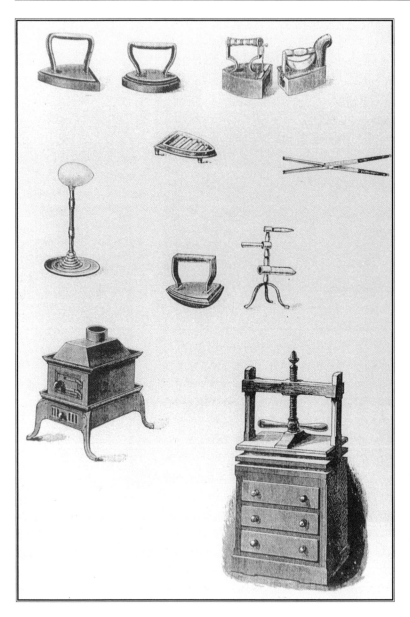

A selection of implements for ironing. From top left: flat, box and charcoal irons; an iron stand and goffering irons; egg, polishing and Italian irons; a laundry stove and a linen press with drawers. From *Cassell's Book of the Household*, c. 1893, vol. 3.

'Smoothing irons are employed to give smoothness to such articles of wearing apparel as do not admit of being wound round a cylinder to be mangled' said one authority'[22] and three basic types were in use. The common flat or 'sad' iron* was pointed at the front and square at the back, but an oval version, rounded at both ends, was thought less likely to damage delicate items. These irons had to be heated in front of a fire or on a specialized laundry or ironing stove and it was a matter of judgement to know how hot they really were.

* 'sad' meaning solid or heavy

The traditional way of testing the heat was to spit on the flat surface. The box-iron resembled the 'sad' iron but had a sliding or hinged back covering a cavity in the body into which fitted a heated iron 'slug' ('shoe', 'bolt' or 'heater'), and it facilitated the job to have two of these – one inside the iron, the other heating on the fire. By the 1840s the box-iron was considered 'old-fashioned' and 'less-used than formerly'[23] although fifty years later it was warmly recommended by Miss Jack, Principal of Edinburgh's School of the Domestic Arts, who wrote: 'They are much liked by some, as they are clean, and keep their heat longer.'[24] A variation was an iron filled with smouldering charcoal which sometimes incorporated a pair of bellows to blow up the embers via a hole in the back but the fumes off the charcoal could cause problems. The third type was the 'Italian iron' (or 'tally' iron) which resembled a short iron poker fitted at right angles to an iron stand. A removable rod was heated, as for the box-iron, and slotted into the hollow 'poker'; articles to be smoothed, such as silk ribbons or flat lace collars, were drawn across the iron rather than pressed.

'Plaiting', a form of pleating for frills or shirt fronts, was done by hand, the fabric being held in place with the fingers and the pleats pressed in with a flat iron. Goffering irons did a similar job and came in various shapes – one resembling a pair of tongs, another like multi-bladed scissors, while a third was a 'goffering stack'. This last consisted of two wooden uprights with a number of horizontal wooden slats running between them; the damp fabric was threaded backwards and forwards between the slats, a top bar was fixed into place to keep it all in place and the pleats set as the material dried. The name 'goffering' was a corruption of the French 'gaufre', meaning a wafer or waffle. In due course, crimping machines came in, to make short work of plaiting or fluting of frills; resembling toy mangles, the material to be pleated was passed between grooved rollers which were heated in the same way as Italian irons.

Also available were polishing irons for shirt fronts, small-headed irons for doing lace, mushroom-topped ones for puffed sleeves or bonnets, egg-shaped ones for awkward corners, long-handled ones for sleeves and bustles – there was no end to the possibilities.

Not until the arrival of self-heating irons was there any appreciable diminution in the labour involved. Many ways of heating the irons were tried, such as paraffin, naphtha, methylated spirits, colza oil or petrol, with varying degrees of success and safety. One of the most efficient methods was the gas-heated iron which was connected to the gas supply by means of an india-rubber tube; they were much in vogue during the 1880s and 1890s and continued to be made into the 1930s. A model designed to run off bottled gas continued in production for another thirty years. The spirit iron heated by methylated spirits was another popular form, produced in Britain in large numbers by the firm of Tilley, better known for their paraffin lamps.

Washing with a 'dolly'; note the tub placed out of doors. From *Cassell's Book of the Household*, *c.* 1893, vol. 3.

The electric iron gradually superseded all these other forms but in 1895 Miss Jack warned her readers: 'Irons heated by electricity are the most recent invention, but they have not as yet come into general use.'[25] Few housewives were able to benefit from them until the 1920s when there occurred a rapid expansion of the supply networks. Early models plugged into a light fitting and, without thermostats, the only way of controlling the heat was by switching the appliance on and off.

At much the same time as ironing was slowly becoming less onerous, some advances were also being made in the actual washing processes and there is no doubt that the task was greatly eased with the introduction of piped water supplies. The development of the wash boiler was one such improvement; the best sorts had a tap to empty the copper although some still had to be filled by hand. Initially, the cast-iron cauldron was set on a brick plinth on which a fire was laid but gradually cauldron and grate combined into one cast-iron unit and, as gas supplies were laid on, so gas-fired washing coppers became a possibility.

The dolly stick and the posser had long been used to push the washing around the tub, thereby forcing water through the material and loosening the dirt. Different localities used different names for these objects and they took different forms too, the most popular resembling a three-legged stool fixed to a long stick with a cross bar to act as the handle. The 'vacuum clothes washer' was a variation of it. The long handle was attached to a perforated metal cone which, when pumped up and down, drove the water through the fabric and sucked it back up again. One innovation of the nineteenth century was the flat board of wood with a ridged, zinc-covered surface against which clothes were rubbed; this was the washboard, probably better known now for its place in the early history of jazz and resuscitated by 1950s' skiffle groups.

Many attempts had been made over the years to invent a machine to do the washing but none were altogether successful. Real advances only became possible when a supply of water was laid on with an efficient means of heating it, together with proper removal and disposal systems for the dirty water and a means of power that was not based on human energy. Until such times housewives had to make do with what was available. Early washing machines required housewife or maid to turn a handle or move a lever backwards and forwards to swish the articles through the water or to motivate paddles to do the job; some machines were given a ridged lining to simulate the washboard; others were provided with mangles to wring out the water as well as smooth out the wrinkles. One type was put on rockers, like a baby's cradle, and the housewife was supposed to sit herself down to rock the washing while doing another chore in the meantime.

However, by the 1890s it could be confidently asserted: 'Amongst the greatest aids to washing at home which can be named are washing machines and wringing machines. It has been truly said that a washing machine is to washing what a sewing machine is to sewing; it does the work in very much less time, and it saves trouble, when people understand it and have got into the way of using it. But when people do not understand it, and do not use it properly, it is only a disappointment.' The article continued: 'Unfortunately, a great many servants have a prejudice against machines; they will not follow the directions given by the makers, and, consequently, they do not give the machines a fair trial.'[26] The fact is, of course, that it was only due to the servant's labour that the machine could work at all. Numerous models were available since 'so much mechanical skill and ingenuity have been exercised in constructing machines to save labour in laundry work'.[27] They came in all shapes and sizes, made by firms such as Messrs Burrell & Co. ('The Alpha', in both large and small sizes), Messrs Bradford's Vowel Machines (including the 'Large E' or their popular 'Y') and Messrs Twelvetrees ('The Villa Washer').

In the 1840s steam-washers, though popular in France, were not considered suitable for domestic use in Britain; yet fifty years later it was reported that the steam-washer was the latest innovation, recently arrived from the USA. The water was heated by gas or coal but its usefulness in a domestic situation was again somewhat limited as it depended on a sufficient supply of the one and a properly constructed chimney for the other. The panegyric ended with the words: 'Of course, when a steam washer is used, clothes have to be mangled, starched and ironed as usual; but the actual washing is made extremely easy.'[28]

The 'Vowel' washing machines, produced by Messrs Bradford in the 1880s, and '90s proved extremely popular. The eight-sided barrels had a corrugated wooden lining and were rotated by means of a handle; they used less water than rival machines. (By courtesy of Ironbridge Gorge Museum Trust)

Yet again, it was the introduction of the electric motor that did most for the hard-worked laundress. Electrically powered washing machines were first produced in the USA early in the twentieth century but were primarily the old-style wooden, hand-operated machines fitted with a separate motor. Not until the 1920s was there a total redesign; a few were imported into Britain but they were costly and, as before, their use was hampered by the lack of electricity supplies to the home and it was not until after the Second World War that they were bought in any numbers. By this time, too, branded soaps and soap powders were on the market, 'Lux Flakes' and 'Persil' being among the earliest. A general shortage of animal fats led to experiments with vegetable oils as the basis of soaps and synthetic detergents, but these in turn were superseded by petroleum derivatives. Spin driers and drying machines were introduced, as were dry-or-steam irons; also being developed were the beginnings of the wide range of non-iron or drip-dry fabrics that have done so much to revolutionize laundry processes and to ease the whole concept of wash day.

The days are now largely confined to the past, when it was asserted that: 'The labour of washing is so disagreeable and injurious to health, that every contrivance which may facilitate it is worth attending to for lessening the manual labour, and even for improving the process itself',[29] for which many a housewife can render up prayers of praise and thanksgiving. Indeed, it is not so long ago that children were taught to sing:

Twas on a Monday morning that I beheld my darling,
She looked so sweet and charming in every high degree.
She looked so neat and charming, oh! A-washing of her linen, oh!
Dashing away with a smoothing iron,
Dashing away with a smoothing iron,
Dashing away with a smoothing iron . . . she stole my heart away.

Tuesday saw 'my darling' a-soaping of her linen, oh! Then came activities such as a-wringing, a-starching, a-hanging, an-ironing; on Sunday 'my darling' actually gets to wear the clothes.

Instead of seeing this as an extremely tedious, long-drawn out method of doing the weekly wash one should, perhaps, after surveying just what was involved, be a little more sympathetic to what women went through in their battle to achieve clean clothing in the past.

CHAPTER EIGHT

The Means of Cooking

'Gentlemen, – Man is a cooking animal.' Thus began the lecture addressed to the fictitious Cleikum Club, but 'Man' was meant only in the generic sense, as in the great majority of households it was women who did the cooking. Indeed, it was a woman whose culinary expertise was central to that same dining club.[1]

Until the development of the kitchen range during the later eighteenth century most cookery was carried out over an open fire which was as likely to be in the centre of the floor as built into a wall under some form of chimney. It mattered little whether it was the only fire in the dwelling, which was most often the case, or whether there was a sequence of fireplaces in a fully equipped kitchen. An open fire could be as versatile as any cooking appliance of today. Food could be roasted, boiled, stewed, fried, grilled (i.e. 'broiled' in eighteenth-century terms), while items could be baked in several different ways.

Cooking vessels could be suspended above the fire, supported on a stand over or near to it, or be placed within the embers. Note the iron fireback to protect the brickwork. (The Weald & Downland Open Air Museum, Singleton)

The open fire burning wood or peat was a method of cooking which dated from the very earliest times and continued right into the twentieth century, coexisting alongside other grates and other fuels. The hearth and its equipment could be as simple or as sophisticated as the household's financial circumstances allowed, although it has to be borne in mind that a locality's fuel supply determined both the way foods were cooked as well as the pots and pans used. Peat, for example, gave out a gentle heat suitable for slow cooking and earthernware pots and it was probably for this reason that Dr Johnson noted on the Isle of Skye, where peat was the only fuel used: 'A dinner in the Western Isles differs very little from a dinner in England, except that in the place of tarts there are always set different preparations of milk'[2] – the former requiring a high temperature while the latter are best suited to a slow heat. When coal took the place of traditional fuels it necessitated a change not only in the arrangements of the grate but also in the utensils; metal vessels, of iron or copper, became essential to withstand the greater heat.

For cooking over an open fire pipkins and skillets, the forerunners of today's saucepans, were given long handles for ease of use and three short legs on the base for extra stability which were only omitted when cooking came to be done on a flat surface. The same extra-long handles could be found on many kitchen implements such as frying pans, grid-irons, girdles, meat forks, toasting forks, skimmers, spoons, ladles and so on, so much so that the approximate age of an article can be gauged from the length of its handle. Another implement was the 'salamander', comprising a long handle with a thick, round or square plate at one end which was heated in the fire until red hot and then held over foods to brown the surface; some had short legs to support them and were used in conjunction with floor-level hearths. An adequate substitute was a 'hot Fire Shovel'.[3]

The well-stocked kitchen would be equipped with many items still familiar today, although made of heavier materials than the contemporary housewife would care to handle and made on a more generous scale, in order to cater for the larger households of the past. A glance at the cookbooks of any period reveals the equipment in use. Sieves and colanders; mixing bowls; wooden spoons; whisks made from birch twigs or hard white rushes; assorted knives for boning, slicing, chopping or carving; graters; string and linen tape for trussing joints or poultry and skewers of metal or wood for similar purposes; moulds for shaping almost any sort of food and tin cases for baking pastries or little cakes; glazed pots for storage; small glasses for serving jellies, syllabubs and other desserts; jugs, bowls, dishes and plates of all shapes, sizes and materials. Less familiar might be the innumerable containers for storage purposes, required to see the housewife through from one year to the next. In other words there was no lack of kitchen equipment for those able to pay for it. As Meg Dods wrote so feelingly: 'We have been so often taken in with wonderful, newly-invented frying pans and infallible gridirons, that we do not venture to recommend any form. We have collected half a garretful of these and other culinary inventions, and on trial found nearly the whole useless, or little improvement on the old-fashioned utensils.'[4]

The old cookbooks reveal the culinary techniques, too. Meat to be roasted needed a fire that was 'brisk' or 'quick' (i.e. hot). Items could be suspended over the fire but were generally cooked in front of it attached to a spit. This was a long rod, sometimes of wood but more often of iron, held between two upright posts placed before the fire and kept turning by a 'turnspit' crouching nearby. Alternatives were devised. A cage-like wheel built into the wall and connected to the spit by chains or ropes would be turned by an animal; sometimes by a goose, as it bore the labour better[5], but more often by a dog and it is said that the basset hound got its name from being the dog most suited to the job – through being 'bas-set' or low slung. Mechanical means of turning the spit were also in vogue, involving either weights or springs. Charles II, escaping after the Battle of Worcester in 1651, was on one occasion disguised as a servant and sent into the kitchen for his supper. Asked by the cookmaid to make himself useful and wind up the jack he shocked her by not knowing how to do such a simple task. However, he retrieved the situation by saying that where he came from 'We seldom have roast meat, but when we have, we don't make use of a Jack'.[6]

Smoke jacks were devised resembling a small windmill at the top of the chimney and were activated by the heat rising from the fire – the hotter the fire, the faster the jack went and the faster the spit revolved. When not in use the jack was liable to start running whenever the wind blew, even after the connecting chain had been slipped off the wheel. 'My wife and I,' Pepys confided in his *Diary*, 'were troubled all night with the sound of drums in our ears, which in the morning we found to be Mr Davys's jack, but not knowing the cause of its going all night, I understand to-day that they have had a

The roasting range at Callendar House, Falkirk is operated by a smoke vane in the chimney. The mechanism to drive the spits acted as the prototype for the more famous one installed thereafter in the Royal Pavilion, Brighton, East Sussex. (By courtesy of Falkirk Museums)

great feast to-day.'[7] Smoke jacks were then relocated in the throat of the chimney directly above the kitchen fire where they were less likely to annoy anyone other than the kitchen staff. The clockwork bottle-jack, so called after its shape, was a later innovation again and the meat dangled from it to roast in front of the fire. This was particularly suited to smaller joints and to the narrower fire-box employed for coal; 'vertical roasting' as opposed to the 'horizontal' previously used.

Meats to be roasted needed plenty of fat in them so most meat was better suited to being boiled or stewed. Wealthy kitchens might incorporate a separately fired stewing stove and vessels placed upon its flat, iron surface would continue to simmer gently. Otherwise stewing would be done in a pot supported over the fire or resting on its three short legs among the embers. Alternatively, a pan might sit close to the fire on a three-legged iron stand called a trivet or be held over the fire in a long-handled iron frame called by the same name, unless in Scotland where the contrivance was known as a cran. The cauldron might also be suspended above the fire with the aid of a piece of rope, or wood, or a chain attached to a conveniently placed beam.

When the hearth shifted from the centre of the room to one wall further advances became possible, regardless of whether there was a properly constructed chimney or a funnel-like wooden structure hanging over the hearth. To take the weight of a pot or pots a horizontal iron bar was attached to a vertical iron post in one corner of the fireplace and this in turn grew into the chimney crane or swee, which swung out and back in the manner of a gate. The pots hung from it on hooks or a length of chain. Over the years more sophisticated means of suspending the pots evolved and it became easier to adjust their height over the fire, but the names of all the bits and pieces changed according to locality and era. The fireplace had its own language. Pot hooks and hangers might be called trammels or cotterels or crooks, with a variant of jibcrooks or racking crooks, while the ratchet hanger looked rather like a saw, curved at one end for hanging over the swee and with a hook and loop at the other which caught over the teeth of the ratchet. The idle-back or kettle-tilter was a device that enabled liquid to be poured from the vessel without having to lift it off the crane. Some of these artefacts were made to the most intricate and decorative designs and, as ironwork was expensive, it was a sign of wealth to have much of it in evidence in the kitchen. However, many managed without such elaborations and if a household was so poor as to have only the one cooking pot its members were not necessarily condemned to eat eternal porridge or broth, although many could afford nothing else. By the ingenious use of earthenware jars and nets or cloth bags assorted foodstuffs could be cooked simultaneously in the same vessel.

There were some places where, even in the eighteenth century, they managed without cooking pots altogether: 'I shall only at present mention one other Piece of their Ingenuity,' said a visitor to the Highlands of Scotland, 'which is, that they can boil a Quarter of Flesh, whether Mutton, Veal, Goat, or Deer, in the Paunch of a Beast, which is prepared by cutting open, and turning outside in, by which it is made clean; then they affix it with Scuars on a Hoop to which they tie a String or a Thong from the Skin of the Beast, by which they hang it over the Fire.'[8] Some twenty-five years earlier another visitor had recorded much the same method, although it was supposedly only in some of the islands that 'the meaner sort of people still retain the custom of boiling their beef in the hide; or otherwise (being destitute of vessels of metal or earth) they put water into a block of wood, made hollow by the help of the dirk, and burning; and then with pretty large stones heated red-hot, and successively quenched in that vessel, they keep the water boiling, till they have dressed their food. It is said, likewise, that they roast a fowl in the embers, with the guts and feathers; and when they think it done enough, they strip off the skin, and then think it fit for the table.'[9] This latter method of cooking was widely practised with peat and similar fuels, with the foodstuffs either being put directly into the embers or else cooked in a vessel sitting in them. The method, though, was not so suited to coal's fiercer heat, while the coal dust clinging to any items cooked directly in the embers was not particularly good for the digestion.

Baking could be done in a number of ways. Bread and pies could be put inside a lidded pan placed over the fire or among the ashes; alternatively items could be placed directly on the hot hearth, covered by an inverted pot and the result was termed 'upset bread'. Another method employed a bakestone, a flat stone supported on a rough-hewn handle. The stone stood upright before the fire so that the surface heated and it was then laid flat, heated side uppermost, and the article to be baked was placed upon it, with or without an inverted pot as a cover. Extra heat could be provided by heaping embers over the pot. Iron versions of these were used in exactly the same fashion in the western parts of Cornwall where they were termed 'pot-ovens'.[10]

Wafering irons resembled iron tongs with rounded ends embossed with a pattern and, after being heated in the fire, the prepared batter was poured in to make the ever-popular waffles and wafers. A grid-iron, girdle or griddle placed over the fire baked many items, such as 'ye oat Clap bread' seen by Celia Fiennes in the vicinity of 'Lake Wiandermer' and described at length. Once it had been kneaded 'as thinn as a paper . . . they have a plaite of jron . . . and so shove off the Cake on it and so set it on Coales and bake it'. Previously she had observed: 'Ye taste of oate bread is pleasant enough and where its well made is very acceptable, but for ye most part its scarce baked and full of drye flour on ye outside.'[11]

Elsewhere, baking might be done in small ovens, as found in Devon and Cornwall: 'They make great use here of Cloume ovens, which are earthern ware of several sizes, like an oven, and being heated they stop 'em up and cover 'em over with embers to keep in the heat.'[12]

Well-to-do households would possess a separately fired bread oven in which all the household's baking of breads, pies, cakes and other items would be done on a set day. Most were constructed of brick or stone but some were made in cast iron before the introduction of the kitchen range with its integral oven. The oven was often sited in a

Although the room is sparsely furnished, the oatcakes are being cooked on the flat surface of a separately fired stove rather than on a girdle over the open fire. Some are drying on the upturned chair and others are draped over the lines above the hearth. From E. Hailstone (ed.), *The Costumes of Yorkshire in 1814*, facsimile edition of 1885. (The Trustees of the National Library of Scotland)

separate bakehouse equipped with meal barrels, dough troughs, bread peels and other relevant articles. The oven was roughly circular or oval in shape, lined with brick or stone, and the entrance was closed with a tight-fitting door of some hardened wood, replaced latterly by one of iron. When baking day came round, once a week or once a fortnight, a fire was lit inside the oven itself and allowed to burn until all the surfaces were hot. The ashes were then raked out, the oven floor swabbed with a damp mop and the door closed until the heat evened itself out, after which the first items were inserted with an oven-peel and the door fitted into place. As the day progressed, so cooked items were taken out and other items requiring diminishing amounts of heat were put in: 'I have known a very large brick oven, heated in the middle of the day with one full-sized faggot or rather more, and a log or two of cord-wood . . . still warm enough at eight or nine o'clock in the evening to bake various delicate small cakes such as macaroons and *mesingues* [? meringues], and also custards, apples &c' wrote Eliza Acton.[13] The residual heat could dry off biscuits or fruits, rags for the tinder box, feathers for bedding and, finally, the kindling for the next baking day.

When the fire lit in the upper chamber of the oven had burnt itself out the ashes were raked through a slot at the front and they dropped on to the floor through the lower aperture. Baking was done in the residual heat of the upper chamber. (The Weald & Downland Open Air Museum, Singleton)

The heat of oven or fire and length of cooking times were for the judgement of the cook and early manuals gave helpful suggestions. Some included instructions such as: 'The water is to remain upon it, no longer than whiles you can say the *Miserere* Psalm very leisurely' or to boil an egg 'whiles your Pulse beateth two hundred stroaks'. In making water gruel (i.e. a variant of porridge) the cook was instructed to 'make it rise in a great ebullition, in great galloping waves'[14] which is much more exciting than today's prosaic 'cook for twenty minutes'. Samuel Pepys observed of his wife's first attempts at baking, shortly after they moved into Seething Lane: 'Found my wife making of pies and tarts to try her oven with, which she has never yet done, but not knowing the nature of it, did heat it too hot, and so a little overbake her things, but knows how to do better another time'.[15] Generally, the housewife 'threw a spittle' on the oven door to judge the temperature, the same technique as was used for laundry irons, but a more genteel version was to throw in a handful of flour. If it went on fire or turned black it was advisable to close the door and wait a while for the oven to cool down.[16]

Many town dwellers bought their breads, pies, biscuits and other items from professional bakers owing to lack of space within their homes and the costs of buying fuel. Indeed, one traveller was of the opinion that no English housewife ever made her own bread: 'They never take the trouble to bake because there is a baker in every parish or village, from whom they can always have new bread,' he wrote.[17] The professionals also baked items prepared by their customers and on Sundays lit their ovens in order to bake joints of meat for those without the means of cooking them themselves – a practice that continued in certain localities until the Second World War. One author, while praising the baker's oven as an economy and a convenience, included a recipe directed at the professionals: *'To grow a shoulder or leg of mutton*: This art is well known to the London bakers. Have a very small leg or shoulder; change it upon a customer for one a little larger, and that upon another for one better still, till by the dinner-hour you have a heavy excellent joint in lieu of your original small one'.[18]

The main hearth, stewing stove and bread-oven were all fired separately, a system that was not only costly to run but extravagant on space and dwindling sources of traditional fuels. Foreigners, such as the American 'Count Rumford', were appalled at the prodigality of English cooks. Alongside these aspects were far-reaching advances in both the coal-mining industry and in the greatly increased distribution of coal, as well as in the use of coal within the iron industry itself. The introduction of a technique employing coke in the production of cast iron led to a huge increase in the number of artefacts readily available to the housewife.

One of the earliest developments was to put an iron box on either side of the grate; these 'hobs' did the job of a stewing stove by allowing foods to continue cooking gently, out of the way of the main cooking area. The next stage utilized the space within the hobs. In 1780 the first known patent was taken out for a cooking range,

A small range suitable for a cottage, a scene familiar in many rural dwellings until the Second World War. (Auchindrain, Inveraray)

devised by Thomas Robinson. This combined a 'range' of cooking methods within the one unit. It had a fire-box open at the top and in front for customary boiling and roasting processes, an oven set on one side with a hinged door and, on the other, a tank for heating water, while the surfaces of both acted as stewing stoves. Early models were not very efficient as the oven heated unevenly leaving foods burnt on one side and raw opposite. The water tank, too, had to be filled by hand and, if this was neglected, there could be a big problem.

The next decade saw improvements in the designs with further progress occurring in 1802 when George Bodley patented a closed-top cooking range. This resembled earlier models in having an open-fronted fire-box but the top became a continuous surface fitted with boiling rings to take pots and kettles. Throughout the nineteenth century and well into the twentieth innumerable designs of cast-iron ranges were manufactured and built into every type of home. They were a byword for the amount of fuel they consumed as well as for the time expended on the daily maintenance and in blackleading them and polishing up the shiny bits.

A totally new concept of domestic cookery was initiated when gas was introduced as the cooking medium. Although gas lighting quickly became popular and reasonably efficient, other uses for gas were slow to be introduced. The first piece of equipment specifically devised to utilize gas for cooking is said to have been a gun barrel bored with holes, made at the Aetna Iron Works in 1824. Thereafter isolated instances of cooking by gas are on record, some of which, such as the exploits of Alexis Soyer, were most successful[19] but in 1844 the situation was summed up thus:

> Among the novelties in the culinary art is the use of coal gas for producing the necessary heat. . . . Some persons have been so sanguine as to suppose that this employment of gas may soon do away altogether with the necessity of open fires in our kitchens, – a hasty opinion evidently founded upon a very superficial and and imperfect acquaintance with the business of an ordinary kitchen. . . . What may be accomplished by future generations we will not endeavour to speculate upon; . . . It will be interesting, however, to describe some of the experiments that have been made with success. The subject is at least amusing, and is really deserving of attention, even should its usefulness prove as limited as we fear it will ultimately be found to be.

Ease of use, ease of getting heat exactly where required, and ease of adjustment of the heat gave gas 'a superiority over every kind of lamp and might almost tempt one to think that methods may some day be invented for applying it with success to culinary purposes with great advantage of convenience on some occasions, if not of economy'.[20]

Meg Dods put it rather more succinctly in the tenth edition (1854) of her celebrated cookbook: 'Some years since we had great hopes of the success of cooking by *gas* which must have been of immense convenience to small families where gas is used for lighting. We regret to say that no great progress has been made: gas cookery is still not only unsatisfactory, but expensive.'[21]

Gas was innovatory in ways in which coal had not been. It was supplied from a central source, beyond the control of cook or housewife, and the fuel used while cooking was not available for the simultaneous heating of water or burning of rubbish. On the other hand it was a clean fuel and easily adjusted by turning a tap, although cooking temperatures still depended on the cook's judgement. Not until 1923 was the first thermostatic control fitted to a gas oven by Radiation Ltd, who called it the 'Regulo', a name still current today.

It was the 1870s and even into the 1880s before gas was accepted as being suitable for cookery and this was due to the impact made on the lighting market by the introduction of paraffin, followed by electricity. Gas companies, therefore, endorsed their fuel for heating and cooking and made many improvements in the design and function of cookers.

An early gas cooker, recognizably the forerunner of today's appliances. From *Cassell's Book of the Household*, *c.* 1893, vol. 1.

Electricity was somewhat swifter in being promoted as a fuel for cooking. In 1891 it was demonstrated at the Crystal Palace and three years later London had its own School of Electric Cookery; in the interim an electric kitchen had gone on show at the Chicago World Fair of 1893.

As with heating, so with cooking. Manufacturing and distribution problems had to be tackled before costs could decline and electricity could be more widely used. The situation was summed up in 1920, as follows:

> Great hopes have been raised in the mind of the general public by the prospect of what is called 'a cheap supply of electricity'. . . . The expectation aroused has been that electricity will displace gas and solid fuel as a means for cooking and heating. While there can be no question of the enormous advantages of electrical power for these purposes – indeed no other form of energy can compare with electricity for combined cleanliness and convenience – yet it must be regretfully stated that unless and until the process of producing electrical power can be completely transformed from the present method, no such general employment of electricity for these purposes is economically possible, either on the ground of national economy of fuel resources or of financial economy to the consumer. . . .
>
> Electricity, therefore, except in very special cases and when financial economy is of very little account, cannot be regarded as a solution of the problems of economy, either for heating or for cooking. Electrical power is supreme for lighting or for the production of mechanical power in small units.[22]

Soon after this was written yet another type of cooking stove came on to the market. This was the Aga, developed in Sweden by a blind physicist and Nobel prize winner. It burned solid fuels such as coke or anthracite and was advertised as needing attention just once a day.

Alongside new fuels and new cookers came new designs for pots and pans. Out went the extra-long handles and the three short legs, no longer needed on the range's flat cooking surfaces. The solid brass, copper and cast-ironware of the previous centuries were gradually set to one side. They had come in a bewildering array of size and shape, been heavy to lift even when empty and those with a bright finish were tedious to polish after every use. To reduce the amount of cleaning ironware had long been tin-coated on the inside and was then black-varnished on the outside. Vitreous enamelled ware became available early in the twentieth century at much the same time as aluminium pans, and both proved popular with housewives since they were so much lighter than earlier utensils, and cooked well, too. Compared with aluminium, stainless steel pans were expensive and not widely used until the 1950s.

In the meantime, other major developments of the period concerned the introduction of oven-to-tableware, for example, 'Pyrex' in the 1920s, as increasing numbers of housewives found themselves running a servantless household and endeavoured to cut down on the time and energy they expended in the kitchen.

CHAPTER NINE

Provisioning the Household

Provisioning the household must have been a major preoccupation for many a housewife. Little imagination is needed to visualize the self-sufficiency of a farmyard setting but what about housewives in towns or remote rural areas? There was also a world of difference between those who were able to exercise choice over their daily fare and those who merely existed on the bare minimum. Time and again observations made about 'the poor' throughout Britain remark on the meagre diet and heavy reliance on a few staple articles such as potatoes, milk or oatmeal.

At one time a reasonable level of self-sufficiency had been feasible. Grazing for a cow, geese and poultry could take place on common ground or be allowed as part of a man's wages. The cow provided milk, cream, butter, cheese – which could be eaten, sold or form part of the rent; at the end of the day it also represented meat, tallow and leather, while the products of geese and poultry took many forms. A pig could be kept on household waste or whatever else might be convenient. Every part of the pig could be eaten – apart from its grunt, or so the saying went – and it gave the household some fresh meat and bacon for the rest of the year. Bread or oatcakes were baked, beer was brewed and lighting produced; fuel was free apart from the labour of collecting it. A strip of garden sheltered a few beehives and supplied vegetables and fruit, or a few herbs, with others coming from the open countryside.

Such a lifestyle was still partially evident in the Oxfordshire hamlet of 'Lark Rise',[1] late in the nineteenth century, whereas one hundred years earlier it had been common as, for example, in South Wales where, it was said, 'every cottager . . . has a little garden, in which he grows his own leeks for pottage, and his potatoes, cabbages, cole-worts, pease, &c. for hodge-podge, &c'.[2] Advances in agriculture and other causes deprived many of their long-established grazing rights and gardens and, without them, they were driven to look for work in the towns, thus becoming paid labourers and buying in their daily food. Arthur Young, on his travels around Ireland, thought it worth noting that there the labourer was still being allowed land for a cow, poultry and potatoes and he debated which system was more advantageous to the wife and children.[3]

For those housewives fortunate enough to have a choice in the matter, food supplies fell into two broad categories: items that had to be acquired from someone else and those that could be home-grown or home-reared, with a narrow dividing line between household and farm. Farmers' wives, along with their household duties, were likely to look after poultry, rear calves, tend any farmyard orphans and sell eggs or surplus products from the dairy. Even in towns many householders kept hens or bees and grew vegetables or some fruit.

'As to my tables, for the most part they are furnished with unbought feasts,' said Sir John Clerk of Penicuik[4], maintaining that, as a countryman, he expected no less. However, his ambitions of self-sufficiency were supported by a well-stocked home farm, kitchen garden, apiary and fish ponds, in all of which he took great pride. For many, though, self-sufficiency was more of a necessity than a philosophical concept.

An early description of the housewife's activities in the garden is to be found in Tusser:[5]

> In March and in Aprill, from morning to night
> In sowing and setting, good husewives delight:
> To have in a garden, or other like plot,
> To trim up their house, and to furnish their pot.
> The nature of flowers, Dame Physicke doth show;
> She teacheth them all, to be knowne to a few:
> To set or to sowe, or else sowne to remove,
> How that should be practiced, learne if ye love.

Herbals were written to help the housewife not only grow the right plants but to teach her when they should be gathered and about their medicinal properties. The emphasis on this branch of a housewife's knowledge had a long history; during the First World War women were exhorted to grow herbs to replace the supplies that had formerly come from Germany and Austria.[6]

Some sixty years after Tusser a little book on gardening appeared aimed specifically at the housewife. William Lawson, a Yorkshire clergyman, gave advice as to soil, situation, layout, size and the need for fencing, and then turned to the cultivation of plants, whether they were for decoration, eating, flavouring or for healing purposes. He described why two gardens were required to grow such 'herbs', a word used then in a much wider sense than today: 'Herbes are of two sorts, and therefore it is meete (they requiring divers manners of Husbandry) that we have two Gardens: A garden for flowers, and a Kitchen garden' he said, because 'that which is for your Kitchins use, must yeeld daily roots, or other herbes, and suffer deformity.' The housewife could put her maids to work in the garden but, says Lawson, when it comes to weeding: 'Withal, I advise the Mistresse, either be present her selfe, or to teach her maides to know hearbs from weeds.'[7]

The frontispiece to *Every Man His Own Gard'ner*, by T. Mawe and J. Abercrombie, 14th edn, 1794, shows that work in the vegetable garden has changed little in two hundred years.

It is often said that fruit and vegetables were not widely grown 'in the early days'. Although it is difficult to be precise as to who exactly ate what, how often or how much, the potential for growing a wide range of plants in the gardens did exist, although the range widened considerably as the years went by. Tusser named about three hundred.[8] In fact, what is now considered to be a 'traditional' kitchen garden has only come about after centuries of geographical exploration as well as influences arriving via trade, immigration, warfare and religion; there was also experimental work with plants of every description, either as a deliberate act or the result of practical observation. The modern strawberry, to take just one example, is a descendant of one found in Virginia and another from Chile, which were hybridized in a French garden but grown on and finally perfected at Islington, near London, in 1826. The history of our garden plants is an adventure story of positively epic proportions. So many everyday food items, thought of as being indigenous, started life elsewhere: parsley, broccoli, carrots, cauliflowers, potatoes, tomatoes, rhubarb, gooseberries . . . There are French beans, Brussels sprouts, damsons from Damascus and Jerusalem artichokes (though not, this time, from the place but derived from the Italian *girasole*); likewise our spinach, thought to be a corruption of 'Spanish' but actually stemming from an Arabic word – possibly arriving by way of the Moorish occupation of Spain.

How quickly such items came to be widely grown is difficult to assess. Many would first be raised in landowners' gardens before being diffused through the population at large. Potatoes were known and grown in Ireland by the end of the sixteenth century and in England at much the same time, but the earliest known references for Scotland are almost one hundred years later. Many similar instances could be quoted, such as the time in 1734 when 'Lochiel of Achnacary in Lochaber' in the Scottish Highlands, served a vegetable soup called hotch potch containing pease, turnip and carrot from his own garden which was accounted 'the first time that these vegetables had been produced in that part of the world'.[9]

A wider range of plants could be grown and their availability prolonged where shelter was provided. Screening on garden walls protected fruit trees at vulnerable times, while heating systems with elaborate flues could be built into the walls themselves. On a smaller scale the gable-end of a house, containing the kitchen fireplace, was often utilized in the same way. Clay pots were used for forcing or blanching individual items, as were glass bell jars (i.e. circular cloches), and cold frames are often portrayed in gardening scenes. 'Hot beds' provided favourable conditions for growing out-of-season plants or otherwise rarely seen delicacies such as melons or pineapples and were created by building up a deep layer of manure, covering it with soil and placing over it panes of glass in a frame. The rotting manure heated the soil and the glass maintained the heat.

A greater use of glass in gardens became fashionable towards the end of the seventeenth century when structures were built to over-winter tender plants, such as orange trees and similar items. These came to be called 'orangeries' but after the plant tubs had been trundled outdoors for the warmer months they did duty as summer houses. Initially, these buildings had very large windows with a solid roof; only later was glass used for the roof as well and from these descend all greenhouses, glass houses, conservatories and so on. However, as a Glass Tax operated from 1695–8 and from 1745–1845 these buildings were costly and so were more likely to be part of a comprehensive kitchen garden with staff, where the housewife was less directly involved.

William Lawson certainly expected his housewife to produce more from her garden than just 'herbs': 'There remaineth one necessary thing to be prescribed . . . which is Bees, well ordered. And I will not account her any of my good House-wives, that wanteth either Bees, or skilfulnesse about them' and so, being a bee-master himself, he devoted a chapter to 'The Husbandry of Bees'.[10] Although some sugar had always been around it remained comparatively expensive and honey was the general sweetening agent and preservative, as well as having medicinal properties; honey also made mead and other variants such as metheglin and hydromel.[11] Beeswax made the best candles and was the basis for polishes and cosmetics, as it still is.

In spite of Lawson's encouragement and the expense of imported sugar, it is strange that references to women keeping bees are sparse until after the upsurge of interest late in the nineteenth century. 'At that date women beekeepers were very scarce,' one Scottish beekeeper recalled in 1940, although there were certainly women who attended, during the day, to the hives of their menfolk, following instructions but having no knowledge of the bees themselves: 'The coming of associations and demonstrations and Shows has led many women to get hives of their own, and to keep the profits of the bees to themselves. What a difference there is now! Women beekeepers are numerous, holding Beemaster, Expert and Honey Judge certificates, and competing at the largest Shows, and even judging at the International Honey Show.'[12]

Poultry also came under the housewife's supervision but were generally allowed to roam at will, scratching a living how and where they could. The sale of eggs provided a little money for the housewife; sometimes poultry, or other commodities such as cheese or fish, were termed 'kain', to be paid as rent, so that behind entries in a housekeeping ledger noting '14 chickens and 2 hens entered as 9' or '20 chickens and a cock as 7' some hard bargaining can be sensed.[13] Poultry provided not only eggs and meat but also feathers for stuffing pillows or cushions and, depending on fashions, as a decoration for hats, while a trimmed hen or goose wing was a neat way of brushing clothes or dusting shelves. The feet, bones and skin boiled up for several hours gave a strong stock which was the base for setting jellies, blancmanges and other delights. When the stock was further evaporated and set in small moulds it became 'Portable Soup', considered to be an essential for travellers as a lump broken off and added to hot water made for an instant soup. Goose grease was important in medical terms, as an embrocation, an ointment or a poultice to ease bad chests; otherwise it softened leather, water-proofed shoes and had a myriad of additional uses as well.

Pigeons were not exactly poultry, nor did they specifically belong to either garden or farm, although some cookbooks included instructions for keeping them. Certainly, once they entered the kitchen as a potential foodstuff they were very much the concern of the housewife or her cook.

Many myths have crept into the subject of the eating of pigeons, but the eighteenth-century cookery books are quite clear as to the type of birds required for the table: 'Take young pigeons', 'take squab* pigeons', the refrain continues, 'Chuse tender Squab Pigeons',

---

* squabs are nestlings still being fed by the parent birds

This handsome 'doocot' straddles the walls surrounding the medieval castle at Dirleton, East Lothian. Inside the 'doocot' the tiers of nesting boxes for the pigeons are clearly visible. A revolving ladder, the potence, gave access to the young birds required by the kitchens.

'Chuse four very young tame Pigeons from the Nest before they have Feathers for flying'.[14] Pigeons will breed when there is sufficient warmth and a plentiful supply of grain or seed for forage; vociferous complaints against their owners speak of the hefty depredations made by the birds in the fields during seedtime (i.e. the spring sowing) and at harvest (i.e. late summer and autumn), while a study of domestic dinner books pinpoints these as being the times when copious numbers of pigeons were appearing on the bills of fare. In other words, it was the young birds that were taken for table use, at the times of year when they were plentiful and when there was no shortage of alternative foodstuffs.[15] Rarely were they eaten in the winter months.

By the mid-eighteenth century such self-sufficiency was becoming less evident even on the largest estates, as witnessed by their domestic account books and similar documents which reveal the range of commodities being bought in.

During the earlier part of the period, the fair was the venue for the more specialized household purchases or for bulk orders. Taking place in a locality once or twice a year and lasting for a number of days – eight or fourteen days being common – the local fair was a scene of the greatest activity. It would attract buyers and sellers from all walks of life and from all parts of the country – and beyond, too, if sufficiently large enough to attract merchants from abroad. Servants and labourers in the area were often granted a holiday so they could attend and those seeking a job went there to offer themselves for hire.

Many fairs had a long history dating back to pre-Reformation times and were held around a significant point in the church calendar or on the local saint's day, which was only to be expected as many had their origins in religious festivals and were actually run by a church or monastery. Fairs were highly profitable to whoever 'owned' them, whether the king, town or local nobleman, seeing that a commission on each transaction was payable by both sides, while traders had to pay for hiring a stall, for building a stall or for using a space on the ground, as well as for hiring the weights and measures they were obliged to use. Hefty fines could also be imposed for assorted misdemeanours. Special courts of justice were set up to officiate in disputes occurring during the life of a fair and these were known as 'pie-powder' courts – a corruption of *pieds-poudrés*, literally the courts of the dusty feet. This was a reference to the fact that some people travelled considerable distances to attend and were unlikely to be found in the area again before the following year.

The serious side of the fair centred on the buying and selling of commodities. Fairs were of a general nature, with a very wide range of goods and services available, but some had become more specialized over the years in areas producing or dealing in certain items, whether it was cloth, wine and spices, salt fish or horses. Following in the wake of the fair were sellers of services – barbers, for example, tooth-drawers or quack doctors; itinerant sellers of hot foods, drinks and much else besides; servants and labourers hoping to find employment; entertainments ranging from strolling players, Punch and Judy booths, 'all the fun of the fair' in fact.

The regular, but infrequent, fair was complemented by the local market which catered for the housewife's ordinary domestic needs. Market day was an important event in the social calendar. Roads leading to the town would be thronged as everyone set off early, some in carts but the majority on foot, taking locally produced goods for sale. Market-bound women in South Wales, it was noted, walked along with a large heavily freighted market-basket on their heads, thus displacing the high-crowned, broad-brimmed hats which they carried for miles either in their hand or tied to an arm or an apron string, so that they could wear their national headdress on arrival.[16]

From the earliest days markets, like fairs, were strictly regulated by the authorities as to the day or days on which they were held, when and where stalls could be set up, the hours at which trading started or finished and the weights and measures to be used. Trading took place in the shadow of a prominent market cross which symbolized the obligation of Christian (i.e. honest) dealing. Small towns might have a general market once a week whereas in a large town, such as Edinburgh, markets could be held on two or three days a week; traders in the same line of business clustered together along the High Street and in the narrow wynds and closes off it, so that for meat the housewife went to one site, for firewood to another, and so on. People speak wistfully of 'the good old days' but trading was done in the open air and goods were on view in wind, sun, rain and snow; haggling was the order of the day, for each and every object, as to its size, weight and quality. Having finally concluded a bargain, wrappings were not provided, small coinage was in short supply and much was counterfeit anyway, and the goods had to be carried home thereafter.

Celia Fiennes made many passing references to market-places and market halls as she travelled the country, such an everyday feature as they were. Near Exeter, she observed: 'Culimton is a good Little market town, and market Cross and another set on stone pillars, such a one was at Wellington but on Brick work pillars'; but, on arrival at Exeter, she was amazed at the sheer scale of the trade conducted in serge*: 'There is an Increadible quantety of them made and sold in the town. There market day is Fryday which supplys with all things Like a faire almost; the markets for meate, fowle, ffish, garden things and the Dairy produce takes up 3 whole streetes beside the Large Market house set on stone pillars, wch runs a great Length on wch they Lay their packs of serges. Just by it is another walke wth in pillars wch is for the yarne.'[17]

Not all markets were so extensive. At the other end of Britain, in Inverness, it was a very different scene: 'Here are four or five fairs in the year, when the Highlanders bring their commodities to market: but, good God! you could not conceive there was such misery in this island. One has under his arm a small role of linen, another a piece of coarse plaiding: these are considerable dealers'. The rest of the goods comprised little more than a few small cheeses, some butter in a bladder, a young goat and maybe a piece or two of wood. The market was not only patronized by the housewife but was also the trading place for merchants and other men of business: 'There they stand in the middle of the dirty street, and are frequently interrupted in their negotiations by horses and carts, which often separate them one from

* a strong, woollen cloth

another in the midst of their bargains or other affairs. But this is nothing extraordinary in Scotland; for it is the same in other towns, and even at the Cross of Edinburgh.'[18]

Contemporary London was different again: 'Nowhere can you see finer markets than in London, especially those of Leadenhall, of Stock Market, and several others; they are vast, covered, and shut in, and in them you can find every kind of butcher's meat, the finest in all the world, and kept with the greatest cleanliness', recorded one foreign visitor.[19]

Everywhere there were the hawkers of goods; everything and anything that could be carried by man, woman, packhorse or donkey, was peddled through the streets, a custom the same visitor considered worthy of comment: 'Besides these large public markets quantities of small vendors go through the streets, especially in the morning, calling out their wares for sale; thus, if you prefer it, you need not leave your house to buy your provisions.' It was said, one hundred years later, that there were as many as 13,000 of these traders in London alone; the scene in Edinburgh was similar although by the 1860s and 1870s their numbers were declining noticeably.[20] In the country areas an assortment of chapmen, hawkers, peddlers, Manchester men, Scotch drapers and so on took their wares to the smaller towns and villages, and this practice continued despite the change in transport from pony and trap or bicycle to the motorized van.

In the early days there were those who surmised that these peripatetic traders dealt in goods other than the ones at the top of their baskets. The fishwives who walked from the coast into Edinburgh each day carrying creels of fish to sell to the town's housewives certainly had this reputation. The lowering of the water level of the Nor' Loch* at the foot of the Castle Rock, the receptacle for much unsavoury rubbish, was also a cause of concern to the town council in 1740 since it permitted goods to be brought in without paying the necessary dues. To protect their revenue the town ordered that the Loch should be filled to its previous level.[21]

Any period when high taxes are levied on desirable commodities, whether they be soap or silk, tobacco or tea, is likely to see an increase in smuggling but, as successful smugglers leave few traces, it is difficult to ascertain just how much was done. Even the Rev. James Woodforde obtained goods this way, though he felt distinctly uneasy about the connection at times. He recorded dealings with one Richard Andrews, curiously described as 'the honest smuggler', over 'a Pound of 9sh. Tea and 3 silk India Handkerchiefs at 5sh. 6d'. On other occasions it was likely to be a consignment of gin or cognac. One

Oysters and fish were just two of the many commodities sold by peripatetic traders. From *The Book of the Old Edinburgh Club*, vol. 2, 1909.

* since drained and turned into Princes Street Gardens

evening at about 9 p.m. a thump was heard at the front door but on going to investigate nobody was around but two casks had been left on the doorstep; a previous time Andrews had 'frightened us a little by whistling under the Parlour Window just as we were going to bed'.[22]

A less nerve-wracking method of obtaining luxuries, or goods unavailable locally, involved sending an order through the post and waiting for one of the many carriers that plied the country to deliver the goods. The *Letters* of the widowed Mrs Purefroy and her son Henry who lived at Shalstone, Buckinghamshire, some 60 miles from London, provide plentiful evidence.[23] So much of what is done today over the telephone is here committed to paper – small transactions as well as a most varied range of commissions to the two men who acted as their agents in London: Mr Robotham, who had married a former servant of theirs, was the licensee of The King's Head, Islington and Mr Peter Moulson was a respectable wine merchant.

The Purefroys can be followed over the years as they persevered in placing orders or requesting the attendance of tradesmen and then seeing from the follow-up letters how often the goods or promised services failed to meet their needs. Letters regarding oysters 'as black as ink', Bohea tea that was full of dust, and hoops that flew off the hogshead of red port as it was unloaded were interspersed with other complaints: 'What fish you sent last week stank & could not be eat' and 'mountain wine . . . so new & sweet that wee cannot drink it'. An account undercharging Mrs Purefroy activated a response similar in style to when she was overcharged or an account was rendered twice: 'I admire you don't keep your books more regular, I suppose if I had lost the receipt & Mr Robotham had chanced to have Dyed – I must have paid the money over again.' The faithful Mr Robotham was charged with diverse commissions, including orders for Hyson and Bohea teas, coffee berries, mountain wine and chocolate, while being thanked at different times for presents of lamb, oranges and lemons, two lobsters and a barrel of sturgeon. In return they sent him gifts of hares and other game, turkeys, butter, cuts of meat and promised some hog puddings when they came to kill their other pig.

Meanwhile, Henry was facing similar problems on the domestic front. On behalf of his mother he wrote of chocolate 'so bitter and high dried that she can't drink it' and of flax 'not fit for her purpose', while consignments of wines and spirits caused endless problems. A sharp reminder was sent to the chimney sweep at 'Bircester' pointing out that as he had promised to come at Michaelmas, some two months before, 'Your not coming is a Disappointment to us' and other arrangements

A grocer's shop of the 1920s fitted with mahogany shelves and counters. Such shops were to be found everywhere until the supermarket made its appearance in the 1960s. (By courtesy of the Museum of Welsh Life)

would have to be made. The sweep came. An order was sent to the brush-maker in Buckingham asking for 'three rubbing brushes to rub parlours with'; payment on an order of nails would be withheld until inspected, seeing that a previous batch had been unsatisfactory; and a gardener from Brackley had not come to thin the cherry trees, as promised, '& pray bring yᵉ Hammer with you wᶜʰ I suppose you took by mistake'. Several years later the same man was asked to supply vegetable seeds '& pray come over soon to prune yᵉ ffruit Trees, for they are grown so scandalously high above yᵉ Walls that I never saw them so in my Life'. It was not only the matter of provisions which caused such problems; the Purefroys were not much luckier when it came to ordering things for the house or items of a personal nature for themselves.

It was only gradually that the housewife 'went to the shops' for her supplies rather than 'did her marketing'. It was grocers, such as Fortnum & Mason established in 1707, who were among the first to trade from a shop instead of a market stall and as the goods were mainly imported (i.e. dried) there was little friction between them and the sellers of fresh produce, although there was some overlap with the apothecaries' wares at one end of the scale and with the chandlers' at the other. Towards the end of the nineteenth century there was an increasing number of shops selling foodstuffs, although the covered markets, which were replacing the old-style open markets, remained popular with working-class housewives until the First World War. They also provided entertainers, such as fortune-tellers and jugglers, in a manner reminiscent of the medieval fair.

A housewife buys her fruit and vegetables from this display, 1925. However, from the size of her basket, she is expecting the greengrocer to deliver her order. (By courtesy of The Hulton Getty Picture Collection Limited)

The concept of multiple shops, with as many as one hundred or more branches spread across the country, was another development in this period; assisted by rapid rail transport and the ability to purchase in bulk, they offered the housewife goods that were both cheap and reliable. Similarly, the Co-operative movement with its dividends and emphasis on honest trading proved popular with the housewife, especially in working-class districts.

Since those days the housewife has seen yet further changes with the huge increase in motorized transport and the concept of 'self-service stores', although the revolution in shopping patterns that lay ahead could only be guessed at in 1950.

CHAPTER TEN

Storage and Preservation of Food

T he housewife did not only have to cope with such imponderables as the availability of provisions in general or scarcity in particular, but the domestic manuals also emphasized the importance of preserving present-day plenty against future needs. Before the days of domestic refrigerators the housewife practised many ways of prolonging the supply of foodstuffs, either in the short term or for a period of a year or more, and some of these are still in use today, albeit more often in commercial hands.

The local name for this cold-store or larder was 'the setlas'. Meat and other items would be kept here; the area under the arched brickwork was even cooler. (Ironbridge Gorge Museum Trust)

One of the simplest, and earliest, of methods utilized the drying properties of wind and sun but this was unreliable in a damp climate. Even so, Scottish housewives could follow recipes for 'Wind-blown fish', 'Rizzard Haddies' or 'To dry Sillocks'.[1] Equally well established was the method of hanging meat or fish in the smoke rising from a fire, where different fuels gave distinctive flavours to the food, and this could be done somewhere out of doors, within the home, or in a purpose-built smoke house. It was often combined with a preliminary salting, either rubbing the article over with salt or immersing it in a brine solution. Sometimes, all three methods were combined in the same item, as for 'Finnan' or Aberdeen haddocks which were given a brief salting, dried in the open air and finished off in the smoke.[2]

Salt, without the smoking afterwards, was often used, especially in areas where salt was readily available, but it required a supply of tubs or crocks in which to store the articles thereafter as items were either layered between dry salt or submerged in strong brine. In the days before turnips and other crops were grown for animal fodder there was an autumnal slaughtering of livestock every year and many a household ate its way, from nose to tail, along the 'mart ox' during the ensuing months. Similarly, the cottager's pig provided not only fresh meat but also a supply of bacon for the ensuing months. To the folk of 'Lark Rise', 'The family pig was everybody's pride and everybody's business,' and the killing was a dramatic occasion for the inhabitants except that 'Laura felt sick and would creep back into bed and cry; she felt sorry for the pig'.[3] Meanwhile, in the story *Cranford* an examination of a bunch of old letters yields one endorsed by the recipient: 'Hebrew verses sent me by my honoured husband. I thowt to have had a letter about killing the pig, but must wait.'[4] Salt beef and salt pork were a fact of life for generations; Belfast exported vast quantities of both whereas Aberdeen was noted for its salt pork. These meats were not limited to the domestic scene but were taken to sea as the mainstay of the sailors' diet, though many were the complaints over its quality and suspicions as to its origins.

Vinegar enhanced with spices was a similarly successful way of preserving items, with the end results generally being called 'pickled'. Almost anything could be treated this way, ranging from lemons to salmon, via eggs, red cabbage, walnuts, mushrooms and so on and so forth.[5] The longevity of such products could be aided by floating a little sweet oil across the surface of the pickle, once cold, but this was only suitable if the container was not to be moved thereafter.[6]

'Potting' was another way of prolonging the life of meats, fish and poultry. This involved cooking the items in a pot with sufficient fat which would rise to the surface in the cooling and, when cold, form an airtight cover to the foodstuffs below. The layer of melted butter covering potted shrimps is a reminder of this but the French-style 'confit' is even closer.

The preservative nature of sugar is probably the most familiar method of all, seeing it is still used by housewives in the making of jams, jellies and marmalades. In 1903 one authority claimed: 'Jam is the most usual method of preserving fruit for winter use. It is the easiest made and easiest kept'[7] but, by then, housewives had been making jam at home for two hundred years or more and certainly since Mrs Eales had published her little book of *Receipts*.[8] The combination of fruit and sugar was well known, with the end products taking many forms. Henry Howard boasted recipes for 'Preserving, Conserving, Candying and Drying Fruits'[9] and the list could be augmented with fruit pastes and cakes,* as well as with fruit cheeses and butters. Howard's method for 'preserving' involved peeling and stoning the fruit which was to be boiled with an equal weight of sugar or in a syrup made from sugar and some of the fruit puréed; by 'conserving' he meant fruits prepared and cooked with sugar in a little water, strained through a cloth; the resultant juices, with spices added, were boiled gently over a fire until thick. In the process of 'candying' fruit was first of all 'preserved', then taken from the sugar and dried off over a slow heat, whereas for 'drying' the fruits were 'preserved' as before but the syrup was washed off before the fruit was dried in a slow oven.

Although small amounts of sugar were imported during the Middle Ages its use increased gradually over the years despite attracting variable taxes from the mid-seventeenth century until 1874. Some 10,000 tons were imported in 1700; by 1754 the figure was 53,270 tons and between 1770 and 1775 it averaged 72,000 tons per year and demand for the product was extending throughout society.[10]

Any commodity seen as expensive tended to be endowed with medicinal properties. The minister of a fictional Ayrshire parish recounts how, in 1787, an upsurge in sugar supplies allied to the innovative planting of gooseberry and currant bushes heralded the fashion of making jams and jellies, hitherto only indulged in by the gentry: 'All this, however, was not without a plausible pretext; for it

---

* Fruit purées stiff enough be dried into flat 'cakes'

was found that jelly was an excellent medicine for a sore throat, and jam a remedy as good as London candy for a cough, or a cold, or a shortness of breath.'[11] Before sugar became an everyday foodstuff honey had been the general sweetening agent and preservative and it was also renowned for its medicinal properties, another reason underlying the connection of sugar with health. Charles Butler, a celebrated beekeeper in his day, expounded at length on 'the singular vertues of (1) Honie, (2) Methe [i.e. mead] and (3) Wax for the use and comfort of man'.[12]

The housewife not only had to obtain all her supplies but had to store them once they were in the house. Items hung from hooks in the ceiling, where the smoke from the fire deterred flies and lessened depredations from rats; the north of England had its bread arks which served the same purpose. Hams and bacon flitches were vulnerable to attacks from an insect that laid its eggs in the meat as it dried so that, for long-term keeping, it was advisable to sift clean dry wood-ash into a chest, sufficiently long to hold the flitch, and to smother the meat completely with the ash. Whether this precaution had been taken by his maids is not known, but Parson Woodforde noted on one occasion: 'Dinner to Day, Ham & Chicken, and a piece of rost-Beef & Apple Dumplins . . . NB: The Ham we had for Dinner to day was almost devoured by the Hoppers getting into it, unknown to me, before it came to Table. The Maids and Nancy [i.e. his niece] knew it before, but said nothing at all to me about it – or not have had it into the Parlour.'[13]

Groceries, candles, soap and other household goods required cool dry storage as did the multitude of jams and pickles and beverages made in due season. A mouthwatering description survives of just such a storeroom, in the north-east of Scotland, where movable frames for planking were laden with every possible sort of jam, dried fruit, biscuits, smoked meats, homemade wines, medicinal liquors and other commodities, to guard against any invasion by unexpected and hungry visitors.[14]

Butter and cheeses from the dairy, in themselves a form of preserving for the winter months, needed specialist storage spaces – butter in the cool, cheeses where the air could circulate around them. If garden produce was not brought across from the kitchen garden each day, where a whole range of storage methods operated, then root vegetables could be kept in bins in an outhouse, while other items might be laid on a stone-flagged floor or hung from the rafters in nets.

Cheeses need to be stored
where the air can circulate
around them. The cheese loft
at Llancaiach Fawr Manor,
Treharris. (By courtesy of
Caerphilly County Borough
Council)

Day-to-day supplies were placed on the marble, slate or stone
shelves of a larder, which was generally built facing north and
given a free flow of air. For a house of any size there might be
several larders, one for what was termed 'butcher's meat', one for
cooked meats, another for fish, game and so on. Meat safes were
also used. These resembled a metal cage with sides of zinc mesh
which would be hung in a cold draughty passageway, or might take

the form of a decorative building in the kitchen court. The method was not infallible, though, as Samuel Pepys had cause to note: 'Then home to dinner, where a stinking leg of mutton, the weather being very wet and hot to keep meat in' – an understandable mishap in June but less excusable on the January evening when they supped with a neighbour 'much against my stomach for the dishes were so deadly foule that I could not endure to look at them'.[15] Cookbooks frequently offered handy hints on 'recovering' tainted meat, stale vegetables, flat or sour beers and other dubious substances and, as just one of that ilk, Hannah Glasse's remedy 'To save potted Birds, that begin to be bad', does not make for comfortable reading.[16]

It was during the course of the eighteenth century that the ice house became the fashionable adjunct for estate owners, not so much to preserve food but as an aid to its preparation; they had first appeared in England during the 1660s. The buildings were carefully constructed of stone or brick to maintain the coldest possible temperature throughout the year. They were either cut into a sloping bank or given an artificial mound of earth over them and trees were planted above to provide currents of air as well as shade. Inside were stacked blocks of ice, or sometimes snow, gathered by the garden staff from a nearby source and layered between straw, bracken or sacking. When required ice would be taken across to the kitchen or dairy to help set the elaborately moulded jellies, creams and blancmanges or to pack around the ice-cream pail. Professional confectioners in towns such as Edinburgh built or rented ice houses on hillsides within easy reach of their premises.

Enormous quantities of ice were imported from North America or Norway during the nineteenth century and stored in insulated warehouses before being sent out to customers for use in an ice chest. These took the form of well-insulated cupboards or chests in which the food was placed along with the block of ice and it was found that placing the ice above the food was more effective, as the natural circulation of air kept the foods colder. The method worked so well that ice chests continued to be advertised throughout the 1920s.

Meanwhile a new method of preserving food was evolving. Many people had tried to preserve foods or liquids by sealing them into glass bottles but the first successful exponent of the technique was the Frenchman, Nicolas Appert, who won the prize offered by

The forerunner of the contemporary refrigerator was the ice chest (or safe, or box), made of wood, lined with zinc and well insulated. Blocks of ice placed inside the lidded upper compartment helped to preserve the foodstuffs on the shelves below. A tap between the cupboards drew off the melted water. (By courtesy of the City of York Museums Services)

Napoleon Bonaparte to whoever could help solve the problem of feeding his vast armies. By 1806 Appert had achieved a wide range of products which were successfully taken on trial by the French Navy and he was awarded a prize of 12,000 francs. However, for soldiers on the move glass bottles were not the most easily transported containers and it was a quirk of fortune that caused an English firm to take the process a stage further by sealing the items inside canisters made of tin, hence the 'tin can' of today. The new method was of benefit to a wider audience than just the housewife. A seafaring man recalled how he was sent to Brazil in 1829 and gave a dinner party on board for the Consul and several others: 'Tinned meats were then in their infancy. I astonished them with a six-pound piece of salmon to begin with, and then with a fillet of veal. They wondered how I became possessed of such a fish, as also of the first rate joint of veal.' The author revealed that an old friend had sent him 'two hampers of good things from Fortnum & Mason's before starting, and these were a part of the lot'.[17]

Canned foods remained relatively expensive until mass-production techniques were employed. Appert did not know why his method worked and it was not until the researches of Louis Pasteur (1822–95) that there was an understanding of the correct methods to follow; in the meantime there were some spectacular disasters and the public was slow to regain confidence in the product. A special tool for opening the tins was equally slow to

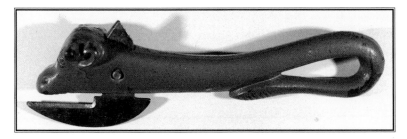

A 'Bull's head' tin-opener, 7 inches in length, *c.* 1890.

develop. Early instructions involved a chisel or 'an opening knife'.[18] Tin-openers materialized about the same time as the corned beef imported from Argentina and were often made in the shape of a bull's head with the handle modelled as the bull's tail.

The nineteenth century witnessed other major changes that would ultimately benefit the housewife and obviate the need for much of her work and worry regarding the preservation and storage of foodstuffs.

The cutting of a network of canals in the eighteenth century had already speeded up the delivery of coal, pottery and other domestic commodities, and of bulky foodstuffs such as potatoes and cheese, but the building of the railways worked momentous changes on the supply system. As early as 1824 the railway's potential to deliver goods at hitherto unknown speeds had been anticipated and it was forecast that it was 'destined, perhaps, to work a greater change in the state of civil society than even the grand discovery of navigation'.[19] By 1850, when the three principal Anglo-Scottish routes were in place, fresh fish and meat could be on sale in London just sixteen hours after leaving Aberdeen. Fresh milk could be delivered to London from as far away as Swindon and Rugby whereas, prior to this, 25 miles on a spring cart with a fast-trotting pony was considered the absolute maximum, while for other towns it was rarely more than 10 miles. The railways eventually did away with 'dry dairies' whereby cows were housed in city-centre byres and milked in front of the customers, although it was many years before such places finally faded from the scene, Liverpool keeping its dairies into the 1950s.[20] Some had been kept in a way that was beyond reproach with a fastidious attention to detail, such as Harley's establishment in Glasgow which became a popular tourist attraction in its day, and the 'Harleian System' was widely copied.[21] Others, though, raised all sorts of questions regarding the health of the cows, cleanliness of the byre, disposal of waste products, hygiene in the dairy and, not least, the quality of the milk.

Town milk had a bad reputation. It was frequently sold with the cream skimmed off, diluted with water (itself of dubious origin) and artificially thickened with a mixture of chalk, egg white and other miscellaneous substances; the cream was extended with wheat flour (already adulterated with chalk, ground bone, bone ash or plaster of Paris) while the colouring of some cheeses came from red lead.

That was only one small part of the housewife's difficulties. The need for the utmost vigilance in the market-place had long been recognized and advice on wise buying was handed out by many domestic manuals and cookery books. Housewives were told how to recognize freshness in the goods on sale and the salient points to be observed when buying fish, whatever the type, while similar observations covered the purchasing of every type of meat, poultry and game. Advice might also be given on the storage of various provisions and what action to take if something was not quite as it should be. It was a narrow divide between the housewife, who might add an extra ingredient to make something last longer or take remedial action in the case of flat beer or tainted meat, and the trader who deliberately altered a foodstuff in order to make a greater profit. In medieval times the authorities had kept a watchful eye on standards so that any trader selling substandard goods was severely punished. As towns grew larger the authorities were unable to be so vigilant and, with an increasing number of people living at a distance from the source of their supplies, so the adulteration of foodstuffs became widespread.

In 1820 the country was shocked by the publication of a young chemist's *Treatise on Adulterations of Food, and Culinary Poisons*: '. . . exhibiting The Fraudulent Sophistications of Bread, Beer, Wine, Spirituous Liquors, Tea, Coffee, Cream, Confectionary, Vinegar, Mustard, Pepper, Cheese, Olive Oil, Pickles, and other articles employed in domestic economy. AND METHODS OF DETECTING THEM',[22] which revealed just how widespread such practices were. Accum's work covered the adulteration of many commodities, the poisonous elements to be found in certain foods, the counterfeit material added to others and various dubious preparation methods utilizing lead or copper vessels. The list was a long one.

The fight to curtail such malpractices was protracted, fought on many fronts and covered numerous aspects of food hygiene now taken for granted: water supply, drainage and cleanliness in premises selling comestibles; the wholesomeness of the goods on offer; the banning of illegal or harmful substances; the enforcement of accurate (i.e. honest) weights and measures and the conditions in which goods were transported. All these aspects, and so many more, benefited the housewife in her day-to-day preoccupations with feeding her household but there was yet one other feature which, in due course, came to revolutionize the supply of foodstuffs and that was through the use of manufactured or artificial ice.

The cooling unit of this early electric refrigerator, *c.* 1927, was so bulky it was placed outside the storage space. (By courtesy of the City of York Museums Services)

Ever since the sixteenth century, when the Venetians found that adding one part salt to two parts snow would enable water to freeze, people had been searching for an alternative way of lowering the temperature artificially and many names could be cited in its development. An American engineer living in London was granted a patent in 1834 and his refrigerating equipment was used by brewers and meat-packers. Incentives for further improvements came from the twin pressures of the ever-increasing demand for ice in the home and from a burgeoning population rapidly outgrowing the country's own food supplies. In February 1880 the S.S. *Strathleven* made history by making the first successful trip with a cargo of chilled beef from Australia; then came meat from New Zealand and the Argentine, followed soon afterwards by eggs and fruit. Initial suspicions soon evaporated and the products found a place in the housewife's shopping basket.

Domestic refrigerators first went on sale in the USA, the Domelre model in 1913 and the Kelvinator the following year, but they were not available in Britain until the 1920s. Two principal systems emerged. The compressor design was initially powered by steam, later by gas or electricity, and the size and noise of the motor combined with the smell of the coolant meant that both were often separated from the insulated unit itself, or sat upon the top of it; the second type was the absorption system which operated with the application of heat from a small gas flame or electrical element on to a refrigerant. Until the early 1930s refrigerators were comparatively expensive and rarely seen outside well-to-do homes but demand grew when manufacturers began making smaller and cheaper models, although production was halted by the Second World War. In the massive house-building schemes thereafter, a small refrigerator in the kitchen was seen as a space-saving idea as it did away with the need for a separate larder.

CHAPTER ELEVEN

Meals and Mealtimes

'He'll be home at dinnertime,' a simple enough phrase in itself but what time will the man be back? Is it in the evening or the middle of the day and what form will his meal take? Similarly with 'tea': does tea follow dinner, precede it or take the place of it altogether? Supper must also be fitted into the equation, as must breakfast, at the other end of the day, but surely there can be no surprises with breakfast, or can there?

Our meals and what we call them are shrouded in many layers of tradition so it is hardly surprising if there is a certain amount of confusion about them. Definitions of the words 'dinner' and 'supper' offer a clue to the problem, since dinner is denoted as the main meal of the day with supper being the last meal of the day, so the reasons underlying that confusion are understandable. However, until comparatively recently dinner and supper were two distinct meals, eaten at separate times.

Some of the background to dinner and dining habits was briefly outlined in Chapter 5, when discussing the position of domestic servants within a household.

The communal life carried on in the medieval great hall was, in time, superseded by newer customs although traces of it lingered well into the nineteenth century. A desire for greater comfort and privacy led increasingly to the withdrawal of 'the family' and any guests of suitable rank into a smaller, more private room for their meals, with a concomitant lessening of ceremonial and the emergence of furniture to suit the changing needs. The lower-ranking members of the household and the servants continued to eat in the (great) hall, which in time became the 'servants' hall' and was resited nearer the domestic offices where they worked. Yet the old-style feudal manner of dining, where a table for the important diners was placed at one end across the width of the great hall with two or more tables set at right angles to it running lengthwise down the room, is still current at the end of the twentieth century and employed at many a formal occasion, whether it be the Lord Mayor's Banquet or a family wedding breakfast.

The dining room of today bears witness to the evolution of our dining habits across the centuries with virtually everything in it having its roots in the medieval great hall. One main table, now generally with a polished surface; the chairs placed at it, with those at each end often having arms to them; the tablecloth, cutlery, plates, glasses laid upon the table, with something to act as a focal point in the middle; and against the walls, where space permits, a serving table and a sideboard for storage and display. How these items took on their familiar shapes and the significant names involved in the process are specialist subjects in their own right and have their own experts to expound on their histories. Space does not allow an in-depth investigation of each here, nor do these histories relate specifically to the life of the housewife although, having said that, she was certainly intimately involved in the outcome and many were as keen to display the latest fashion of fork, chair or soup tureen as to be seen wearing the latest hairstyle or dress.

At the same time it should be remembered that concepts of this nature would be totally alien to innumerable households who were dependent on a few basic necessities for their very survival; their food would be eaten squatting around the fireplace with everyone dipping into the one pot or eating from a dish placed upon the floor, as witnessed in many places: 'Mark the Irishman's potatoe bowl placed on the floor, the whole family upon their hams round it, devouring a quantity almost incredible, the beggar seating himself to it with a hearty welcome, the pig taking his share as readily as the wife . . . No man can often have been a witness of it without being convinced of the plenty and, I will add the chearfulness, that attends it.'[1] Dorothy Wordsworth touring Scotland found similar conditions from time to time as on 'Friday September 2d', when she entered a small hut lived in by four women and some children: 'They had just taken from the fire a great pan full of potatoes, which they mixed up with milk, all helping themselves out of the same vessel, and the little children put in their dirty hands to dig out of the mess at their pleasure.' It is hardly surprising to learn that though sorely in need of refreshment she had not the heart to eat anything.[2] Equally, there were others as, for example, prosperous farmers in Wales and in England who ate simply but well, relying on their own produce and buying in few commodities from outside.[3]

For those who could afford it, it was customary to eat two or three meals in the day. Some folk did without breakfast designed, as its name suggests, to break the overnight fast and as variable in composition as the habits of those eating it. Not until the mid-seventeenth century could it be accompanied by tea, coffee or chocolate and it was some while before these newly imported drinks supplanted the usual beer or ale. At the other end of the day there was supper and this could be as light or substantial, as intimate or formal, as the occasion demanded. Between them came dinner, at this time served around midday. It was the principal meal of the day which was served with a certain formality and elegance, with servants in attendance, and it was the gradual variations in the patterns of dining that caused changes to the style and content of the other meals.

For at least half of the period under review dinner stayed relatively unchanged. If Samuel Pepys (and his wife too, of course) had been invited to dine with Lady Grisell Baille and her husband, Parson Woodforde and the niece who stayed with him, alongside Dorothy Wordsworth, a sprinkling of Jane Austen's heroines and the capable, but fictitious, Meg Dods, they would all have been familiar with the way the meal was put on the table. Other things about the dinner might have surprised them but the presentation of the meal would not. Dinner to them consisted of one or more 'courses'. A course comprised an assortment of dishes including soup, fish, meat, vegetables, sweet things and pastry and a wide variety of cooking styles – boiled, roasted, served plain, in sauce and so on – put on the table at the same time, the number of dishes roughly corresponding to the number of people eating. The day Samuel Pepys and his wife invited six guests to dine with them the *Diary* recorded with some pride: 'I had for them, after oysters, at first course, a hash of rabbits, a lamb, and a rare chine of beef. Next a great dish of roasted fowl, cost me about 30*s.*, and a tart, and then fruit and cheese. My dinner was noble, and enough.'[4] Additional dishes of lesser significance might also have been served as Pepys remarked that his wife had been up before daylight to go to the market and had 'bought fowls and many other things for dinner'. The menu, or bill of fare, as it was called then, fits well with some of Meg Dods' suggestions for 'Family-Dinners or Small Parties': a first course of baked pike and a roast leg of mutton, both with appropriate sauces, along with stewed celery and mashed turnips, was to be followed by veal cutlets in vol-au-vents, young peas, dressed lobster, ratafia cream and ducklings.[5]

Servants would be in attendance to fetch and carry plates or cutlery, to remove dishes no longer required and to pour wine and other drinks as necessary. The diners served each other and could choose what they wanted to eat; they did not necessarily taste every dish upon the table. For the record, food that was not eaten was not wasted; it could well reappear at the table the next day in a different format[6] while some dishes went to serve the senior servants, the 'heads of department', who ate separately from the rank and file.

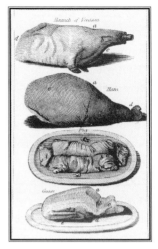

Directions for carving venison, ham, sucking pig and goose as shown in *A New System of Domestic Cookery*, by a Lady, 1818.

Joints and poultry were carved at the table by the host and hostess and carving was a necessary accomplishment for both sexes well into the nineteenth century: 'Carving is justly esteemed one of the minor arts of polite life,' wrote Meg Dods, 'To carve quickly and neatly requires a good deal of practice . . . There are awkward grown-up persons, having, as the French say, *two left hands* whom no labour will ever make dextrous carvers; . . . One objection to allowing juvenile practice is, that young people haggle provisions; but they might surely be permitted sometimes to try plain joints and cold things, which would soon bring in their hands.' Elsewhere, apropos roast pig, she expressed the wish that 'the practice of having this dish carved by the cook were universal; for, in this fastidious age, the sanguinary spectacle of an entire four-footed animal at table is any thing but acceptable. Like the larger poultry, pig is also very troublesome to the carver.'[7] Practice did not always make perfect, though. One man fondly remembered the occasion when a chicken arrived unexpectedly on his lap 'and the lady, with a sweet smile, saying "Would you kindly give me back that chicken?" '[8]

Once the company had finished with the first course it was cleared away and a fresh array of foodstuffs was brought in, similarly varied but of a lighter consistency – roast partridge and orange custards, for example, as opposed to the boiled beef and vegetable broth of the first course. Lesser households made do with a one-course dinner while there were, it has already been said, many who had no such choice in the matter and ate frugally throughout the year.

The 2nd Earl of Hopetoun thought it an unnecessary extravagance to serve two courses: 'In the latter years of his life, a second course never appeared at his table, for having observed that it had become a frequent practice in gentlemen of rather small fortunes to have two courses, in hopes that his example would have the effect of putting a stop to a custom at once ridiculous and ruinous in them, his Lordship abstained from that luxury; and calculating how much was saved by the retrenchment, added the amount to his other bounties

A rare example of a page from a manuscript Dinner Book of 1754–5. The household was divided into four 'tables' for dinner, the first table being for the family and their guests and the others being for the different grades of servants. Dinner on Monday 16 June was particularly elaborate with the two courses being followed by a dessert of eleven dishes. An epergne held pride of place in the centre of the table. (Hopetoun Papers Trust)

to the distressed.'[9] Those days were still in the future (he died in 1781) as surviving dinner books of the 1750s show exactly what was being served to his lordship's table and reveal that one-course dinners occurred only rarely, generally when Lord and Lady Hopetoun were away from home.

A fashionable dinner of one or two courses would then be followed by a separate dessert course, the climax to the meal, when the tastiest or rarest foods were eaten from the prettiest porcelain dishes and the most expensive wines drunk from the finest glasses. There was also a therapeutic element about it, as many of these items were considered to have a beneficial effect on the digestive processes.

Although dessert followed dinner it was seen as being separate from the actual meal and did not emanate from the kitchen, a situation which stemmed from its origins. Initially, the dessert filled the short space of time taken to clear the great hall after dinner to prepare it for the next activity. The VIPs of the household withdrew to a small room and spent the time in conversation (which gave this room its name of parlour, from *parler*, to speak) and in taking a glass of wine and a nibble of something 'to go with' (which in time became the dessert, after *desservir*, to clear the table). The English originally knew this as a 'banquet' and only changed the name when all things French became fashionable later in the seventeenth century, whereas the Scots were using the term 'dessert' at a much earlier date. The foods eaten at this point, such as fresh and dried

Fruit-based dishes were popular items for dessert and were presented in many ways. From E. Acton, *Modern Cookery*, revised edition, 1857.

fruits, items cooked in syrup or preserved in sugar and anything that was rare and costly, came not from the kitchen but were provided by the housewife. Gervase Markham listed a skill in 'Banquetting Stuffe' as one of the essential branches of the housewife's knowledge: 'For albeit, they [i.e. these items] are not of generall use, yet in their due times, they are so needfull for adornation, that whosoever is ignorant therein, is lame, and but the halfe part of a compleat Hous-wife.'[10] When she ceased to have an interest in concocting such delicacies in her own still-room, responsibility for them was shifted on to the housekeeper, her deputy.

To begin with, the banquet or dessert was eaten in a room other than the one in which dinner had been eaten; or in a 'garden house' or 'banqueting house' out in the grounds, or even up on the roof or in a small room in a tower, as at Laycock Abbey in Wiltshire, with a commanding view over the surrounding countryside. Gradually dessert came to be eaten at the same table as the dinner, but only after all traces of the previous courses had been removed; even the tablecloth was whisked away to reveal the polished surface of the newly fashionable mahogany dining table. After a short time spent over the dessert the ladies would 'withdraw' to the withdrawing room. The origins for this custom are obscure and it seems to have happened quite suddenly in the closing years of the seventeenth century, possibly as a result of the fashion for drinking tea and coffee which swept the country about that time. The ladies left the table

The three-storey tower built at
Laycock Abbey, Wiltshire,
c. 1550. It contains two small
'banqueting rooms', one above
the other, in which a dessert or
banquet could be enjoyed.

early in order to prepare the tea for the menfolk who would join
them when it was ready. Left on their own, though, the menfolk
settled down to some serious drinking after which hiatus they might
or might not be capable of joining the ladies for tea or coffee and a
further nibble of cake or biscuit. By Victorian times the table
settings had become so elaborate that it was far too complicated to
remove everything, so only the unwanted items such as salts and
peppers and surplus utensils were removed before the dessert was set
out, the practice still followed in the 1990s.

Over the years a later and later hour for dinner came into vogue: Lady Grisell Baillie early in the eighteenth century would be eating at about 2 p.m.; some fifty years later Parson Woodforde and his friends were dining at about 4 p.m.; by the start of the next century the hour was nearer 6 p.m., even 6.30 p.m., but it was not without a certain amount of protest and a determination to resist the advancing dinner hour.[11] This later timing was affecting peoples' appetite for supper. It was noted that 'the lateness of modern dinner-hours has now, almost universally, changed suppers from a solid meal into a slight shewy refreshment'.[12] The Scots, though, were reluctant to be parted from their convivial supper parties and the comment was made: 'Early dinners begat suppers. But suppers are so delightful, that they have survived long after dinners have become late. . . . Supper is cheaper than dinner; shorter; less ceremonious; and more poetical. The business of the day is over; and its still fresh events interest. It is chiefly intimate associates that are drawn together at that familiar hour, of which night deepens the sociality. If there be any fun, or heart, or spirit, in a man at all, it is then, if ever, that it will appear.'[13]

If folk had little appetite left for supper it was quite otherwise between breakfast and dinner, especially when the hours between the two meals began to lengthen noticeably. The slight gap which before had been pleasantly filled with a glass of sweet wine like madeira and a slice of plain cake, known by the name of the wine it accompanied, became a much longer gap; the wine and cake were augmented by fruit, by a little cold meat and in time was recognized as 'nuncheon', later to be 'luncheon' and a full-scale meal, though never as lengthy or as elaborate as dinner. Meanwhile, as the fashion for taking luncheon developed, so dinner could be delayed even further, until by the 1920s dinner was described as being 'invariably at 8 o'clock'.[14]

There was yet another development. Now that dinner was so much later there was a gap between luncheon and dinner. It was said that the custom for taking tea in the afternoon was started by the then Duchess of Bedford (supposedly Anna, d. 1857, wife of the 7th Duke), who arrived to stay at Belvoir Castle one time bringing with her some tea, then an expensive item, and inviting the female guests to drink it with her in her boudoir.[15] On the other hand it is easy to see how such a custom might also have evolved from the time when tea, being a newly introduced and costly substance, appeared as part of the dessert course; later, it separated from the dessert and was drunk a short while afterwards which, in the days when dinner was a midday meal, would put it half way through the afternoon.

```
                    M E N U.
      2188.—SERVICE  A  LA  RUSSE  (November).
                    ——•◇•——

      Ox-tail Soup.      Soup à la Jardinière.
      ═══════════════════════════════════

  Turbot and Lobster Sauce.   Crimped Cod and Oyster Sauce.

      Stewed Eels.   Soles à la Normandie.

    Pike and Cream Sauce.   Fried Filleted Soles.
      ═══════════════════════════════════

 Filets do Bœuf à la Jardinière.  Croquettes of Game aux Champignons.
                    ▬▬▬▬

    Chicken Cutlets.  Mutton Cutlets and Tomata Sauce.
                    ▬▬▬▬

      Lobster Rissoles.    Oyster Patties.
                    ▬▬▬▬

   Partridges aux fines herbes.   Larded Sweetbreads.
                    ▬▬▬▬

      Roast Beef.    Poulets aux Cressons.
      Haunch of Mutton.    Roast Turkey.
   Boiled Turkey and Celery Sauce.    Ham.
      ═══════════════════════════════════

      Grouse.    Pheasants.    Hare.

    Salad.   Artichokes.   Stewed Celery.
                    ▬▬▬▬

 Italian Cream.   Charlotte aux Pommes.   Compôte of Pears
                    ▬▬▬▬

  Croûtes madrées aux Fruits.    Pastry.    Punch Jelly.
                    ▬▬▬▬

            Iced Pudding.

              — ————

          Dessert and Ices.
```

Mrs Beeton offers suggestions for a dinner à la russe suitable for November. It was a novelty to have only one type of dish at a time and to have servants handing it round to each person in turn. From *The Book of Household Management* [n.d. but 140th thousand].

Whatever its origins, afternoon tea became a meal in its own right and the simple cup of tea came to be accompanied by a wide assortment of breads, biscuits, cakes, pastries and savouries and the housewife was able to show off to the full her skills in baking. Once afternoon tea had become a meal for fashionable folk those lower in the social scale tried to copy it but were hindered by their long working hours; so, for them, dinner was maintained as the midday meal while supper was adapted to incorporate the new meal and the hybrid was called 'tea' by some and 'high tea' by others.

The description of Scotland as 'the land o' cakes' has come to refer to the housewives' prowess in baking with wheaten flour, although the 'cakes' originally meant were oatcakes. The housewives of Wales were equally competent and Welsh teas, eaten between 4 and 5 p.m., were spectacular: 'Cream-cakes, home-made preserves, fresh water-cresses . . . daintily toasted cream cheese served with buttered toast, jellies, blancmange, custards, several kinds of tartlets, and a variety of cakes, especially small round ones, . . . Then there are pikelets, and bakestone cakes, which, to a certain extent, resemble muffins, only the Welsh cake is larger.'[16] As tea was becoming a full-blown meal in its own right, so changes were taking place in the service of dinner. The style of dining current in polite society for almost two hundred years was described as *'service à la francaise'*; the alternative style, *'à la russe',* was coming into fashion by the 1850s and in the next decade Mrs Beeton was sounding a warning to her (mainly middle-class) readers: 'Dinners à la Russe are scarcely suitable for small establishments; a large number of servants being required to carve, and to help the guests; besides there being a necessity for more plates, dishes, knives, forks, and spoons than are usually to be found in any other than a very large establishment. Where, however, a service à la Russe is practicable, there is, perhaps, no mode of serving a dinner so enjoyable as this.' She pinpointed the difference between the two styles by stating: 'The dishes are cut up on a sideboard, and handed round to the guests, and each dish may be considered a course. The table for a dinner à la Russe should be laid with flowers and plants in fancy flowerpots down the middle, together with some of the dessert dishes. A *menu* or bill of fare should be laid by the side of each guest.'[17] Previously the centre of the table had been taken up with something important in the way of food and the two formats, food and flowers, amalgamated into that indispensable adjunct, the Victorian epergne. It took time for new ideas to filter down through the social scale and when a former servant girl returned to the hamlet of 'Lark Rise' and placed a vase of flowers on the table it caused much merriment among her family.[18]

The new style of presentation had originated, as the name would imply, in Russia and had been observed by the famous chef Antonin Careme[19] when working for Czar Alexander I at St Petersburg, although he doubted whether it could be adapted to French cuisine. It did eventually become the vogue, although there must have been a rather confusing period for dinner guests with some households clinging on to the traditional ways while others slipped happily into the new style immediately. In its turn this has become the 'traditional' way and is the presentation still met with, though somewhat modified, when eating in formal circumstances late in the twentieth century.

While there were some advantages in the new style it was far more laborious and time consuming to have the servants handing round the dishes to each guest individually, changing the plates and putting sauceboats on the table, removing them afterwards and so on and, with each dish or pair of dishes forming a course, many diners found the meals extending interminably: 'Board . . . it ought to be spelt bored!', wailed one despairing voice, 'Never was a more solemn torture created for mankind than these odious dinner parties.' Caught between a garrulous neighbour on the one side and an unresponsive one on the other and cut off by a huge epergne from those sitting opposite, there was only an occasional glimpse to be had of an irritable, solemn host at one end and a most anxious hostess at the other. 'Upon my word, two whole hours of this, with the most laboured attempts at conversation all round, in a darkened room with a servant perpetually thrusting something across my shoulder, exciting each time a fresh alarm of a shower of sauce or gravy . . . really is this society?' The reply comes: 'Perhaps not; but that is no reason why a dinner-party properly selected and properly served, should not be as pleasant a meeting as any other.'[20]

From the housewife's point of view menu-making for this type of service was certainly far more complicated as the dishes all had to balance or contrast with each other, with regard to colour, style of cooking and method of presentation. Advice on such matters was available from many cookbooks and domestic manuals which often included diagrams showing sample dinners and suppers or how to set out the dishes of dessert to achieve a proper balance. The housewife's problems were one thing; preparing and serving all the dishes in their correct order, with appropriate garnishes and sauces, must have been a daily nightmare for the average cook and kitchen-maid. No wonder Mrs Beeton could foresee problems ahead for households of smaller means. By the 1920s Lord Ernest Hamilton was writing: 'For let it not be forgotten that the number of dishes which it was obligatory on the host to have handed to his goggle-eyed guest was laid down by statute. From this rule there must be no parsimonious departure. Even to an ordinary small family party the dinner served consisted of soup, fish, two entrées (one after the other), joint, game, sweet and savoury, followed by an elaborate course of cheese, toast, butter, radishes, celery, and mustard and cress, the special function of which was supposed to be to clear the palate for the good wines to come.'[21] In his opinion everyone ate their way through the menu in an unashamedly greedy way and constantly talked about and thought about food.

Amazingly, in view of the luncheons, teas and dinners that were being served – and eaten – breakfast was also becoming a more solid affair. Previously it had generally been a rather lighter meal, based on bread or rolls spread with butter and accompanied with something to drink, although it varied enormously depending on personal preference, circumstance or what the day had in store. In the country rounds of beef and substantial joints would be placed upon the sideboard.

Dr Johnson, that severest of critics, had nothing but praise for the Scottish breakfasts he met with: 'The breakfast, a meal in which the Scots, whether of the Lowlands or the Highlands, must be confessed to excel us. The tea and coffee are accompanied not only with butter, but with honey, conserves, and marmalades. If an epicure could remove by a wish in quest of sensual gratifications, wherever he had supped, he would breakfast in Scotland.'[22] Others before him had made similar observations, especially as to the serving of conserves and marmalades at this meal,[23] which seems to have been an innovation of the Scots. Marmalade was the anglicized version of the Portuguese 'marmelada', a sweetmeat of puréed quinces (*Cydonia oblonga*) cooked with honey or sugar, which was imported from Portugal and eaten in the dessert course as it was considered to have medicinal properties. Housewives wanted to make their own and, as quinces can be reluctant to ripen in Britain, they substituted other locally plentiful fruits – apples, gooseberries, cherries and so on, as well as imported oranges and lemons. In due course marmalade changed from being a stiffish substance that could be cut with a knife to being a softer mixture eaten with a spoon. It continued to be a dessert item in the south[24] long after it was being used as a breakfast spread in Scotland and produced commercially by such firms as Keillers of Dundee. The surge in marmalade's popularity coincided with the repeal of taxes on citrus fruits and sugars in 1860 and 1874 respectively.[25]

In the 1820s it was observed: 'That change of manners which has introduced late dinners, and superseded hot suppers, has very much improved the modern breakfast', and a long list of cooked dishes for eating both hot and cold was appended.[26] In addition to the sausages, eggs, grilled fish, hams, cold game pies and so on, baskets of rolls, breads and scones were served as were assorted jams and marmalades. Within the next forty years the repetoire for breakfasts had expanded still further, if the description of two meals taken in Wales can be trusted: 'In about twenty minutes after I had ordered it my breakfast made its appearance. A noble breakfast it was; such indeed as I might have read of, but had never before seen. There was tea and coffee, a goodly white loaf and butter; there were a couple of eggs and two mutton chops. There was broiled and pickled salmon – there was fried trout – there were also potted trout and potted shrimps. Mercy upon me! I had never previously seen such a breakfast set before me

By the 1890s breakfast was becoming an elaborate meal offering a selection of dishes. From *Cassell's Book of the Household, c.* 1893, vol. 1.

nor indeed have I subsequently. Yes, I have subsequently, and at that very house when I visited it some months after.' The second description extols Welsh hospitality in similar terms: 'What a breakfast! pot of hare; ditto of trout; pot of prepared shrimps; dish of plain shrimps; tin of sardines, beautiful beef-steak; eggs, muffin; large loaf, and butter, not forgetting capital tea. There's a breakfast for you!'[27] By the end of the century one further item could be added, 'that very common dish to be met with at many breakfast-tables – tinned lobster. Some people are very fond of tinned lobster at breakfast', or so said one authority.[28]

This type of breakfast, needless to say, required lengthy preparations in the kitchen beforehand and the right sort of equipment upstairs to ensure it kept hot, as in many households family and guests tended to arrive in their own time. A decline in domestic staff coupled with a less-leisured pace of life as more men commuted to work from the suburbs saw a gradual simplification of the breakfast menu, but even in 1923 Mrs Beeton's 'Specimen Menus for simple Breakfasts' were still including porridge, two hot dishes and one cold dish winter and summer alike, stewed fruit, rolls, toast and bread with butter and marmalade, and a choice of tea or coffee with hot and cold milk.[29] Interestingly, shredded wheat and rolled oats are suggested as possible alternatives to the familiar porridge.

Since that date the trend towards lighter breakfasts has continued, the pace of life has speeded up considerably and a concern for 'healthier eating' is prevalent. Whatever the cookbooks and the experts might suggest about suitable foodstuffs for breakfast it is the most individual of meals and the one at which people find it hardest to change their accustomed preferences.

CHAPTER TWELVE

Drinks

No meal would have been complete without a drink to accompany it either as an aid to the eating or for the pleasurable effect of the liquid itself but, equally, there were many other occasions on which something to quench the thirst was a requirement. It seems almost unbelievable that there was a time when there was no tea, no coffee and no chocolate in the British way of life, yet that is the way it was until the middle years of the seventeenth century. In the early days drinks for general consumption were produced from readily available basic commodities. Barley and oats were turned into ale, honey was the basis for mead and sweetened other beverages, apples were crushed for cider; while milk, buttermilk and whey were widely drunk and many herbal infusions were prepared which nowadays are considered only in a medicinal context.

It was the Normans who brought with them the habit of drinking wines (i.e. from grapes) and then had to import the wines to support their habit and, as the Norman hierarchy superseded the indigenous Saxons, the drinking of imported wines carried a social cachet for many a long year. Wines were drunk by whoever could afford to buy them but ale was the beverage drunk on a daily basis by the great majority of the population. For many centuries it was considered to be one of the housewife's duties to make or to supervise the regular brewing of ale and other drinks for her household. Gervase Markham certainly thought so and listed it as yet another of the 'vertues' required of his housewife, and many cookbooks thereafter included chapters on the subject. For those housewives living in crowded conditions in towns and lacking the space for a brewhouse in which to store the various barrels, tubs, troughs and other pieces of bulky equipment involved in the operation, ready-made products were widely available.

The names 'ale' and 'beer' were synonymous until Tudor times but once hops came to be the preferred flavouring-cum-preservative what was made with them became 'beers' while those without hops were 'ales'. They would be made to different strengths for different purposes: strong for the master and his guests, a second quality for general use and a weaker brew, later called 'small beer', to be drunk by children and servants. In the days before supplies of water were both regular and clean, ale was the general purpose drink and servants were given a generous daily allowance;[1] women servants drank it too but tended to be allocated a smaller amount.

Over and above the straightforward brews, the ale or beer could be augmented, and doubtless improved, in numerous ways.[2] A gentle warming and the addition of spices, sugar and butter created 'buttered ale'; extra flavour could be gained by incorporating juniper berries, or a mixture of bay leaves, coriander and caraway seeds; or the ale could be supplemented with a fortified wine like sack (i.e. a type of sherry) along with raisins and cloves, and 'cock ale' was produced by literally steeping a cockerel's body in the brew to 'strengthen' it. Ale was also an ingredient in many caudels and possets (eaten warm as part drink, part food) which were sweetened, spiced, augmented with eggs and cream and sometimes thickened with ground almonds or breadcrumbs. Samuel Pepys gave his guests a supper consisting of 'a good sack posset' and some cold meat after the generous dinner given them earlier in the day.

A week or so later it was cider that Pepys, having ordered a new pair of boots, was drinking with his shoemaker and his wife 'they broaching a vessel of syder a-purpose for me'.[3] The orchards of Kent presumably provided Londoners with a ready supply, but housewives in the apple-growing areas would make their own ciders which would replace the staple ales and beers. Some of the old horse-powered cider presses have survived; the horse walked round and round in a circle while harnessed to a yoke attached to a beam that turned a rough-hewn stone wheel within a circular trough, thereby crushing the apples to release the juices. Scotland's first gardening book, published in 1683 specifically 'for the climate of Scotland', is also the country's oldest known cookbook. In it can be found instructions for the making of cider and 'the making of Perry differs not from that of cyder'.[4] The need for the total cleanliness of all the equipment is stressed as is the advantage of using barrels that have already stored white wine or sack.

Another recipe given here is for the making of metheglin, a
variant of mead incorporating flavourings over and above the basics
of honey and water. 'Take one part of Clarified Hony and eight parts
of pure Water and boyl well together in a Copper vessel till the
consumption of the half; but while it boyls take off the scum, and
when done boyling and beginnes to cool, tun it up, and it will work
of itself [i.e. ferment]; as soon as done working, stop it very close.
Some advises to bury it under ground three moneths, and that to
make it lose both smell and taste of Hony and Wax, and taste very
like Wine. I use to add dry Rosmary and sweet Marjorum in
boyling.'⁵ Metheglin was still much made in late nineteenth-century
Wales, according to one authority: 'The wives of today . . . make the
"meth" in the same way as it was made in the Middle Ages'; and,
later, as if to corroborate the statement, are the words 'and . . . their
honey cannot be rivalled'.⁶

Doubtless it was honey that formed the basis of other beverages,
too, in the early days although many of the surviving recipes for
them, whether printed or manuscript, have sugar in conjunction
with the other ingredients; it may well have been the change from
being honey-based to sugar-based that caused the recipes to be
written down in the first place. By the seventeenth century the
housewife could be utilizing a wide variety of garden fruits as they
became ready – cherries, apricots, mulberries, white or red
currants, gooseberries, raspberries or quince, for example – and the
end-results were called 'wines' after the imported, fashionable type
made from grapes. Those same Welsh housewives who were
making their metheglin also made 'rhubarb wine, prepared from
an ancient recipe, . . . as good and sparkling as champagne',
although it would be interesting to know just how 'ancient' that
recipe was, as the type of rhubarb currently eaten is a more recent
import than that used earlier for medicinal purposes. Wines were
made from other locally available ingredients such as cowslips,
elderberries, clove-gilly flowers or sage, and from imported raisins
and oranges.

Orange wine seems to have been particularly popular in Scotland
with numerous domestic accounts specifying purchases of either the
oranges for it or the sugars. Lady Grisell Baillie recorded a payment
of £3 2s 6d [stg] 'For 30 dusone oranges, 20 dusone limons at 15d p.
duson, out of which I had 8 gallons orrange wine and large twelve
gallons of pansh and 2 dusone oranges beside to preserve'⁷ but, in
addition, there would be the cost of the sugar and the eggs with

which to clarify it and the barm (i.e. yeast) to ferment the mixture. Later recipes, as for example Hannah Robertson's in 1767, advise adding 'four bottles of French white-wine or two bottles of good mountain: some use Rhenish wine'; and similar instructions continue into the next century.[8]

Housewives were also instructed how to make many refreshing non-alcoholic drinks such as barley water; apple or lemon water; white-wine whey; orgeat; orange- or lemon-ade; and raspberry vinegar. These drinks also included a wide range of semi-medicinal preparations which encompassed numerous broths, teas, milks and jellies, alongside water gruel, barley gruel, toast and water, 'a refreshing Drink in a Fever' and a 'Soft and fine Draught for those who are weak and have a Cough'.[9] It is difficult to know just how many of these products were actually made or when they were drunk because being homemade they rarely feature in the domestic records. There is no such problem about the wines, beers and spirits that were bought in as these were recorded twice – once when they came into the house and again when the bottles were drunk in the dining room.

Wines were being imported from many corners of Europe and a wide variety of both white and red featured significantly on the dinner table in households of a certain standing. How much influence the housewife actually had in the matter of choice is uncertain as the purchase of wines tended to be regarded as 'a man's job' or was left to the discretion of the house steward or butler. The 3rd Duke of Hamilton was accustomed to choosing the household's wines from the merchants of Glasgow himself, but after his death in 1694 samples were sent up to the palace for the widowed Duchess Anne to consider.[10] Gervase Markham would have thought this only right and proper, even though the scope of his book was limited to England: 'It is necessary,' he stated, 'that our English house-wife be skilfull in the election, preserving, and curing of all sorts of Wines, because they be usuall charges under her hands, and by the least neglect must turn the Husband to much losse.' The housewife was carefully instructed as to the choosing of wines of different sorts, how to 'help' or 'remedy' any defects, and 'of what countries Wines are by their names'.[11]

Both Mrs Purefroy and her son were writing to their suppliers either to order further consignments or to express dissatisfaction with what had been sent. 'I desire you will send my Mother 8 gallons of Canary in a runlet, she desires of all things it may not be on the

Stoneware and earthenware jars were used to store many commodities in the days before glass bottles became widespread. These three were used for liquids. (Gwent Rural Life Museum).

fret [i.e. ferment], for the last you sent was like bottled Cyder and flew all about yᵉ cellar & broke yᵉ bottles. Besides yᵉ Physicians say wine on yᵉ fret is very prejudicial to her health.' A later consignment proved satisfactory as Henry was able to write: 'The last Canary did not ferment or fly at all'.[12] His mother wrote expressing her annoyance at 'a very rotten hogshead . . . Severall hoops flew of(f) when wee unloaded it; it is wonderfull it did not break on coming'. Another of her letters reproached the supplier about 'the mountain wine, it is so new & sweet that wee cannot drink it; my son drinks it for the Gout in his Stomach & I drink it with water. I wonder at the mistake because you always used to send us dry mountain wine' and she asked to exchange it for something more to their liking.[13]

For long enough the wine, in casks, was brought across the Channel in the autumn before the winter storms or else in the spring when the weather had quietened somewhat. Either way, the wines were drunk in an immature state and were not intended for long-term keeping, hence the need to 'help' them along with the addition of spices, orange peel and other substances. Bottles were somewhat squat in shape, made to stand upright upon their base and the mouths were closed over with a piece of leather or parchment held on with packthread until such times as corks came to be used. Then the shape of the bottles changed to a longer, slimmer line suitable for storing on their sides so that the wine remained in contact with the cork. While bottles could be refilled many times corks had to be purchased new each time, as domestic accounts reveal, and that essential artefact the corkscrew was invented.

Wines for home use were generally bought in the cask and bottled by the customer, although a purchase might be shared between neighbours or friends which sometimes led to trouble. Mrs Purefroy had to reprimand her friend Mrs Price for the fact that the latter's daughter-in-law had failed to pay for their share of a consignment of sack and there was an undercurrent of ill-feeling over the way it had been divided up, owing to the fact that one of the Price's bottles had broken when filled.[14]

It is surprising, though, to find that Hopetoun House, some 12 miles from Edinburgh, was making numerous purchases of wines and ales already in the bottle; the household was certainly large enough to absorb any number of casks. Breakages in transit were frequent, three or four out of a batch of four dozen being nothing untoward, though the day thirteen were broken in one such delivery must have been a disaster.[15] Alternatively, if lesser quantities were required, people could buy their wine by the jugful. Whenever a new cargo of wine arrived in Leith it was the custom for a cask to be drawn through the streets of Edinburgh and anyone who paid a small sum could claim a 'taster', with no limits being put on its size.

The housewife, or her cook, found many opportunities for adding wine to the dishes being cooked and augmented the soup with sherry, fish dishes with white wines, meat gravies and sauces with wines in general, while needing no excuse to pour alcohol into almost any sweet confection.

Spirits such as brandy, rum and, in Scotland, whisky, 'provided the latter have no smoky or *peat-reek* flavour',[16] also had a place in the kitchen, though the housewife generally seems to have had less use of

A page from a manuscript Dinner Book recording the number of bottles stored in the cellars and how much was drunk over a four-day period in July 1755. The list includes two clarets, two ports and other wines from France, as well as Spain and Portugal. 'Inglis', 'Napiers', and 'Sheriffs' refer to the importers or the wine merchants. Also detailed are ale and beer, lamp oils, vinegars and spa water from Hartfell, near Moffat. (Hopetoun Papers Trust)

gin, at least for culinary purposes. A number of beverages made at home had their starting point in a bottle or two of brandy in which the fruit, their kernels or peels were steeped and the end results went under the name of 'ratafias' or 'fruit brandies.' Raspberry Brandy required the juice of the fruit to be boiled with sugar and then, after skimming and cooling, mixed with an equal amount of brandy and bottled, though the recipe concludes: 'Some people prefer it stronger of the brandy'.[17]

Other drinks, too, were employed as the basis for a homemade product. The making of a 60-gallon cask of 'British Port' began with 'eight gallons of port wine, genuine and unadulterated,' to which was added 40 gallons of good cider and the cask was to be filled up with French brandy, which must have taken about 10 or 12 gallons; space had to be left for juice from elderberries and sloes to give the required degree of 'roughness' and the whole was coloured with cochineal. The cider, though, was optional and could be replaced by 'turnip juice or raisin cyder . . . and instead of French brandy, brandy spirits'.[18] There might have been an excuse for substituting the brandy, seeing that this particular recipe was published after some twenty years of war against France, but that could hardly have been a valid reason for the substitution of the cider.

Later in the century Mrs Beeton needed port wine to make up the drink called 'Negus' which, rather surprisingly, she regarded as suitable for children's parties. The name came from a Colonel Negus (d. 1732) who devised the mix, and it was based on a pint of port diluted with twice as much boiling water and with sugar, lemon juice and nutmeg to taste. This amount was considered sufficient for a party of nine or ten children.[19] Other recipes for it replaced the port with sherry or any sweet white wine.

The housewife's repertoire of homemade beverages was extensive and cookbooks continued to include information on the subject throughout the period but, despite this, by the 1820s the habit of brewing beer at home was diminishing. William Cobbett inveighed against this untoward development and quoted the words of a 'large farmer, in Sussex,' who, in 1821, claimed that forty years earlier 'there was not a labourer in his parish that did not brew his own beer; and that now, there is not one that does it, except by chance the malt be given him'. Cobbett blamed their plight, among other things, on low wages, heavy taxes on barley when turned into malt and the increased taxes upon hops, to which he might have added a severe shortage of fuel. 'These have quite changed the customs of the English people as to their drink' he wrote. They still drank beer but it was commercially produced and drunk in a public house rather than at home.[20] The situation is underlined by contrasting two cookbooks. The one dating from the early nineteenth century (i.e. pre-Cobbett) contains recipes 'to brew very fine Welsh Ale', 'Strong Beer, or Ale', 'Excellent Table Beer' and instructions 'To Refine Beer, Ale, Wine, or Cider'; Mrs Beeton, on the other hand, some forty or so years later, while including recipes for homemade wines and other beverages, gives no guidance on brewing beer or ale at home.[21]

If home brewing was decreasing at this time, the consumption of tea and coffee was increasing among every social class – and Cobbett held equally strong opinions on the evils of tea drinking.

That triumvirate of drinks – tea, coffee and chocolate – came into Britain within a few years of each other, during the mid-seventeenth century. They came from totally different regions of the world. Chocolate was taken from Mexico to Spain, coffee was Ethiopian/Arabian in origin, while tea was brought to the west from China. Their ready acceptance and popularity is often attributed to the fact that they arrived during the period of the Civil War and its aftermath. It was not a happy time. Many estates had been confiscated, their owners either dead or in exile; feasting and merrymaking were banned; anything that smacked of luxury was frowned on. In Scotland it was even forbidden to celebrate Christmas Day.[22] The new drinks were non-alcoholic and maybe came as a little welcome relief in a period of austerity.

The Spanish found chocolate being drunk in Mexico and cocoa beans were taken back to Spain in the earlier part of the sixteenth century where, for a while, their origins were kept a closely guarded secret. As its use spread throughout the Spanish Empire so it became more widely known and it came into Britain via The Netherlands, at that time in Spanish hands. It remained as a drink until 1828 when the scientific process that enabled it to be made into a foodstuff was developed. Until then it was used only as a drink although, just occasionally, that might become the basis for a cream or jelly for dessert.[23] If the household drank chocolate frequently it was possible to make a batch in advance that would last a week or more. The cake of chocolate had to be broken up or grated and added to boiling water; off the fire it had to be 'milled' (i.e. frothed up with a special implement) and then put back over the fire until it came to the boil. It had then to be poured into a basin and set to cool in the larder. 'When wanted, put a spoonful or two into milk, boil it with sugar and mill it well. This, if not made thick, is a very good breakfast or supper' the recipe concluded.[24] On the other hand a cookbook of similar date warned that chocolate should never be made in advance but, when wanted, equal quantities of good new milk and water should be boiled, the scrapings of chocolate and sugar added, and the whole milled well and rapidly so that it was served thoroughly mixed with the froth on the top. Only if it was needed for 'a delicate person' could a batch be made in advance.[25]

Coffee probably arrived by way of merchants who traded with the countries of the eastern Mediterranean although differing stories are told of its introduction into Europe; its English debut was witnessed by John Evelyn soon after he went up to Oxford in May 1637: 'There came in my time to the College one Nathaniel Conopius, out of Greece . . . He was the first I ever saw drink coffee; which custom came not into England till thirty years after.'[26] His timescale is a little awry as the first English coffee house was established in Oxford in 1650 with London's first coming two years later. The coffee was drunk Turkish style, a tiny amount of liquid but sweet and strong. It was not long before the mixture was diluted somewhat and served in a distinctly British style, a trait remarked upon by foreign visitors at a surprisingly early date. The Frenchman, Faujas de St Fond, waxed lyrical about the hospitality he met with at the Duke of Argyle's table at Inveraray, with lavish dishes, exquisite wines and everything of the highest calibre but, even so, he was forced to admit there was one element that failed to live up to the rest: 'At last they proceeded to the drawing room, where tea and coffee abound . . . the tea is always excellent, but it is not so with the coffee: . . .Their coffee is always weak, bitter, and completely deprived of its aromatic odour.'[27] Exactly the same accusation was made against the coffee served in England and travellers were warned that they should always specify how many cups were to be made with half an ounce of coffee, 'or else the people will probably bring them a prodigious quantity of brown water'.[28] Some fifty years later Meg Dods agreed that the reproach was entirely justified and that it was due either to an insufficiency of material or to a lack of freshness in it.[29] Notwithstanding such criticisms coffee drinking was taken up enthusiastically. Coffee houses sprang up everywhere and acted as meeting places for merchants and traders as well as centres for the dissemination of the day's news, so the drinking of coffee acquired distinctly male overtones. No such overtones attached to tea drinking, the third in the triumvirate which, although fashionable for both men and women to begin with, went in quite the other direction and came to be considered a feminine pursuit.

An early reference to tea is to be found in Pepys' *Diary* on 25 September 1660, when he recorded: 'And afterwards I did send for a cup of tee (a China drink) of which I never had drank before.'[30] It was indeed 'a China drink' and its introduction to Europe is generally credited to Jesuit priests returning to Portugal and to ships of the Dutch East India Company bringing back supplies of the leaf to sell in Amsterdam. In England the tea-drinking habit was made all the more fashionable after Charles II married a Portuguese princess, well-accustomed to drinking it.

It was not only the tea itself that was imported but also the tiny porcelain cups and saucers from which to drink it, as well as the diminutive teapots in which it was made and the little lacquered tea tables on which to set the items. One thing led to another. What with the craze for collecting chinese porcelain, potters endeavouring to discover the secrets behind the manufacturing process and silversmiths creating a range of spoons, sugar tongs, jugs, bowls, caddies and such like used in conjunction with it, the drinking of tea was ideally suited to become a pursuit of the wealthy, and leisured, classes.

Tea was an expensive substance initially but as more was drunk the price began to drop and the habit spread further afield, both geographically and socially. It was supposedly introduced into Scotland in 1680 by Mary of Modena, wife of James Duke of York, while residing at Holyroodhouse.[31] It was 1702 before Lady Grisell Baillie purchased a 'tee pot' as well as little tea cups, a small 'yetlen [i.e. cast iron] kettle' and spirits of wine to boil it; three years later she bought two dozen china plates, the same number of tea and chocolate dishes, and a tea pot and basin imported from Holland; the following year 'a pot for milk to tee' was added.[32] It was after her marriage in 1749 that Hannah Robertson was recalling, with some pride, in a late (i.e.10th) edition of her book, 'I remember to have been almost the first person who possessed at that time and in that part of the country [i.e. Perthshire], an entire tea equipage of plate, which I received from the relations of both families.'[33] Tea drinking was spreading throughout society; domestic servants expected an extra payment in their wages for tea and sugar and labourers were accused of drinking weak tea instead of wholesome soups or home-brewed beer. The evil consequences of tea drinking were denounced on all sides, as were its effects on peoples' morals, and all the country's major problems were ascribed to it. So dominant was the drink that almost any infusions made from plants – rose-hips, sage, raspberry leaf and so on – were designated as 'teas' and even a light soup made of meat was called 'beef tea' or 'chicken tea' as appropriate.

CHAPTER THIRTEEN

Pastimes and Pleasures Around the Home

Cooking, cleaning, fetching water and fuel, making candles, washing and ironing, producing food from the garden, looking after poultry, pigs or bees, going to market to sell products of her own making or to buy in what was required, supervising servants, caring for children and other dependants – in such a busy life so filled with the practicalities of running a household there can have been few moments left over for anything that could remotely be called leisure, let alone pleasure. Yet even the busiest housewife must have found some parts of her life enjoyable, while for others the pendulum had swung the other way and because the domestic work was done by others they had more hours of leisure than they knew what to do with.

The pastimes and leisure activities of the town housewife would not necessarily be the same as those enjoyed by her rural sister, although for some of her activities it mattered little where she happened to be. Similarly, there must often have been some overlap between domestic duty and pastime, as between pastime and pleasure; what was pleasurable one day might well, depending on circumstance or mood, have seemed like a duty the next.

In the early days long hours were spent spinning wool or flax, which would then be sent to the local weaver to be made into different grades of cloth for household or family use. Equally long hours were spent in the basic sewing of garments, hemming of household linen, or smocking of shirts and under garments at yoke and cuffs to ensure a better fit, though the best known examples of the genre are the heavy cotton or linen working 'smocks' of the labourer. Many a housewife took pride in the neatness of her work

150

and found the repetitive work therapeutic, while giving her a quiet lull in which to reflect on other matters. Maybe it was in those quieter moments that she ordered her thoughts for bringing her account book up to date or writing up the sermon she had heard the previous Sunday; maybe too, she considered the wording of a recipe acquired from a neighbour which she wanted to add to others in her collection or turned phrases in her mind as they came together in poetry or song. Chores to some, no doubt, but a pleasurable occupation for others who might enjoy the opportunity to practise their writing or their arithmetic, while making certain their daughters saw how these things should be done.

In certain quarters such homespun practices were deemed old fashioned surprisingly early, while elsewhere they continued into the next century. Writing in 1729 under the name of 'a lover of his country' one Scot deplored the changing times: 'Where I saw the Gentleman, Lady and Children, dress'd clean and neat in home-spun Stuffs, of her own Sheep's growth and Women's Spinning, I now see the Ladies dress'd in French or Italian Silks and Brocades, and the Laird and his Sons in English broadcloth. Where I saw the Table serv'd in Scots clean fine Linen, I see now Fleemish and Dutch Diaper and Damask.'[1]

For those with less leisure and even less money, who knew to the last penny where every coin had gone, the order of the day was not so much making from new as mending, turning and making over. The housewives of 'Lark Rise' were thrifty out of necessity and were grateful for any clothing that came their way from their daughters out in service and made full use of every garment until it fell apart.[2] Their contemporaries across the Welsh border had the reputation of being not only thrifty but exceedingly industrious too: 'When not engaged in household work, they devote their time to knitting, sewing, and repairing, and sometimes to patchwork, in which they generally are adepts. The patchwork counterpanes are most neatly made, and quilted in fanciful designs.'[3] Patchwork quilts, now considered items of beauty in their own right, were a means of using up scraps of fabric to produce something of worth out of next-to-nothing; heavier materials from outworn clothing were cut up into strips about an inch wide and made into 'hooked' or 'prodded' rugs with the aid of a tool that pulled the strips through a hessian backing; the designs tended to be simple and bordered with black. The rugs took pride of place in front of the hearth or stopped the draught from under a door and added a touch of warmth to a stone floor along with some colour to the room.

Patchwork was a means of utilizing even small scraps of material to produce something that was both useful and attractive. The chamber pot under the bed was a necessity when the privy was across the yard or at the bottom of the garden. (Ironbridge Gorge Museum Trust)

In certain parts of the country, such as Yorkshire, everybody knitted – both men and women. The story is told of a woman living in Cotterdale who was accustomed to walk the 3 miles to her local market carrying on her head the weekly output of goods knitted by her family and she knitted as she went along. She continued to knit while selling her goods and returned home, still knitting, carrying on her head the necessities for the family and the supply of worsted for the following week's work. 'She was so expeditious and expert, that the produce of the day's labour was generally a complete pair of men's stockings.'[4] As already noted (see Chapter 4) Welsh women were frequently to be seen knitting as they walked home from fetching water, the pitcher balanced upon their heads.[5]

Those whose housekeeping duties were less onerous often took an active pleasure in beautifying their homes with their needle and specimens abound of the extremely fine work that such women could produce. Queen Mary, wife to Dutch William, set an example by being a noted needlewoman and at Hampton Court Celia Fiennes observed 'the hangings, Chaires, Stooles and Screen the same, all of satten stitch done in worsteads, beasts, birds, jmages and ffruits all wrought very ffinely by Queen Mary and her maids of honour.'[6] The origins of the familiar 'picture' sampler of Victorian days are to be found some two hundred or so years before, when girls were taught how to work designs and motifs in different stitches and threads on a strip of cloth as a 'sample' against the day she would marry and leave her own home. With the spread of printing came pattern books giving similar information in printed form; in due time the sampler was worked to a stylized design and became a benchmark in a girl's education. She also stitched a whitework sampler using white thread on a plain linen background, a style of sewing which ultimately led to other forms such as Ayrshire lace, sewed muslin and 'Irish flowering'; and also English whitework, otherwise called 'Coggeshall work' after the place in Essex where much of it was done, and broderie anglaise.

Sir Joshua Reynolds' painting of 'The Ladies Waldegrave' shows the three young sisters engaged in tambour work, a style of embroidery fashionable at the time. (The National Gallery of Scotland)

Some styles of needlework became very fashionable for a short period and portraits of the well to do might show the ladies engaged in such work: 'Netting', for example, where a gauge was used to create a framework of net which was afterwards filled in with stitches; or tambour work, called after the tambour or drum used to keep the material taut on which the embroidery was done with a hook pulling a continuous thread through the fabric. The Ladies Waldegrave, the three beautiful young great-nieces of Horace Walpole, were painted by Sir Joshua Reynolds doing this work. In the centre of the painting is Laura, winding the skein of silk; on her right Maria is holding it; while Horatia on her left holds the tambour frame.[7] This style of embroidery was quick to do and many collars, cuffs, caps, shawls and wedding capes were worked in this way, while babies' and children's garments were decorated in assorted styles and techniques.

For housewives with the time, inclination and ability to do the work, the scale of a project was no bar to their ambition: sets of canvas-work backs and seats for stools, chairs and sofas were hand-stitched; designs were worked for fire or pole-screens or for setting into panels on the walls; they even tackled hangings for the tall, four-poster beds which required curtains that drew all the way round, a pelmet and other pieces for the canopy above, a valance to put over the mattresses, and a coverlet for the bed itself. One such set of seventeenth-century bed hangings was created by the lady of the household in the early days of the Civil War when her husband was elsewhere on the King's business; while her house was surrounded and under seige from the Parliamentary forces she personally directed the defence, putting up a most spirited counter-attack, meantime stitching a charming set of bed hangings. Almost inevitably, the story ends with the dashing Prince Rupert riding to the rescue![8]

Embroidery and sewing, although necessary skills, were not for everyone; for many girls drawing and painting were part of their education and they were able to spend many happy hours so engaged. Painting, varnishing, staining and graining in the way of interior decoration was to be encouraged seeing that, by the late nineteenth century: 'Everything is nowadays made so easy for the amateur . . . that many people think far less of the trouble of decorating a room in all its details than of that involved by the arrival of a small army of work-people to execute the task for them'. At the same time a warning was sounded: 'The beginner must not be disappointed if his first attempts do not equal the work done by a professional decorator.' If all that was too daunting then it was possible to paint on glass, porcelain, pebbles and shells; on wood, leather, metalwork and American cloth; on mirrors and fans. It was also possible to paint on every imaginable textile, whether silk, satin, velvet, linen or canvas, employing techniques from the straightforward oils or water colours to crewel, pennon and oxydinia painting.[9] Subject matter was a personal choice, but although left to the artist it was to be considered carefully, whether it related to portraits, miniatures, landscapes or something nearer to hand such as garden flowers. In fact the flowers from the garden had a habit of surrounding the housewife indoors. Ranging from the humble bowl of pot-pourri to the finest porcelain, flowers were everywhere. Paintings of flowers to hang on the wall were always popular; flowers were painted on to china and porcelain, engraved on glass or silver, and collected as jewellery or tiny *objets d'art*; flowers of every description were woven into lace or damask and appeared on fabrics, whether hand embroidered or professionally woven and dyed; flowers, both real or artificial, surmounted hats or were discreetly placed to enhance a neckline or waist; they were favourite motifs in interior design, rioting across ceilings in swirls of plasterwork, tumbling down wood panelling or forming swags across the marble hearth. Ladies were often portrayed in paintings with a pot of flowers placed on a table or window ledge and baskets or bouquets of flowers in their laps or artfully placed nearby.

The growing of things in a garden is creative and therapeutic in the same way as embroidery or painting. William Lawson, the Yorkshire clergyman, certainly assumed that women would take an interest in the garden and wrote his book accordingly[10] (see also Chapter 9). Even if the housewife did not personally dig and delve she would surely have had her say as to what should be grown, how it should be tended and when it should be gathered. Despite the fact that gardening was considered to be a very feminine interest and many women derived great pleasure from their gardens, it is curious that few women wrote on the subject until well into the nineteenth century even though they were not shy of appearing in print on other topics.

There were some who had ambitions too large for a mere garden. Helen Hope, who was aged eighteen when she married the 6th Earl of Haddington in 1696, was one who worked on the grand scale planting trees and her husband gave her full credit for turning his own interests in that direction. In time he became known as one of the greatest planters of the period. She started on a small scale and he was pleased with what she did; then she persuaded him to let her create woodland over 300 Scots acres of rough moorland, although everyone said the scheme was impracticable. When husband and wife failed to agree on a focal point for the project they called in three friends to arbitrate on the matter and ended up with a design featuring three focal points.[11] Her initiative was later commemorated in verse:

'Watering my flowers.'

Thus can good wives, when wise, in every station,
On man work miracles of reformation:
And were such wives more common, their husbands would endure it;
However great the malady, a loving wife can cure it:
And much their aid is wanted; we hope they use it fairish,
While barren ground, where wood should be, appears in every parish.[12]

A garden could supply not only fruits, vegetables and herbs for the table but also plants for medicinal and cosmetic purposes. Many plants, or parts of plants, were pressed into service; the housewife was expected to have ready to hand a store of remedies that might be needed by her family at any moment and to supply her own cosmetics and creams. Long hours would be spent by the housewife in gathering together and preparing the materials in her still-room and in

From the 1905 edition of M.R. Mitford's *Our Village*, illustrated by H. Thomson.

The housewife needed herbs for different purposes within the house. Clockwise from top left: lemon balm, parsley, southernwood or wormwood, tarragon, lavender, lungwort and rosemary.

concocting the mixtures as advocated. Much information would be passed from mother to daughter, from housewife to housewife, but many herbals and other printed materials were available to those who could read them and had the money to buy them. The housewife could read works by John Parkinson, Nicholas Culpeper or Elizabeth Blackwell, among other authors, and learn from them about the plants themselves and how to grow them, which parts should be used, when to gather them and about their 'vertues' or what they were supposed to be good for. Cookery books also contained recipes for these items, and continued to do so for many years to come, under such chapter headings as 'Cookery for the Sick' or 'Various Receipts',[13] whereas in earlier days the latter were unequivocally entitled 'Beautifying Waters, Oils, Ointments, and Powders, to adorn and add Loveliness to the Face and Body'.[14] The dividing line between remedy and cosmetic was frequently slim as, for example, in mixtures intended 'To take away Sunburn' or 'To make the hair grow thick'. No such ambiguity existed in the directions for 'A sweet scented Bath for Ladies: Take of Roses, Citron-peel, sweet Flowers, Orange-flowers, Jessamy, Bayes, Rosemary, Lavender, Mint, Penny-royal, of each a sufficient quantity, boil them together gently, and make a Bath; to which add Oil of Spike six Drops, Musk five Grains, Amber-greese three Grains, sweet Afa one Ounce'. After putting that little lot together it is not altogether surprising that the recipe ends with the words, 'let her go into the Bath for three Hours'.[15]

How those three hours were to be spent is not on record; maybe some singing would have helped to pass the time. Music and singing played a significant role in many people's lives and certainly formed part of a girl's education; long hours were spent learning and practising various instruments and at social gatherings everyone was expected to contribute. Many women sang while they did the chores, though most especially in Wales where such habits were still common late in the nineteenth century: 'Music and singing in the homes, even of the poorest people, were general . . . . The harp and the fiddle were the instruments used, and to accompaniments of these, the men and women, the lads and maidens, sang the songs of Wales, and, sometimes, the wild roundelays of the age. . . . Singing and song are as natural to the Welsh as to the birds that fill the woodlands of Wales. From their cradles to their graves, songs and hymns are to be heard. The Welsh mother nursing her babe in the rocking-chair, or old-fashioned oaken cradle, sings the songs of her land, as she rocks to and fro. The Welsh housewife sings while she works – the men sing to their horses, the lads sing to the oxen, and the milkmaids sing to the cows.'[16]

The Scots also, one hundred years earlier, had been credited with much the same musical ability and their dancing had also been praised, but only when it concerned Scottish reels and Scottish airs. 'The Scotch ladies,' said an English visitor, 'will sit totally unmoved at the most sprightly airs of an English Country Dance; but the moment one of these tunes is played, which is liquid laudanum to my spirits, up they start, animated with new life, and you would imagine they had received an electrical shock, or been bit by a tarantula. A Lady, who, for half an hour before, has sat groaning under the weight of a large hoop and a corpulent habit of body, the instant one of these tunes is applied to her ear, shall bounce off her seat, and frisk and fly about the room to the great satisfaction of all the spectators.'[17]

As for other energetic pursuits, walking was always popular, if not a practical necessity for getting from one place to another. Some women walked long distances for pleasure, as did Elizabeth Grant and her friends when staying in Edinburgh for the winter;[18] the women of the Welsh Vales similarly walked long distances, unlike their counterparts in the hills.[19] An early nineteenth-century writer merely asserted that 'moderate exercise in the open air claims to be noticed' and observed that too much sedentary occupation and frequenting of public diversions would whittle away enjoyment 'for

The original caption reads: 'The flannel tennis dress . . . is as nearly perfection as can be obtained for its purpose; . . . The loose jacket is easily slipped on and off between the setts; and the slight drapery in front of the skirt, while taking off from the excessive plainness, in no way impedes the movements of the wearer.' From *Cassell's Book of the Household*, *c*. 1893, vol. 4.

the freshness of a pure atmosphere, for the beauties and amusements of the garden and for those "rural sights and rural sounds" which delight the mind unsubdued by idleness, folly or vice'.[20] Be that as it may, by the end of the century a domestic compendium included a chapter on 'Outdoor Games and Exercises'[21] which were beneficial to health, 'although of a less distinctly athletic character than those mentioned in a previous article' (i.e. one which dealt with cricket, rowing, hare-and-hounds and football, among other sports).[22] They could also be the focus of a pleasant afternoon's entertainment, with suitable refreshments laid on and seating provided for the onlookers.

Lawn tennis came first, 'because it is so essentially a family pastime; for whatever the game of the future may be, or however soon tennis may become as old-fashioned, not to say obsolete, as croquet itself, it is at the present day first favourite with both sexes and all ages'. Battledore and shuttlecock was described as 'an excellent game if played out of doors . . . usually considered quite a children's pastime, but children of larger growth may often engage in it with advantage'; badminton was supposedly similar only 'played with proper racquets across a net, according to certain rules'; croquet was said to be 'not without its advantages from the social point of view'; while archery was described as 'eminently a game of skill, and one that healthfully absorbs the whole attention'. Not so much for the home, although described, was hockey 'one of the most ancient ball-games we have any history of'; hockey on the ice 'a splendid game' and hurley, 'an Irish modification' of it with significant differences. Golf, which had long been played in Scotland, had only recently become popular in England and abroad: 'Golf is essentially a man's game', concluded the entry, 'though there is no reason why resolute hardy girls may not play it. Its chief recommendations consist in the long delightful walk to the links, in the walking entailed during the game, in the pleasurable excitement maintained throughout, and in the breathing of bracing sea or country air, which never fails to induce an excellent appetite.'

Returning to the garden there was bowls, another very ancient game much played in Elizabethan times, and many a bowling green became, in due course, the lawn tennis court; and quoits, played with iron rings of differing weights. Curling was the last to be explained, 'a more wholesome happy winter game than this would be difficult to imagine. . . . broadly likened to a game of billiards on the ice, and certainly it entails as much scientific skill' and though it was not to be considered as a pastime for the ladies they would always be welcome as spectators or else might engage in skating upon the ice. The economical Scots combined the curling rink with the lawn tennis court, the article observed: 'In Scotland a lawn-tennis ground is often made in a hollow, with banks all round, so that in winter, as soon as frost comes, it can be flooded, and thus turned, in one night into a curling pond.'

The bowling greens lasted longest in Scotland, where they were a focal point of the hospitality provided at many an old house. The two Misses Grant were in the capital for the visit of George IV in 1822 and with so many friends to see and activities to fit into each day they were hard pressed to visit their old friends at Craigcrook Castle, at that time a few miles outside the city. Yet they walked around the gardens there until dinner time and then again until tea; they chatted to their fellow guests and to the gardener and his wife, as well as to some favourite animals; they admired the beds of roses, the creepers on the house walls, and made use of the swing for half an hour, all to the background of the bowling matches being played on the green beyond the garden wall. It was a format repeated on many a summer Saturday.[23]

Animals, both real and mythical, featured in domestic life in much the same way as flowers did. In the early days there might have been a symbolism about what was depicted in conjunction with a person – an

The nature of cats has changed little over the years! (Ironbridge Gorge Museum Trust)

owl to represent wisdom, for example – but many family groups or domestic scenes throughout the period include a bird cage, or a dog, cat or parrot, which have the appearance of being family pets; men were portrayed with their horses and their dogs. 'Cranford's' Mrs Jamieson had a pampered pet dog, but Miss Betsy Barker had her beloved Alderney cow 'which she looked upon as a daughter'. This animal had inadvertently fallen into a lime pit and lost its hair, so was clad thereafter in an outfit of dark grey flannel for all of 'Cranford' to see.[24]

The passage of years does not mask the feelings expressed in an account of the loss of a much loved dog: 'My poor little pug is gone the way of all canine flesh; I wept as I saw him stretched motionless on the floor, and when I saw him laid on the ground; but his loss was the less to be regretted as he was asthmatic, paralytic, half-blind, three-quarters deaf, and nearly thirteen years old.'[25] Yet in spite of so many sentimentalized portrayals of children and animals during the Victorian era the housewife is warned in no uncertain terms that it is her responsibility to see that all animals kept in the house are treated well: 'The mistress of a house in which animals are unkindly treated, is guilty of *a very great sin*; and till she has taken care that the dog has his daily exercise and water, and that the cat and the fowl, and every sentient creature under her roof, is well and kindly treated, she may as well, for shame's sake, give up thinking she is fulfilling her duties.'[26]

When outdoor activities were not possible the housewife could find many ways of passing the time indoors with the family. Apart from the solitary pleasures obtainable from books, letter writing or various forms of handiwork, there were music and singing, charades, reading aloud, whist or other card games where permitted, backgammon or dominoes, chess, draughts, story telling, puzzles and jigsaws, acrostics, games such as Blind-Man's-Buff or Hunt the Ring and others of the genre.[27]

Those pastimes needing artificial light, elbowroom or special equipment and skills might be beyond folk of lesser means. When the light of the fire was the principal illumination the short space between the last meal of the day and an early bedtime, for such folk tended to rise with the sun, might be spent with the household gathered around the fire. A few passages from the Bible might be read, or an article from a journal; the women might knit, the maids do some mending, and the menfolk do simple jobs that needed little light, all the while talking over the day's events or discussing past times.

CHAPTER FOURTEEN

Pastimes and Pleasures Outside the Home

For the housewife living in a town there were many opportunities for pleasurable outings and for socializing with others but the country housewife might have to find a reason for getting herself to a venue that offered such delights. To present a daughter of marriageable age to society might well be accounted a valid justification or a suggestion to visit friends or relations; otherwise the housewife might have to invoke 'reasons of health' and propose 'taking the waters' somewhere.

'Off we drove in our little pony chaise, drawn by our old mare.' The two girls were to spend the day visiting the grounds of an old house. From the 1905 edition of M.R. Mitford's *Our Village*, illustrated by H. Thomson.

Visits to friends took up much time, and visitors might settle in for weeks or months at a time, or merely stop off *en route* to somewhere else. Longer journeys, as between London and Edinburgh, might be made by sea as it was often a faster and cheaper way to travel. For other journeys women rode pillion behind husband or manservant or travelled in some form of horse-drawn vehicle; those who wished to do so could ride. The first edition of Celia Fiennes' *Journeys* was entitled *Through England on a Side-Saddle* and there is a long-standing notion that she was the original 'fine lady upon a white horse' of the nursery rhyme about Banbury Cross. One time, when the weather had been wet and the track was slippery, her horse's feet failed 'and he Could noe wayes recover himself, and soe I was shott off his neck upon the Bank, but noe harm I bless God and as soone as he Could role himself up stood stock still by me, which I Looked on as a Great mercy – indeed mercy and truth all wayes have attended me'.[1] She certainly had her adventures along the way.

It somehow seems strange that 'stately homes' have always been 'open to view' and anyone passing by and interested in a house could request to be shown round. It was customary for the housekeeper to conduct visitors round the house, while the gardener performed the same task for the grounds; both expected to be well tipped for their services. Celia Fiennes was frequently going around other people's houses and commenting on their choice of decor or the style of furniture. At 'My Lord of Exeters Burly house' she found rooms leading one from the other, at least twenty of them in sequence, each room differing, 'and most fine Carving in the Mantelpieces, and very fine paint in pictures, but they were all Without Garments or very little, that was the only fault, the immodesty of ye Pictures, Especially in My Lords appartment.' After an exceedingly thorough inspection, which evidently included climbing up to a viewing platform on the roof, Celia Fiennes ends her description by saying: 'The great variety of the roomes and ffine works tooke me up 2 full hours to go from one Roome to another over the house. The Bowling-green, Wildernesse nor Walke I was not in, being so great a tract of ground, but you see it all at a view on ye top of ye house.'[2] This expectation of being able to see round any house of importance continued through into the nineteenth century, as demonstrated in the celebrated scene in *Pride and Prejudice*[3] where Elizabeth Bennett and Mr and Mrs Gardiner, her uncle and aunt, visit Mr Darcy's mansion in Derbyshire in the belief that he is absent and are shown round by his devoted housekeeper, only to be surprised by the unexpected arrival of the owner.

The healing properties of Harrogate's water were recognized in the sixteenth century. Many other spas were developed throughout Britain in the years that followed and some became exceedingly fashionable.

The first English 'spaw' was at Harrogate where the waters were said to resemble those of the original town of Spa in present-day Belgium. It was followed by Tunbridge in 1606 and Epsom in 1618, although both Bath and Buxton with their hot springs had been exploited by the Romans. Tunbridge Wells was brought to prominence after a visit from Queen Henrietta Maria in 1630 when she had been joined by the king and the rest of the court. Her daughter-in-law, Catherine of Braganza, came in 1663 seeking much the same cures and the entire court arrived in 1665 to escape the plague raging in London. Bath came into fashion after Queen Anne stayed there and the place was developed as a fashionable resort, with shops, libraries, public gardens, concert rooms, and other places of public entertainment under the strict control of a master of ceremonies. The Scottish spa at Moffat was another early one, first mentioned in 1650 though reasonably well established by that date. Sir John Clerk of Penicuik (1676–1755) paid it an annual summer visit for fifty years and took bottles of the water away with him for drinking at home; unflattering comments on the 'knot of Hovells' would suggest the fashionable facilities were still lacking in 1709.[4] The Minister of Ettrick, on the other hand, took a course of the water in his own home to which he attributed his sudden and considerable illness; he found the drinking of a daily dose of three English quarts of water a wearisome business.[5] The 2nd Earl of Hopetoun was often in the vicinity of Moffat overseeing his Dumfriesshire estates but, it was said, although he occasionally rode to the well in order to maintain its fashionable status he himself, on medical advice, paid an annual visit to Buxton.

The custom of submersing the patient, or the afflicted part of the patient, into waters credited with medicinal or holy powers was not new. It had been practised since pre-Christian times and the places were subsequently 'christianized' by being dedicated to a local saint. Celia Fiennes on her travels visited Holywell in Wales, of which she thought rather poorly: 'At Holly well they speake Welsh, the inhabitants go bare foote and bare leg'd – a nasty sort of people',[6] but its origins were colourful enough. The place was named after the famous Well of St Winifred, a saintly woman whose head was cut off by a thwarted Prince Cradocus because she had spurned his advances. 'The head rolled down hill, and at the spot where it stopped, there sprang up a stream of water which has continued ever since. The head was replaced upon the shoulders and St Winifred lived for fifteen years afterwards.'[7] Towards the end of the eighteenth century another traveller observed, 'The spring boils with vast impetuosity out of a rock . . .The waters were almost as sanitive as those of the pool of Bethesda . . . all infirmities incident to the human body met with relief'. By the time he was visiting it he thought there were fewer pilgrims than previously and that 'Few people of rank at present honour the fountain with their presence'.[8]

The practice of bathing in the water was superseded by drinking the water at its source. Neither Samuel Pepys nor Celia Fiennes were happy at the thought of sharing a bathing place with a whole lot of afflicted people. 'Methinks,' records the *Diary*, 'it cannot be clean to go so many bodies together in the same water'.[9] Celia Fiennes, meanwhile, had something else to worry about for, as she said at Holywell, she could not have bathed without curtains to hide her from the stares of passers-by in the street and people watching from nearby buildings 'for ye wett garments are no Covering to ye body'.[10] For those worried on this score it was the custom to be wrapped in a thick towel and carried in a sedan chair back to one's home or lodgings. There evolved the alternative practice of drinking the waters at their source or in a 'pump room' as at Bath or Harrogate, although submersion was still practised in the nearby baths.

The latest modes in bathing costumes (French style), designed by Marshall and Snelgrove, London, *c.* 1893. English women were advised that the best material for a costume was undoubtedly flannel or serge as anything else, when wet, would cling to the figure and in all probability give the wearer a chill. From *Cassell's Book of the Household, c.* 1893, vol. 3.

Different kinds of waters were suited to treating different types of ailment and the water's composition varied according to its mineral content, the four principal characteristics being chalybeate (iron), sulpherous, acidulous and saline.[11] From using saline water out of springs was but a step to the concept of the health-giving properties of sea bathing and sea air, which came into fashion after George III visited Weymouth in 1783. His son, later to be Prince Regent, began building his Marine Pavilion at Brightelmstone soon afterwards and resorts such as that developed at Brighton, along with Llandudno, Scarborough, Tenby, Ramsgate, and numerous places around the coast became noted for the healthy air and enjoyable lifestyles they provided. A description of Blackpool, in about 1788, painted an unflattering description of the surrounding moor and low cliffs of earth: 'It consists of a few houses ranged in line with the sea, and four of these are for the reception of company'; taking 30, 60, 80 and 100 guests respectively.[12] Somewhat earlier a visitor to

Edinburgh spoke of how the ladies drove in their carriages to the sands at Leith and Musselburgh and paraded backwards and forwards 'after the manner of Scarborough, and other public places of sea-bathing resort',[13] but by 1795 the beach had acquired bathing machines 'with steady horses and careful drivers'; the mile-long sands and water that was both clear and strong were described as being 'very retired'. So famous did the beach become over the years and so popular that the town earned the compliment of daily becoming more like Edinburgh-super-Mare.

The concept of seaside holidays and day trips was greatly encouraged by the building of the railway networks in the nineteenth century, especially those to places within easy reach of any large industrial centre. The impact can be gauged by the fact that in 1849 at Chatsworth, Derbyshire the first summer after a railway had been constructed, some 80,000 visitors were shown round the house despite the railway line terminating some 3 miles away. The 'day tripper' had arrived, although Samuel Pepys in his day had already been complaining of the hordes thronging Epsom, Barnet, Clerkenwell or Sadlers Wells, all watering places within easy reach of Londoners.

Although the objective for going to such a place was to effect an improvement in someone's health by bathing in or drinking the medicinal waters, such places became centres of social life generally, with a rather leisured atmosphere and plenty of opportunities for enjoyable activities, many of which could also be found in major towns across the country.

Much socializing centred around meals. Dinner might well be followed by music, singing or cards and everyone was expected to contribute their talents to the occasion. An evening 'rout' or 'drum' was another possibility – both forms of large parties in private houses, the latter so called because hostesses 'drummed up' the maximum number of guests. Dancing could take place at private gatherings in houses with a room large enough for the purpose; otherwise public 'assemblies' were organized in some central venue, large enough to hold a crowd. An 'assembly' was merely a gathering of people and it could be a dancing assembly or one for cards or music and so on. Many towns in the eighteenth century acquired purpose-built assembly rooms with all relevant facilities, but in smaller towns or larger villages the local inn would be pressed into service. In Bath and the most important social centres the assemblies were strictly run with a code of rules and a master of ceremonies. In

Conducted to the top of the room.

'Conducted to the top of the room.' That evening, shy Fanny Price opened the dancing with the eligible Mr Crawford as her partner. From J. Austen, *Mansfield Park*, 1897, illustrated by H. Thomson. (The Trustees of the National Library of Scotland)

Edinburgh a group of aristocratic ladies acted as 'Directresses' and the assemblies there had the dual purpose 'both for polishing the youth and providing the poor'; the young folk learnt how to behave in society under the watchful eye of the evening's directress and the profits were put to charitable purposes, almost £6,500 being distributed to good causes over twenty-five seasons.[14] The dancing comprised two hours of minuets followed by the country dances and tea and other, simple refreshments were on offer.

Transport to and from the assembly rooms for the ladies of the party might well be by sedan chair, an enclosed seat carried on poles between two chairmen. These conveyances were supposedly called after the French town of Sedan, although a derivation from the latin verb *sedere*, to sit, is also possible, but the 'litter' carried between horses or on men's shoulders had been in use much earlier. The sedan was first seen on the streets of London early in the seventeenth century and derogatory remarks were made about men becoming as servile as horses but, as on so many other occasions, what was considered laughably eccentric became perfectly acceptable in due course. Some households maintained their own but chairs were available for hire in many towns, like a modern taxi, and the fares operated in a similar way, being based on a combination of distance and time. The chair was the ideal form of transport in the narrow, twisting streets of so many medieval towns and took up relatively little space when not in use. When building spread far beyond the old town walls, streets became not only wider but straighter while houses became more spacious with space for stabling nearby, and it was then that horse-drawn vehicles became the fashionable alternative and the sedan chair faded into the past.

They were disappearing about the time that life in genteel 'Cranford' was portrayed by Mrs Gaskell. Rumours were flying through that small community about a gang of robbers operating locally, so that an invitation to take tea from an old friend living along an unlit lane, ominously referred to as 'Darkness Lane', caused some trepidation. Although Miss Matty was glad to be shut into the sedan chair, she was also fearful that, if the little party was attacked *en route*, the chairmen would run away and she would be left at the mercy of the robbers. Fortunately no such mishap occurred and they arrived back home safe and sound.[15]

Chairs could be hired for transport to other venues, too, such as musical events, visits to friends, theatres and for going to church on Sundays; hospitals used them to convey sick patients and an eminent Scottish judge was in the habit of sending his wig home in one when it rained, while he himself enjoyed the walk.[16]

Concerts and other musical events were always popular. Singers and musicians toured the country and gave public and private recitals; music societies were formed whose membership was mainly amateur but also contained a scattering of professionals, and they would give several performances a year to their fellow members and guests. Music and dancing combined in the 'ridotto', but the 'masquerade' was more of a masked assembly, with the guests wearing masks for the first part of the evening.

Busy at the pianoforte.

After dinner, everyone was expected to contribute towards the entertainment of their fellow guests. From J. Austen, *Mansfield Park*, 1897, illustrated by H. Thomson. (The Trustees of the National Library of Scotland)

The theatre was enjoyed by many, although it was frowned on in certain quarters – partly on account of certain religious values, partly on account of the supposedly dissolute life of those performing on the stage. Under Charles II the theatre in London blossomed; his mistress, Nell Gwyn, began her career selling oranges in the theatre but reputedly won the King's heart by declaiming a witty ditty from the stage while wearing a hat the size of a coachwheel. Theatre-going became the fashionable pastime for every layer of society. Countless theatres were built all over the country, both in established towns and in the newly developed spas or seaside resorts, and the widest possible range of theatrical performances was staged. Many celebrated stage personalities of the day, of the calibre of Mrs Sarah Siddons and Mrs Dorothea Jordan, began their careers in the provinces and then set off for fame and fortune in London, while continuing to tour thereafter. When Sarah Siddons arrived in Edinburgh, just a year after her triumph in London, so many people wished to see her, including a large number of ministers attending the General Assembly of the Church of Scotland which happened to be meeting at the time, that the Assembly's sessions had to be rescheduled.

There were other things to watch as well, such as conjurers, or acrobats or dancers; in the seventeenth century an elephant was walked around the country and records of payments 'to see the elephant' crop up in contemporary domestic accounts.[17] By the end of the eighteenth century Astley's Amphitheatre could be added to the list of Londoners' entertainments. Astley himself was a former cavalry officer who was given his horse as a leaving present. He began by giving equestrian displays in the fields near Southwark and then in a canvas-covered ring; after this was destroyed by fire the amphitheatre was built and the displays included clowns, acrobats, swordsmen and jugglers, alongside melodramas and the ever-popular equestrian displays. The place was rebuilt on several occasions and was functioning until 1893.

There were exhibitions of a different nature that today would be set up in art galleries or museums. In 1851, under the auspices of the Royal Society of Arts and the Presidency of Prince Albert, the Great Exhibition was held in London's Hyde Park, which all the world flocked to see, greatly aided by the railways. Further exhibitions were subsequently held at regular intervals both in London and other venues around the country.

Not everything happened indoors; outdoor recreations became very fashionable in the nineteenth century. Sports have already been spoken of in relation to the housewife around the home but they certainly lent themselves to outdoor entertaining; archery was exceedingly popular, as were tennis parties. Hunting and other equine pursuits were attractive to some; race meetings up and down the country attracted the crowds. The origin of the Epsom course where the Derby is run is said to be connected with the crowds of folk who went to drink the waters at Epsom and had time on their hands.

Spas and other towns established public parks and gardens where people could enjoy walking in the fresh air, with music provided from a central bandstand. They provided an opportunity for people to see others and to be seen; the late-afternoon promenade in London's Hyde Park was very much part of the Season and everyone paraded up and down, either on foot, on horseback or in horse-drawn vehicles. Pleasure gardens had long been known in London and many took to calling themselves 'tea gardens' when that drink became popular; folk paid an entrance fee, walked around and then drank a cup of tea and ate bread and butter. Vauxhall, Marylebone and Ranelagh Gardens were all famous in their day, although there were others as well. The gardens were lit after dark when dancing, concerts and firework displays were the entertainments provided, along with food and drink.

Eighteenth-century Edinburgh with its two gardens tried to emulate London, but without much success: the Scottish Ranelagh was rather more fashionable than the Comely Gardens which were described by Edinburgh's own historian as 'A wretched attempt to emulate Vauxhall for which neither the climate nor the gardens were adapted.'[18] The gardens were open twice-weekly during the summer but when an English visitor went there he found the place deserted, the musicians playing in the ruins of a former pigeon house; he learnt afterwards that the gardens were considered 'unfashionable' and were therefore not patronized by 'fashionable folk'.[19]

Over and above the varied social life a visit to town, for the average housewife, meant shops and shopping on a grand scale. The smaller towns might have their shops and dressmakers and milliners, but it was not the same as seeing the fashions for herself. The fictional 'Cranford' was some 20 miles from the nearest town and after the Misses Barker had retired from their genteel millinery establishment the residents relied on the principal shopkeeper 'who ranged the trades from grocer and cheesemonger to man-milliner as required'. He told his customers he went straight to Paris 'until he found his customers too patriotic and John Bullish to wear what the Mounseers wore' when he changed the venue to London, where he had seen Queen Adelaide only the week before wearing exactly the same cap as the one in front of them on which she had been complimented by the King.[20]

Almost any town offered opportunities unrivalled by anything the housewife's own locality could provide but purchases made in London carried a cachet of their own. Miss Hutton understood this fact well enough when she wrote appealing for help to:

Mr D — at London.

Birmingham, May 14, 1781.

I am going to trouble you with a commission. Not to buy me a new silk; nor yet that highest pinnacle of female ornament, a new cap; but a fashionable, plain, black riding hat, without either feathers or lace. One might suppose that one plain hat would be very like another; yet there is a style, a manner, in a London hat which our untutored hats in the country cannot equal. My father has given me a habit of scarlet broad-cloth, and I am ambitious to look as well in it as I can.

Next to having my hat fashionable, I wish to have it soon; for I cannot wear my habit without it. . . . I am going with my mother to Aston (Derbyshire) next Monday, and the habit is as necessary for the journey as the hat is for the habit.

My brother says I must send you the circumference of my 'sappy pate' which, strange to tell, is twenty-three inches. It is the reverse of *multum in parvo*. I forget whether you understand Latin.[21]

For those who were unable or unwilling to travel to London themselves there had always been ways round the problem. Mrs Purefroy and her son relied on the two men acting as their agents there and were accustomed to requesting either them or their wives to hunt out a very wide and varied assortment of purchases, such as a second-hand sedan chair, a book on the therapeutic waters of Scarborough possibly written by a Dr Shaw, and a brass fender measuring 3 feet at the very least. Mixed in with requests for coffee berries, tea and 2 gallons of 'sallet oyl', which she had heard was very cheap in London, they were asked to buy, at diverse times, enough white satin material to make a petticoat and gown for herself, a fashionably hooped petticoat from a certain warehouse and a hat of fine leghorn straw. There was also a commission regarding a suit of mourning for her son Henry to wear following the Queen's death in 1737, even though Henry was frequently writing on his own behalf.[22]

A more personal alternative had involved making use of family or friends travelling to London or, indeed, any large town, and anyone setting off was likely to be provided with a long list of 'wants' for those back home. In the seventeenth century Anne, Duchess of Hamilton (1656–1716) had relied upon the Duke to make certain purchases for her on his frequent visits to London, with mixed results; his taste did not always match hers and on one unfortunate occasion when nobody could tell him what was meant by a 'sallantine' he had to send a letter off to the Duchess, back in Scotland. A tart rejoinder explained that he had misread her writing and what she had asked for was a 'palantine', a furry tippet or scarf.[23] Samuel Pepys, a contemporary of hers, recorded with some pride in his *Diary* the many occasions on which either he or his wife bought or wore new clothes, and he also noted innumerable purchases of the other articles necessary for the fashionable lifestyle to which they aspired, culminating in a fine coach and a pair of horses.

London had always been able to provide merchandise of every description in a manner unrivalled anywhere else and the period witnessed an enormous increase in the number of goods readily available. As travelling became easier more women were able to make the journey for themselves and enjoy the temptations of the London shops, a habit that was greatly expedited by the building of the railway networks.

At the end of the eighteenth century a new concept of shopping was established in the former Schomberg House in Pall Mall. It was the 'department store', so called because the goods for sale were offered in different 'departments'. Hats and dresses in one, fabrics in another, jewellery and ornamental objects in a third and so on; upstairs there was a large room where customers could buy light refreshments and see the latest in furnishing fabrics; on the floor above were the workrooms. It was a successful format and one that was to be followed by numerous retailers down the years, with many well-known names surviving until after the Second World War.

However, every visit to the capital or other centre of social activities had to end at some point and, laden down with purchases and memories, the housewife would make the journey home, with heavy heart or happy anticipation, to resume her duties among her own family; while maybe taking the opportunity to regale her country friends with tales of the sights to be seen and the people met with while away.

CHAPTER FIFTEEN

The Housewife in the Wider World

> Take weapon away, of what force is a man?
> Take huswife from husband, and what is he then?
> As lovers do covet, together to dwell,
> So husbandrie* loveth, good huswiferie well.
> Though husbandrie seemeth, to bring in the gains,
> Yet huswiferie labours, seem equall in pains.
> Some respite to husbands, the weather may send,
> But huswives affaires, have never an end.[1]

A t a time when some 90 per cent of the people were directly involved with the land, Tusser was formally acknowledging the contribution that women made to the well-being of the household. The needs of the household must, indeed, have seemed as if they had 'never an end' and for many a housewife those domestic concerns must have absorbed most, if not all, of her time, whether or not she was doing the work herself or seeing that the work was done correctly by others. Fuel and water had to be found and carried home; the wherewithal for lighting had to be provided; homes and clothing required cleaning and laundering; servants needed supervising; and the subject of food must have been a perennial concern, whether home-grown or bought in, over-abundant in times of plenty or scarce at times of dearth, whatever the quantity or quality it had to be stored, preserved, cooked and served to its best advantage and according to the household's current standards. The housewife had also to maintain a store of beverages suitable for the formal dinner, for the unexpected visitor or for comfort in times of sickness, while other preoccupations concerned the provision of

* the work of a farmer, farm business

domestic textiles and clothing and keeping a well-stocked medicine chest in case of sudden illness or accident. Many a housewife would offer her services and homemade remedies to a neighbour in times of trouble or to someone who came knocking on the door. It was considered a matter of Christian charity to do so, linked to the concept of grace and the giving of alms.

Over the years the housewife's workload did change, slowly and not necessarily with an immediate change for the better, nor was such change consistent to all housewives at all times. For the aristocratic lady living in a spacious town house and the shepherd's wife on a Welsh hillside change came at different times and might well mean different things. A supply of cold water brought into the dwelling might be thought of as heaven sent to the one; whereas to the other, what were servants for if not to fetch and carry that sort of thing and what she really wanted was a steady, reliable housekeeper to maintain order. Throughout the period some housewives were living an almost medieval lifestyle, fetching in water and firewood and growing all their own foodstuffs, whereas others were able to get the benefits of any advances, technological or otherwise, rather sooner.

One of the most outstanding developments must have been the provision of a water supply into a dwelling, courtesy of labour carried out by someone else, which meant that the housewife no longer had to find a source of supply or to carry home containers of water from a distance; the quality of that water was also coming under control. A readily available supply of water eased the burden of keeping the household washed and fed and the home clean. Of comparable importance was the provision of cesspits and sewers to remove the household waste thereafter. The supply of fuels, again from an external source, led to heating and lighting being taken out of the housewife's hands. Where once she was expected to assist in the cutting and stacking of peats and gathering of firewood, along with its transport home, the provision of paraffin, gas and, eventually, electricity, with which to heat rooms and to cook, obviated that sort of drudgery altogether. Equally, these fuels did away with the necessity for the labour (and smell) involved in making tallow candles or rush-lights as well as the daily chore of cleaning and filling oil and paraffin lamps; instead, heat and light could now materialize almost instantaneously with the minimum of effort. Both housework and laundrywork involved much physical labour but both were undoubtedly eased where piped, and possibly heated, water was laid on and further revolutionized with the advent of electricity to power the equipment, though there were always some chores that remained beyond such help.

Turning to cooking and food, the range of available foodstuffs widened considerably over the period, the increase being linked to geographical exploration, the exchange of commodities with other nations and the advances made in methods of agriculture and horticulture, among other reasons. Cookery books took cognisance of the fact and included recipes for making desserts from imported oranges or pineapples; others dealt with newcomers such as potatoes, tomatoes, turkey or macaroni; and they adapted instructions for 'marmalades' to ingredients that were more readily available. The growth of British influence in India was reflected in the proliferation of recipes for curry and pilau, chutney and kedgeree, and it is the reason why many British men in the past relished such foods, yet turned up their noses at French cooking with its sauces, assuming that the sauce was a disguise for something that was 'off'. French styles of cooking and presentation also found a place in the cookbooks, although some authors, such as Hannah Glasse, fought a spirited battle against these foreign ways. New varieties of wines and spirits, along with non-alcoholic drinks, came in from widely differing regions of the world and, in the case of tea, gave Britain the focal point of a new meal. Housewives or their cooks had to contend with new foods, new styles of cooking stoves, a change in fuels and, latterly, a new format for presenting those meals at the dinner table.

By the time the nineteenth century was nearing its end it was becoming apparent that fewer girls and boys were entering domestic service but, conversely, with the advent of motorized transport, the telephone, commercial laundries and dry cleaners, electricity and other domestic aids, fewer servants were required to help in the home anyway. Houses were built taking this into account; more compact styles were in evidence and there was therefore less to keep clean. A simpler domestic routine was forced upon the hard-pressed housewife, not only around the house generally but most obviously in the kitchen where the style of cooking was simplified and the number of dishes served at the average dinner party somewhat reduced; although the number of courses remained unchanged the practice of offering a choice of dishes within each course was no longer essential.[2]

If domestic life within the house changed between 1650 and 1950 it is fair to say, speaking in terms of the broadest generalizations, that the housewife herself also changed during those years.

In 1650 the housewife was very much an active, hands-on housewife, occupying herself personally with many of the domestic chores or working closely with her servants. Gervase Markham had enumerated the skills required of the housewife; over and above those skills, he laid down guidelines for her behaviour: 'Our English Hous-wife' he observed, 'must be of chast thought, stout courage, patient, untyred, watchfull, diligent, witty, pleasant, constant in friendship, full of good Neighbour-hood, wise in discourse, but not frequent therein, sharpe and quicke of speech, but not bitter or talkative, secret in affaires, comfortable in her counsels, and generally skilfull in the worthy knowledges which doe belong to her Vocation.'[3] In being the 'mother and mistris of the family [i.e. household] . . . where from the generall example of her vertues, and the most approved skill of her knowledges, those of her family may both learne to serve God, and sustaine man, in that godly and profitable sort which is required of every true Christian'.[4] By the 1750s the housekeeper was already in evidence and well-to-do ladies were gladly handing over many of their duties to this paid employee. Meanwhile, the housewife who carried on working in her still-room or insisting on her servants spinning wool or flax for homespun clothing was becoming rarer, although she still existed. One such specimen was encountered in 1788 when Miss Hutton was travelling around the country with her mother who was in indifferent health: 'The progress of the arts,' she wrote to a friend, 'even the art of cookery, is from south to north. We have here* the wife of the rector of Rochdale, a gentlewoman of the old school, in person and manner resembling a good fat housekeeper, who, I dare say, never heard of a curry in her life, yet is excellently skilled in pickling shrimps, potting herrings, raising goose pies, and flourishing in pastry.'[5]

A century later and the housewife had relatively few domestic duties to attend to herself, apart from supervising her many servants; to do the work herself was considered to be demeaning to her husband's status and denying employment to someone else. Domestic manuals instructed her how to fill her time with schemes for self-improvement and with pastimes such as reading or fancy stitchery, painting or collecting botanical specimens. Her prime duty was to make an attractive home for her husband, a refuge from the outside world, and to make herself his worthy companion and chosen friend.[6]

* i.e. staying in the same lodgings in Blackpool

Frontispiece of *Instructions in Gardening for Ladies*, 1840. Jane Loudon (1807–58) wrote the book to encourage and assist women in the garden and it proved immensely popular. Although gardening was considered eminently suitable as a feminine occupation, it was surprising that it took so long for women to write on the subject.

By 1950 things had changed again; the housewife was learning to live without paid help, food was still scarce in the aftermath of the Second World War when 'make do and mend' – making every possible use of whatever there was – recalled a lifestyle closer to the seventeenth century rather than midway towards the twenty-first. During the 1940s many folk took to keeping hens, for the sake of their eggs and the extra meat, or took up beekeeping on account of the honey to eke out the meagre sugar ration (although, it has to be said, there was an added attraction in the sugar allowance provided for feeding the bees each autumn which did not always make it into the hives . . .); it was a time when flower gardens were dug up and turned over to vegetable and fruit growing, and 'bottling' the produce took up many hours in the late summer and autumn; the hedgerows were plundered for crab-apples and rose-hips to provide much needed vitamin C formerly provided by imported oranges and other fruits; and folk scavenged for firewood to make up the limited amounts of fuel available.

If work within the house changed over the years, as did the role of the housewife, then it is true to say that attitudes to domestic work also changed as time went by. From being the all-important guiding force, the lynch-pin of her household, whose example was there to be followed by everyone, the housewife became a supernumerary figure, with too few real duties and too much time on her hands, which she was accused of filling with idle chatter and a few pastimes. She was hardly to be blamed for the situation; meaningful education was denied to her seeing as she was a girl and likely to be married. The work the housewife had previously done herself was now done by servants, so that any work carried out within the house was perceived to be of lowly status. Even when the housewife was without servants and single-handedly maintaining a domestic routine, working within the home never regained its former status.

'The idea of careers for girls is quite of modern origin' noted the compilers of *Cassell's Book of the Household* in the 1890s: 'Half a century ago it used to be taken for granted that the one career open to a girl was that of wife, mother, and mistress of a household; and individuals who failed to achieve what was supposed to be woman's vocation by marriage, were looked down upon and pitied by their neighbours and acquaintances. Moreover, the women who worked for a living were regarded as anomalies; and even if they attained success, they were believed to have simply made the best of a misfortune, rather than to have merited approval.'[7] The article continued by saying that 'this theory of women's work has been rudely shaken' and gave the example of the census returns of 1831 and 1881. The former included only one question relating to women's occupation and that was 'domestic service', whereas in the latter year 330 occupations were being followed by women and throughout the census returns there were only 70 in which women did not participate.

The article is too dismissive of women's employment outside the home and glosses over the fact that many women were distinguished or celebrated one way or another. To take just one example out of the numerous possibilities, actresses of the calibre of Mrs Dorothea

Jordan and Mrs Sarah Siddons[8] were idolized by the theatre-going public, audiences flocked to see them perform at venues throughout the country and their portraits were painted on many occasions. Whatever their personal lives may have been there was no way in which their adoring public 'regarded them as anomalies'.

Even with only the basic domestic skills women still managed to earn themselves a living, of sorts, for women's pay was consistently set at a lower rate than for men, but some then made use of their experience to move on to other things. Domestic servants were always in demand and, if a girl was good at the work, she could rise through the ranks to be cook or housekeeper in a wealthy household with servants to assist her; to become a lady's maid was another option if she was able to sew and do fine laundrywork. These skills could provide a living in the outside world as well, for professional laundresses, dressmakers, milliners and many others of that ilk. Before the Industrial Revolution changed the pattern of employment countless women were able to contribute to the family income while in their own homes by selling the products of their own making from knitting, sewing, spinning and other handiwork of this nature.

After fifty years' combined experience of domestic service Mr and Mrs Adams put it all to good use when they wrote a handbook for servants of every rank, whereas Hannah Glasse at an earlier date had confined herself to writing about the female staff. Her contemporary, Elizabeth Raffald, who gave birth to sixteen daughters in eighteen years, established Manchester's first registry office for domestic servants alongside her cooked meats and confectionary shop. Women cooks went on to write innumerable cookery books, some of which are still highly regarded today, and the reasons for writing them were as diverse as the books. Hannah Robertson needed to make some money for her old age; Mrs Rundell claimed she was writing for the sake of her daughters when they were leaving home and it was only by chance that it came to the eye of a publisher; Eliza Acton, on the other hand, offered a little volume of 'further fugitive verses' to a publisher and was told to go away and write a cookbook instead, which she did – most successfully. Women ran cookery schools or sewing classes and wrote their books to help their students. Others might set themselves up in a large house in order to take in lodgers; the fictitious Meg Dods, of cookbook fame, was based on the character of a genuine innkeeper in the Scottish Borders, while the real author of the book was Mrs Christian Isobel Johnstone, a writer of novels and a literary journalist.

Writings of every sort seem to have fitted in well with women's household duties, possibly as a result of housewives honing their skills in letter-writing as a means of keeping in touch with distant family and friends, and many women's work appeared in print. The letter format was a good starting point, whether portraying life in far-flung Scotland or far-away Turkey, and from there it was but a step to journals, memoirs or reminiscences of visits to distant parts and one step more to books advising travellers on how to travel. Poetry was another favourite format, often taking domestic themes as its subject; for one thing, lines and rhythms could be turned over in the mind in the quieter moments while attending to other matters and then it needed less in the way of paper, ink and writing time than the average novel. Were the likes of Jane Austen, Mrs Gaskell and the many others who turned out a copious supply of full-length novels really to be considered as 'anomalies'? There were those whose work went beyond novels and poetry and turned to writing plays for the theatre, or to philosophical or scientific theses. Margaret, Duchess of Newcastle was an early example who tried her hand at most forms, while others specialized in one form or the other and won renown for their achievements.

Women gifted with artistic talents were able to put them to good use. Elizabeth Blackwell illustrated a treatise on medicinal plants[9] and engraved the plates and coloured them herself thereafter in order to raise money when her husband was imprisoned for debt. Mary Moser was a flower painter and a Foundation Member of the Royal Academy. Mary Beale, whose husband gave up his own job to further her career, was a portraitist, and Maria Cosway a miniaturist who travelled extensively and set up a school for girls in Italy after being widowed; Hester Bateman headed a dynasty of silversmiths and Anne Damer worked in marble producing portrait busts and animal pieces.

Although Markham had considered it every housewife's duty to be skilled in physic and surgery there were some women who were more than ordinarily blessed in this line. Not only did they carry out 'good works' by looking after their neighbours and ameliorating the lot of any of the sick or poor who came to the door but they also bequeathed money to establish alms houses, religious foundations and other charitable institutions. Others took a more vociferous line. Elizabeth Fry, mother of innumerable children, visited women in prison and ameliorated their conditions and treatment by dint of her demands; Josephine Butler canvassed for the more humane treatment

St Mary's Cathedral, Edinburgh. The Misses Walker left their entire fortune to the Episcopal Church in 1870 on condition that the Diocese of Edinburgh built a cathedral. Services were being held in the nave by 1879.

of prostitutes; Caroline Norton campaigned for the rights of divorced women; while the founding of the Royal Hospital at Chelsea for veteran soldiers, 'the Chelsea Pensioners', is often credited to Nell Gwyn (undoubtedly a mother, though it is hard to think of her as a housewife), who badgered Charles II until he agreed to provide amenities for the veterans.

The Lady Anne Halkett won acclaim for tending the wounds of soldiers who trudged past her gates after one of the Civil War battles and it is on this account that she was once described (rather over-enthusiastically) as having served as 'an army surgeon on the royalist side'. Such was her reputation that patients came to her from far and wide for the rest of her life and she treated men, women and children alike, and also women in childbirth. She also found the time to write a large number of devotional meditations.[10] Some women specialized in midwifery and wrote text books on the subject, as did Jane Sharp and Mrs Cellier, although for a while the women lost out to the male obstetricians who denied them access to formal medical training and qualifications.[11] It was not until Princess Charlotte, daughter of the Prince Regent, that a member of the royal family employed a male 'accoucheur' and Queen Victoria followed her example; until then, royal births for many a long year had been supervised by midwives.

In fact education generally, or the lack of it, was seen by the women themselves as being the key to their difficulties. Without education they were unable to exercise much choice in their lives, they were looked upon as second-class citizens and yet they were barred from obtaining that education.

It had not always been like that. Some sixteenth-century women were famed throughout Europe for their learning as were some in the early part of the seventeenth, but by the end of that century women were protesting at the changed situation and proposing ways to improve their lot. As early as 1673 Bathsua Makin, one-time tutoress to Charles I's children and more especially to the Princess Elisabeth, wrote *An Essay to Revive the Ancient* Education of Gentlewomen*, which outlined the benefits that would accrue to both piety and motherhood.[12] It was intended that such an education would be fitted round the existing tenets of housewifery and accomplishments designed to attract a husband; neither she nor those who came after were asking for public careers for women, only for the means to make women better companions to their husbands, better mothers to their children and better able to cope on their own if they remained unmarried or were widowed. Mrs Makin put her theories into practice by setting up a school near London where pupils spent half their time on accomplishments such as writing and accounts, the other half on Latin, French and so on. Others followed her example in demanding that girls should be given a formal education.

Women have always been involved in education, teaching their offspring until ready for a tutor or for school but, beyond that, they often ran schools, or assisted their husbands in the running; some offered a sound education, some were horrendous. Women with only a smattering of learning ran 'dame schools' in their own cottages

*i.e. former

where they taught a modicum of reading and writing for a tiny fee; and in due course many others became the governess in a family, both at home and abroad.

Their opportunities for education changed for the better during the eighteenth century, in parallel to the improvements made in the schooling of boys, but it was often the case that women who wished to study 'academic' subjects had to do so on their own. It was an uphill struggle to win the right to a university education for women and,

Girton College, Cambridge, the first institution devoted to the higher education of women, was established through the determination of Emily Davies (1830–1921).

186

exactly two hundred years after Bathsua Makin's treatise, Girton College, Cambridge, the first of its kind in Britain, opened its doors in 1873.[13]

The fear that girls might become too learned and scare away a potential husband was very real to mothers and daughters were to be discouraged at all costs from showing themselves to be 'blue stockings'. For husbands, the fear was rather that an educated woman would become too immersed in her studies and neglect her domestic duties and his comforts. Women have always had this balancing act in their lives and have had to be ready to put their own work to one side in favour of domestic concerns. Jane Austen combined writing with her household duties but preferred to work in a room with a squeaky door so she had warning of any interruption. Mary Somerville, after whom Somerville College, Oxford was named, was a self-taught mathematician and astronomer of international repute who as a child had been forbidden a candle at bedtime lest she used it to read by and instead had memorized mathematical problems and worked them out in her head. Her second husband was most supportive of her work and by rigorous organization of her day she managed to combine her academic studies with her accepted domestic duties. By so doing she would have merited the approval of one Scotsman who said 'that there was no objection to the blue stocking, providing the petticoat came low enough down'.[14]

Few women, however, have been so fortunate and many have found their studies interrupted by domestic duties. Florence Nightingale spoke scathingly of 'the great god dinner' and the three whole hours expended every day on eating and asked how women could achieve anything with that sort of disruption in their daily life? An earlier age had witnessed the sight of Mary Astell, an extremely learned lady, opening an upstairs window to shout down to potential visitors that 'Mrs Astell was not at home'.[15]

The progress made in women's education and the subsequent advances made in their position in society gradually changed the perception of women in the home, but allied to this were also the considerable changes that were taking place both inside and outside the home. Slowly but surely so many of the duties previously considered to be part of every woman's life were gradually whittled away, to be provided by other people or by other means. As her duties have diminished and become less onerous so the perception of her role has also weakened, to such an extent that, in the closing years of the twentieth century, the dignity of the housewife's calling has been seriously eroded and the full-time housewife is on the way to being an endangered species.

Yet, in many respects the demands on a housewife at the end of the twentieth century are similar to those on her predecessors three hundred years ago. She may work with different materials and have different sources of help available to her, the servants replaced by electricity, but the requirements of a household have changed relatively little. Cleaning, cooking, washing and ironing, the buying and storing of foodstuffs, the care of dependants, gardens and animals, all these activities remain to be done, along with any charitable work and the housewife's own personal interests. The housewife's life is, indeed, a patchwork of activities that somehow has to be fitted together, whether she works full time within the home or is in paid employment outside it.

Across the years, one generation of housewives has been followed by the next, each rising to the challenge of whatever the fates might send and accepting the reversals with fortitude. Many found great strength in their religious beliefs, for the biblical 'three score years and ten' was very much a reality for much of the period; there were those for whom even that was unattainable while few mothers saw all their children grow to adulthood. The inevitability of death was softened in the belief that it was not an end but the start of another, better existence.

Let the last word go to Margaret Cavendish, Duchess of Newcastle, whose mind was given over to philosophical speculation and the writing of plays rather than to the domestic skills, as being a 'spinster of poetry' if not a 'spinster in housewifery':[16]

Soule, and Body

Great Nature She doth cloath the Soule within,
A fleshly garment which the Fates do spin.
And when the Garments are growne old, and bare,
With Sicknesse torn, Death takes them off with care.
And folds them up in Peace, and quiet rest,
So laies them safe within an Earthly Chest;
Then scoures them, and makes them sweet, and cleane,
Fit for the Soule to wear those cloaths agen.[17]

Notes

Where the place of publication is London, this has been omitted.

Chapter One

1. I. Beeton, *Book of Household Management*, (Ward, Lock & Tyler, n.d. '140th thousand'), p. 1
2. *Proverbs* 31: 27, but the full passage runs from 10 to 31
3. G. Markham, *The English House-wife*, 5th edn, (John Harrison, 1637), title page
4. R. Scott-Moncrieff (ed.), *Household Book of Lady Grisell Baillie*, (Edinburgh, T. & A. Constable, 1911)
    H. Graham, *Group of Scottish Women*, (Methuen, 1908), p. 110
5. G. Eland (ed.), *Purefroy Letters*, (2 vols, Sidgwick & Jackson, 1931)
6. B. Marshall (ed.), *Memoirs of Lady Fanshawe*, (John Lane, 1905)
    Margaret, Duchess of Newcastle, *Life of William Cavendishe, Duke of Newcastle to which is added the true relation of my birth, breeding and life*, C.H. Firth (ed.), (John Nimmo, 1886)
    i.e., R. Lonsdale (ed.), *Eighteenth-Century Women Poets*, (OUP, 1989)
7. S. Pepys, *Diary*, H.B. Wheatley (ed.) and the Rev. Mynors Bright (tr.), (9 vols, George Bell & Son, 1893)
    J. Woodforde, *Diary of a Country Parson*, J. Beresford (ed.), (5 vols, Humphrey Milford, 1924)
8. E. Grant, *Memoirs of a Highland Lady 1797–1827*, Lady Strachey (ed.), (John Murray, 1898)
9. C. Hutton, *Reminiscences of a gentlewoman of the last century*, Mrs C.H. Beale (ed.), (Birmingham, Cornish Brothers, 1891)
    G. Jekyll, *Old West Surrey*, (Longmans, Green & Co., 1904)
    i.e. *Within Living Memory Series* [by individual county], (Countryside Books, 1994) i.e., Cumbria, Shropshire etc.
10. M. Dods (pseud.) *Cook & Housewife's Manual*, 3rd edn, (Edinburgh, Oliver & Boyd, 1828)
11. E.C. Gaskell, *Cranford*, a reissue, (Macmillan & Co.,1898)
    F. Thompson, *Lark Rise to Candleford*, (OUP, 1945)
    J. Galt, *Annals of the Parish*, 2nd edn, (Edinburgh, T.N. Foulis, 1911)
12. F.M. Eden, *The State of the Poor*, (3 vols, J. Davis, 1797)
    H. Mayhew, *London Labour & London Poor*, (4 vols, Griffin, Bohn & Co., 1852–61)
13. C. Fiennes, *Through England on a Side-Saddle*, (Field & Tuer, 1888)
14. S. Johnson, *Journey to the Western Islands of Scotland*, new edn, (Edinburgh, Mundell & Son, 1798)

J. Boswell, *Journal of a Tour to the Hebrides with Samuel Johnson*, 2nd edn, (Charles Dilly, 1785)

15. D. Wordsworth, *Recollections of a Tour made in Scotland AD 1803*, J.C. Shairp (ed.), 3rd edn, (Edinburgh, D. Douglas, 1894)
    E.I. Spence, *Sketches of Scotland*, (2 vols in 1, Longman, Hurst et al., 1811)
16. The 'Ladies of Llangollen' were Lady Eleanor Butler (1739–1829) and Miss Sarah Ponsonby (1755–1831), who ran away from their homes in Ireland in 1788 and lived thereafter at Plas Newydd, Llangollen
17. Four Schoolmistresses, *Through North Wales with a Knapsack*, (Keegan Paul, Trench & Truber, 1890)
18. M. Trevelyan, *Glimpses of Welsh Life & Character*, (John Hogg, 1894), preface
19. C. de Saussure, *A Foreign View of England*, Mme van Muyden (ed. & tr.), (John Murray, 1902)
    F.A.F. de la Rochefoucauld-Liancourt, *A Frenchman in England in 1784*, J. Marchand (ed.) and S.C. Roberts (tr.), (CUP, 1933)
20. P. Kalm, *Kalm's Account of his visit to England . . . in 1748*, J. Lucas (tr.), (Macmillan & Co., 1892), p. 327
21. T. Tusser, *Five Hundreth Pointes of Good Husbandrie*, (Wm. Seres, 1590), p. 127
    Trevelyan, *Welsh Life & Character*, p. 27
22. E. Haywood, *Present for a Servant-Maid*, (T. Gardner, 1743)
23. By a Lady, *New System of Domestic Cookery*, new edn, (John Murray, 1818), pp. xxiii–xxvii
24. Ibid. and also:
    The Female Instructor, (Liverpool, Nuttall, Fisher & Dixon, *c.* 1811)
    S. & S. Adams, *Complete Servant*, (Knight & Lacey, 1825)
    Mrs J. Sandford, *Female Improvement*, 3rd edn, (Longman Brown et al., 1847)
25. Grant, *Memoirs*, p. 180
26. R. Bradley, *The English Housewife in the 17th and 18th Centuries*, (Edward Arnold, 1912), pp. 39–40
27. R. Strachey, *The Cause; a short history of the women's movement in Great Britain*, Appendix 1 – 'Cassandra' (Bath, Cedric Chivers, 1974)
28. H. Robertson, *Young Ladies School of Arts*, 2nd edn, (Edinburgh, Wal. Ruddiman Junior, 1767), Part II, p. xii

Chapter Two

1. Wordsworth, *Tour*, p. 183
2. J. Torbuck, *Collection of Welsh Travels & Memoirs of Wales*, (J. Torbuck, 1738), [2]: 'A Trip to North-Wales,' p. 18
3. Tusser, *Pointes*, p. 135
4. G. Bourne, *Change in the Village*, (Duckworth & Co., 1912), p. 35
5. W.H. Hudson, *A Shepherd's Life*, (Methuen & Co., 1910), p. 225
6. F.M. McNeill, *Scots Kitchen*, (London & Glasgow, Blackie & Son Ltd, 1929) p. 32
7. B.P. Capper, *Statistical Account of England & Wales*, (T. Geoghegan, 1801), pp. 66–72; also W.T. Comber, *Inquiry into the State of National Subsistence*, (T. Cadell & W. Davies, 1808), Appendix XXV, p. 52
8. Eden, *The Poor*, vol. 1, 525; 496; 548
9. W. Cobbett, *Rural Rides*, new edn (2 vols, Reeves & Turner, 1885), vol.1, p. 381

10. Fiennes, *Through England*, p. 132
11. Torbuck, *Welsh Travels*, Pt 2, p. 9
12. Eden, *The Poor*, vol. 2, p. 394
13. Mr & Mrs Hall, *Ireland; Its Scenery, Character &c.*, (3 vols, How & Parsons, 1841–3), vol. 2, pp. 263–4
14. Wordsworth, *Tour*, p. 95; p. 135
15. Fiennes, *Through England*, p. 219
16. Johnson, *Journey*, p. 176
17. T. Pennant, *Tour in Wales*, (Henry Hughes, 1778), pp. 16–17
18. Fiennes, *Through England*, p. 146; p. 153
19. T. Pennant, *Wales*, p. 16
20. R. Meade, *Coal & Iron Industries of the United Kingdom*, (Crosby Lockwood & Co., 1882), p. 296
21. Kalm, *Kalm's Account*, pp. 7–8
22. Woodforde, *Diary*, vol. 1, p. 339; vol. 2, p. 56; vol. 4, p. 302; vol. 5, pp. 109–10; p. 306; p.120
23. Kalm, *Kalm's Account*, p. 138
24. R. Chambers, *Traditions of Edinburgh*, (Edinburgh, W. & R. Chambers, 1912), p. 152
25. Fiennes, *Through England*, pp. 153–4
26. A. Young, *Tour in Ireland*, (2 vols, Dublin, Whitestone, Sleater et al., 1780), vol. 2, Pt. 2, p. 35; p. 36
27. A.H. Barker, *Domestic Fuel Consumption*, (Constable & Co., 1920), p. 104

Chapter Three

1. F.A. Pottle (ed.), *Boswell's London Journal*, 1762–3, Yale edn, (Wm. Heinemann Ltd, 1950), p. 224
2. S. Dowell, *History of Taxation and Taxes in Britain*, 2nd edn, (4 vols, Longman, Green & Co., 1888), vol. 4, pp. 306–10
3. O. Mackenzie, *A Hundred Years in the Highlands*, (Edward Arnold, 1921), pp. 37–8
4. Fiennes, *Through England*, p. 137; also T. Webster, *Encyclopedia of Domestic Economy*, (Longman, Brown &c, 1844), p. 98
5. E. Hewlett, *Cottage Comforts*, 4th edn, (Simpkin & Marshall, 1827), p. 90
6. S. Johnson, *Dictionary of the English Language*, 6th edn, (2 vols, W. Strahen et al., 1778), vol. 2, see 'rush candle'
7. G. White, *Natural History of Selbourne*, (B. White & Son, 1789), pp. 197–9
8. C. Butler, *The Feminine Monarchie*, 2nd edn, (J. Haviland, 1623), C.10. Pt 3., p. 24
9. By a Lady, *Domestic Cookery*, p. xxxviii
10. *The Habits of Good Society*, new edn, (John Hogg, 1890), p. 336
11. Dods, *Manual*, p. 491
12. H. Glasse, *Servant's Directory*, (Ldn, for the author, 1760), pp. 61–2
13. E.S. Eckford & M. Fitzgerald, *Household Management*, (Sir Isaac Pitman & Sons Ltd, 1920), p. 48
14. Ibid., pp. 45–7
15. Lord Ernest Hamilton, *Old Days and New*, (Hodder & Stoughton, 1924), p. 91
16. Eckford & Fitzgerald, *Household Management*, p. 39; p. 43

Chapter Four

1. Fiennes, *Through England*, p. 41
2. J.H.B. Browne, *Water Supply*, (Macmillan & Co., 1880), *passim*
3. Thompson, *Lark Rise*, pp. 8–9
4. White, *Selbourne*, p. 3
5. Hudson, *Shepherd's Life*, p. 40
6. Bourne, *Change*, p. 34
7. Hutton, *Reminiscences*, p. 52
8. J. Colston, *Edinburgh & district water supply*, (Edinburgh, Colston & Co., 1890), p. 43
9. *Whitakers Almanac*, (Joseph Whitaker, 1920), p. 394
10. Fiennes, *Through England*, p. 41. Other examples of donkey wheels can be seen, as at The Weald and Downland Open Air Museum, Singleton, Chichester, Sussex, and also at Burton Agnes Hall, nr Bridlington, Humberside
11. J. Evelyn, *Diary 1620–1706*, Globe edn, (Macmillan & Co., 1908), p. 346
12. Fiennes, *Through England*, p. 45
13. J. Ray, *Complete History of the Rebellion*, (York, John Jackson, 1749), p. 304
14. F.M. McNeill, *Scot's Cellar*, (Edinburgh, Reprographia, 1976), p. 5; a geological fault provided an underground trough and the breweries were established along its line
15. Colston, *Edinburgh water*, p. 49
16. H. Cockburn, *Memorials of his Time*, (Edinburgh, A. & C. Black, 1856), pp. 334–5
17. Fiennes, *Through England*, p. 307
18. As per *Within Living Memory* Series, i.e. Cumbria
19. Browne, *Water Supply*, pp. 48–51

Chapter Five

1. Markham, *House-wife*, title page; see Ch.1
2. Beeton, *Household Management*, p. 8
3. Adams, *Complete Servant*, title page
4. Ibid., p. 5
5. Gaskell, *Cranford*, p. 259; but see also pp. 236–7; p. 109; p. 5
6. Adams, *Complete Servant*, pp. 5–6
7. Ibid., p. 295
8. Kalm, *Travels*, p. 327
9. Adams, *Complete Servant*, p. 369
10. J.P. Wood, *Antient and Modern State of the Parish of Cramond*, (Edinburgh, John Paterson, 1794), p. 154
11. For greater detail concerning such increments see, for example, J.J. Hecht, *The Domestic Servant in Eighteenth Century England*, (Routledge & Keegan Paul, 1980), pp. 153–76
12. Ibid., p. 37
13. Beeton, *Household Management*, p. 9
14. D.M. Stuart, *English Abigail*, (Macmillan & Co., 1946), p. 23
15. Baillie, *Household Book*, pp. 273–80
16. Ibid., p. 280
17. *Purefroy Letters*, vol. 1, p. 147
18. Stuart, *English Abigail*, p. 47
19. Pepys, *Diary*, vol. 4, p. 427; vol. 3, p. 100; vol. 8, p. 276

20. Woodforde, *Diary*, vol. 1, p. 273; also A. Fea, *After Worcester Fight*, (J. Lane, The Bodley Head, 1904), p. 184
21. Pepys, *Diary*, vol. 6, p. 270
22. S.O. Addy, *Evolution of the English House*, (Swan Sonnenschein & Co., 1898), p. 58
23. Thompson, *Lark Rise*, p. 376
24. J. Colston, *The Domestic Servant of the Present Day*, (Edinburgh, Colston & Son, 1864), pp. 8–10
25. Dowell, *Taxation & Taxes*, vol. 3, pp. 215–23
26. La Rochefoucauld-Liancourt, *Frenchman in England*, p. 25
27. *Purefroy Letters*, vol. 1, p. 136; p. 139
28. Colston, *Domestic Servant*, p. 16

Chapter Six

1. Sandford, *Female Improvement*, p. 119
2. Attributed to J. Wesley (1707–88), although used by others, too; occurred originally in the writings of Rabbi Phineas ben Yair
3. de Saussure, *Foreign View*, p. 157
4. Kalm, *Kalm's Account*, pp. 12–13
5. La Rochefoucauld-Liancourt, *Frenchman in England*, p. 25
6. de Saussure, *Foreign View*, p. 177
7. E. Burt, *Letters from the North of Scotland*, new edn, (2 vols, Gale, Curtis & Fenner, 1815), vol. 1, pp. 86–7
8. Wordsworth, *Recollections*, p. 20; p. 157
9. Boswell, *Tour*, p. 13
10. Young, *Ireland*, vol. 1, p. 4; p. 6
11. Torbuck, *Welsh Travels*, 1, p. 55
12. K.K., *Wales and its people*, (Simpkin, Marshall & Co., n.d.), p. 53
13. White, *Selbourne*, p. 199
14. Glasse, *Directory*, p. 32
15. W. Grant (ed.), *Scottish National Dictionary*, (10 vols, Edinburgh, Scottish National Dictionary Association, 1933–76), vol. 2, 'C', p. 18
16. Baillie, *Household Book*, pp. 274–5
17. Glasse, *Directory*, p. 37; p. 24
18. Webster, *Domestic Economy*; *Cassell's Book of the Household*, special edn, (4 vols, Cassell & Co., n.d. but *c.* 1893)
19. Glasse, *Directory*, pp. 23–42, 'The House-maid'
20. Beeton, *Household Management*, p. 990
21. S. Whatman, *Housekeeping Book*, T. Balston (ed.), (Geoffrey Bles, 1956), p. 40
22. Glasse, *Directory*, pp. 26–33
23. *Cassell's*, vol. 2, p. 249
24. Woodforde, *Diary*, vol. 2, pp. 29–30; pp. 252–4
25. Pepys, *Diary*, vol. 8, p. 44
26. Adams, *Complete Servant*, pp. 233–5
27. de Saussure, *Foreign View*, p. 157
28. La Rochefoucauld-Liancourt, *A Frenchman in England*, p. 41
29. See, for example: Adams, *Complete Servant*, pp. 393–4
30. Beeton, *Household Management*, p. 965

Chapter Seven

1. General Register Office, *Census 1951; England & Wales, Housing Report*, (HMSO, 1956), pp. xcviii–cxii
2. Burt, *Letters*, vol. 1, pp. 43–4
3. Webster, *Domestic Economy*, p. 1084
4. Young, *Ireland*, vol. 2, p. 35
5. Baillie, *Household Book*, pp. 279–80; also *Purefroy Letters*, vol. 1, p. 153
6. Glasse, *Directory*, pp. 45–6
7. Fiennes, *Through England*, p. 136
8. Webster, *Domestic Economy*, p. 1075
9. Glasse, *Directory*, p. 49
10. Adams, *Complete Servant*, p. 294: 'Two ounces of pearl ash, to a pound and a half of soap, will make a considerable saving'
11. Webster, *Domestic Economy*, p. 1078
12. Dowell, *Taxation & Taxes*, vol. 4, pp. 317–22
13. Adams, *Complete Servant*, p. 294
14. P. Stubbes, *Anatomy of Abuses*, F.J. Furnivall (ed.), (2 vols, New Shakespere Society, 1877–9), Pt. II, pp. 51–2; p. 70
15. Pepys, *Diary*, vol. 1, p. 288; vol. 4, p. 12
16. Thompson, *Lark Rise*, pp. 512–13
17. Woodforde, *Diary*, vol. 5, p. 198; also *Purefroy Letters*, vol. 1, p. 153
18. Baillie, *Household Book*, pp. 278–80
19. Pepys, *Diary*, vol. 1, p. 288; vol. 3, p. 294
20. Wordsworth, *Recollections*, p. 265
21. Spence, *Sketches*, vol. 1, pp. 75–6
22. Webster, *Domestic Economy*, p. 1087
23. Ibid.
24. F.B. Jack, *Art of Laundry Work*, 3rd edn, (Edinburgh, T.C. & E.C. Jack, 1898), p. 21
25. Ibid., p. 22
26. *Cassell's*, vol. 3, p. 10
27. Ibid.
28. Ibid., p. 14
29. Webster, *Domestic Economy*, p. 1090

Chapter Eight

1. Dods, *Manual*, p. 28
2. Johnson, *Journey*, p. 93
3. A. Macdonell (ed.), *The Closet of Sir Kenelm Digby, Knight, Opened*, (Philip Lee Warner, 1910), p. 228
4. M. Dods, (pseud.) *Cook & Housewife's Manual*, 10th edn, (Edinburgh, Oliver & Boyd, 1854), pp. 130–1
5. V. Mandey & J. Moxon, *Mechanick Powers*, (for the authors, 1696), p. 72
6. Fea, *After Worcester Fight*, p. 127
7. Pepys, *Diary*, vol. 1, p. 282
8. Ray, *Complete History*, p. 377
9. Burt, *Letters*, vol. 2, p. 252–3
10. R. Pococke, *Travels through England*, J.J. Cartwright (ed.), (2 vols, printed for the Camden Society, 1888), vol. 1, pp. 135–6

11. Fiennes, *Through England*, p. 161; p. 156
12. Pococke, *Travels*, vol. 1, p. 135
13. E. Acton, *The English Bread Book for Domestic Use*, (Longman, Brown & Co., 1857), p. 105
14. *Sir Kenelm Digby*, p. 132; p. 203; p. 138
15. Pepys, *Diary*, vol. I, p. 282
16. Acton, *Bread Book*, pp. 106–7
17. Kalm, *Kalm's Account*, p. 327
18. Dods, *Manual* (1828), p. 115
19. Alexis Soyer (1809–58), famous French chef and keen promoter of gas for cooking; introduced it into the kitchens of the Reform Club, London in 1841. He went to Scutari in 1855 to reorganize the victualling of hospitals in the Crimea and also improved the military's cooking facilities
20. Webster, *Domestic Economy*, p. 836
21. Dods, *Cook and Housewife's Manual*, 10th edn, (1854), p. 88
22. Barker, *Domestic Fuel*, pp. 153–4

Chapter Nine

1. Thompson, *Lark Rise*, pp. 10–19
2. Eden, *The Poor*, vol. 1, p. 553
3. Young, *Ireland*, vol. 2, Pt 2, pp. 30–2
4. Sir John Clerk of Penicuik, *Memoirs, 1676–1755*, J.M. Gray (ed.), (Edinburgh, T. & A. Constable, 1892), p. 238
5. Tusser, *Pointes*, p. 79
6. A.B. Teetgen, *Profitable Herb Growing and Collecting*, (Country Life, 1916), p. vii
7. W. Lawson, *New Orchard & Garden* (John Harrison, 1638), p. 86; p. 97
8. Tusser, *Pointes*, pp. 74–6
9. P. Neill, *On Scottish Gardens & Orchards*, (Edinburgh, not detailed, 1813), p. 64
10. Lawson, *Orchard & Garden*, p. 98
11. Many cookery books carry recipes for mead but *The Closet of Sir Kenelm Digby, Kt . . . Opened*, Anne Macdonell (ed.), 1910, contains over 100 of them
12. The Rev. J. Beveridge, *A Veteran Beemaster Looks Back*: address delivered to the Edinburgh & Midlothian Beekeepers' Association, 16 November 1940, p. 16. The situation in Scotland is outlined in Una A. Robertson's, 'Where have all the women gone?', *The Scottish Beekeeper*, 1988, p. 26
13. Hopetoun Papers Trust, South Queensferry, (ms) *Dinner Book 1754–5*
14. C. Carter, *Complete Practical Cook*, (W. Meadows et al., 1730), pp. 86–9; Martha Bradley, *The British Housewife*, 2 vols (S. Crowder & H. Woodgate, c. 1770), vol. 1, p. 177; p. 638
15. For a fuller investigation into the subject see Una A. Robertson, 'Pigeons as a Source of Food in Eighteenth-Century Scotland', *Review of Scottish Culture*, IV (1988), pp. 89–103
16. Mr & Mrs Hall, *Book of S. Wales, the Wye & the Coast* (Arthur Hall, Virtue & Co., 1861), pp. 299–301
17. Fiennes, *Through England*, pp. 206–7
18. Burt, *Letters*, vol. 1, p. 50
19. de Saussure, *Foreign View*, p. 171. A market had flourished at Leadenhall from the fourteenth century onwards but the site was rebuilt after the Great Fire of 1666. Beef was sold in the first court; other meat, poultry, fish and cheese in the second; and the third was given over to fruit and vegetables

20. H. Mayhew, *London Labour & London Poor* (4 vols, Griffin, Bohn & Co., 1852–61), vol. 1, pp. 4–5; also *The Book of the Old Edinburgh Club*, 35 vols (Edinburgh, T. & A. Constable, 1909), vol. 2, pp. 177–222

21. D. Robertson & M. Wood, *Castle & Town* (Edinburgh, Oliver & Boyd, 1928), p. 23

22. Woodforde, *Diary*, vol. 1, p. 282; p. 197; vol. 2, p. 292; vol. 1, p. 201

23. *Purefroy Letters*, vol. 1, pp. 61–97; vol. 2, pp. 214–38

Chapter Ten

1. McNeill, *Scot's Kitchen*, pp. 118–19

2. Mrs Dalgairns, *Practice of Cookery*, 2nd edn (Edinburgh, Cadell & Co., 1829), p. 53

3. Thompson, *Lark Rise*, pp. 11–12

4. Gaskell, *Cranford*, p. 84

5. See, for example, Dalgairns, *Cookery*, pp. 392–403; also By a Lady, *Domestic Cookery*, pp. 178–85

6. Dalgairns, *Cookery*, p. 42

7. 'Vera', *Middle Class Cookery*, (London, R.S. Cartwright, *c.* 1903), p. 153

8. Mrs M. Eales, *Receipts*, reprinted from 1733 edn by Prospect Books, 1985

9. H. Howard, *England's Newest Way*, 3rd edn, (Chr. Coningsby, 1710), title page; also pp. 111–18

10. Dowell, *Taxation & Taxes*, vol. IV, pp. 17–33

11. J. Galt, *Annals*, pp. 173–4

12. Butler, *Feminine Monarchie*, C.10, Pt 3

13. Woodforde, *Diary*, vol. v, p. 235

14. Mackenzie, *A Hundred Years*, p. 39

15. Pepys, *Diary*, vol. 8, p. 58; vol. 4, pp. 15–16

16. H. Glasse, *Art of Cookery*, 5th edn (Mrs Ashburn, 1755), p. 259

17. D. Bonner Smith (ed.), *Capt Boteler's Recollections*, (Navy Records Society, 1942), pp. 236–7

18. *Cassell's*, vol. 2, p. 166

19. D. Bremner, *Industries of Scotland* (Edinburgh, A. & C. Black, 1869), pp. 86–7

20. H. Hill, 'Liverpool – Last Stronghold of Town Cowkeepers' in *Dairy Engineering*, vol. 73, April 1956, pp. 107–10

21. W. Harley, *Harleian Dairy System*, (James Ridgway, 1829)

22. F. Accum, *A Treatise on Adulterations of Food, & Culinary Poisons*, (Longman, Hurst et al., 1820), title page

Chapter Eleven

1. Young, *Tour in Ireland*, 1780: vol. 2, pp. 33–4

2. Wordsworth, *Tour*, pp. 156–7

3. W. Davies, *General View of Agriculture & Domestic Economy of N. Wales* (Sherwood, Neely & Jones, 1813), p. 356

4. Pepys, *Diary*, vol. 3, p. 13

5. Dods, *Manual*, pp. 59–60

6. Adams, *Complete Servant*, p. 220

7. Dods, *Manual*, p. 37; p. 40

8. C. Cooper, *The English Table in History & Literature* (Sampson Low, Marston & Co., 1929), pp. 199–200

9.   Wood, *Cramond*, p. 155
10. G. Markham, *English House-wife*, p. 122
11. H. Cockburn, *Memorials*, pp. 33–4
12. Dods, *Manual*, p. 70
13. Cockburn, *Memorials*, pp. 40–1
14. Hamilton, *Old Days & New*, p. 69
15. Cooper, *The English Table*, p. 202
16. Trevelyan, *Welsh Life*, pp. 157–8
17. Beeton, *Household Management*, (n.d., '140th thousand'), p. 955; p. 954
18. Thompson, *Lark Rise*, p. 165
19. M.A. (Antonin) Careme, 1784–1833, is considered the founder of 'la grande cuisine française'. He worked for, among others, Prince Talleyrand for twelve years and the English Prince Regent for two years, but found the fogs depressing. He worked in St Petersburg, in Vienna, in Paris; and for the Princess Bagration and Baron de Rothschild. He wrote several learned works on the history and theory of cookery
20. *Habits of Good Society*, new edn, (John Hogg, 1890), p. 300
21. Hamilton, *Old Days & New*, pp. 67–8
22. Johnson, *Journey*, pp. 92–3
23. i.e. W. MacKintosh, *Essay on Ways and Means*, (Edinburgh, Mr Freebairn, 1729) p. 230; also D.W. Kemp (ed.), *Tours in Scotland by Richard Pococke* (Edinburgh, T. & A. Constable, 1887), p. 3
24. By a Lady, *Domestic Cookery*, 1818, p. 211: 'Orange Marmalade . . . Lemon Marmalade do in the same way; they are very good and elegant sweetmeats'
25. Dowell, *Taxation & Taxes*, vol. 4, p. 40; pp. 27–8
26. Dods, *Manual*, p. 71
27. G. Borrow, *Wild Wales*, (3 vols, John Murray, 1862), vol. 2, pp. 211–12; vol. 3, p. 36
28. *Cassell's*, vol. 2, p. 167
29. *Mrs Beeton's Family Cookery*, 1923, p. 827

Chapter Twelve

1.   See, for example, Hecht, *The Domestic Servant*, pp. 113–14
2.   For much interesting material on drinks in the seventeenth century see: O. Mendelsohn, *Drinking with Pepys*, (Macmillan & Co., 1963)
3.   Pepys, *Diary*, vol. 3, p. 14; p. 26
4.   J. Reid, *The Scot's Gard'ner*, (Heriot's Bridge, David Lindsay & Partners, 1683), pp. 120–1
5.   Ibid., p. 123
6.   Trevelyan, *Welsh Life*, p. 27; p. 28
7.   Baillie, *Household Book*, p. 90
8.   Robertson, *Young Ladies School of Arts*, 1767, Pt I, p. 103; also Dods, *Manual*, p. 459; in England see Glasse, *Art of Cookery*, p. 291; *Female Instructor*, p. 534
9.   By a Lady, *Domestic Cookery*, pp. 286–9
10. R. Marshall, *The Days of Duchess Anne*, (Collins, 1973) p. 100
11. Markham, *English House-wife*, pp. 155–66
12. *Purefroy Letters*, vol. 1, p. 73; p. 76
13. Ibid., vol. 1, p. 76; p. 80
14. Ibid., vol. 1, pp. 77–8
15. Hopetoun Papers Trust, South Queensferry, (ms) *Dinner Book 1754–5*

16. Dods, *Manual*, p. 447
17. By a Lady, *Domestic Cookery*, p. 256
18. *The Female Instructor*, pp. 531–2
19. Beeton, *Household Management*, p. 890
20. W. Cobbett, *Cottage Economy*, stereotype edn, (C. Clement, 1822), pp. 11–12
21. By a Lady, *Domestic Cookery*, pp. 247–9; Beeton, *Household Management*, (n.d. 140th thousand)
22. *Old Edinburgh Club*, vol. 16 (1928), p. 38
23. By a Lady, *Domestic Cookery*, p. 193
24. Ibid., p. 284
25. Dods, *Manual*, p. 467
26. Evelyn, *Diary*, p. 6
27. B. Faujas de St Fond, *Travels in England, Scotland and the Hebrides*, (2 vols, James Ridgway, 1799), vol. 1, pp. 254–7
28. C.P. Moritz, *Travels in England*, (Humphrey Milford, OUP, 1924), p. 32
29. Dods, *Manual*, p. 466
30. Pepys, *Diary*, vol. 1, pp. 249–50
31. Chambers, *Traditions*, p. 344
32. Baillie, *Household Book*, p. lviii
33. H. Robertson, *Young Ladies School of Arts*, 10th edn (Edinburgh, J.Tod, 1806), p. 39

Chapter Thirteen

1. MacKintosh, *Ways and Means*, p. 229
2. Thompson, *Lark Rise*, p. 19
3. Trevelyan, *Welsh Life*, p. 156
4. E. Hailstone (ed.), *Costumes of Yorkshire in 1814* (Leeds, R. Jackson, 1885) pp. 95–6
5. Hutton, *Reminiscences*, p. 52
6. Fiennes, *Through England*, p. 305
7. The Ladies Waldegrave: Their father died in 1763 and their mother Maria, illegitimate daughter of Sir Edward Walpole, subsequently married Prince William Henry, Duke of Gloucester
8. Sir W. Dugdale, *Baronage of England* (2 vols, Thos. Newcomb, 1676), vol. 2, pp. 251–4. Through the marriage of a daughter, Emelia, to John Earl of Atholl, the bed hangings can be seen in the Derby Room at Blair Castle, Blair Atholl
9. *Cassell's*, vol. 4, pp. 72–83; pp. 128–40; p. 233; p. 244
10. Lawson, *Orchard & Garden*
11. Sir W. Fraser, *Memorials of the Earls of Haddington*, (2 vols, privately printed, 1889), vol. 1, pp. 244–5
12. Ibid., p. 260
13. By a Lady, *Domestic Cookery*, p. xix; p. xx
14. Howard, *England's Newest Way*, p. 180
15. Ibid., p. 189: 'oil of spike' is generally taken to be *Lavendula spica* but 'sweet afa' is not so obvious
16. Trevelyan, *Welsh Life*, p. 23; p. 105
17. E. Topham, *Letters from Edinburgh 1774–5*, (J. Dodsley, 1776), p. 263
18. Grant, *Memoirs*, for example, p. 296; p. 299
19. Trevelyan, *Welsh Life*, p. 157

20. *Female Instructor*, p. 176
21. *Cassell's*, vol. 3, pp. 142–52
22. Ibid., vol. 3, pp. 71–85
23. *Old Edinburgh Club*, vol. 31, (1962), p. 107
24. Gaskell, *Cranford*, pp. 8–9
25. Hutton, *Reminiscences*, p. 192
26. *Cassell's*, vol. 1, p. 101
27. Ibid., vol. 4, pp. 83–4

Chapter Fourteen

1. Fiennes, *Through England*, p. 233
2. Ibid., pp. 52–4
3. J. Austen, *Pride and Prejudice*, (George Allen, 1894), pp. 308–9
4. J. Taylor, *Journey to Edenborough in Scotland*, (Edinburgh, William Brown, 1903), p. 149
5. T. Boston, *Memoirs of the Life, Times and Writings of Thomas Boston*, new edn, (Edinburgh, Oliphant, Anderson & Ferrier, 1899), pp. 390–1
6. Fiennes, *Through England*, p. 150
7. K.K., *Wales & its People*, p. 15
8. Pennant, *Wales*, pp. 28–36
9. Pepys, *Diary*, vol. 8, p. 45
10. Fiennes, *Through England*, pp. 149–50
11. For further reading see: P. Havins, *The Spas of England*, (Robert Hale & Co., 1976) and also: R. & F. Morris, *Scottish Healing Wells*, (Sandy, Alethea Press, 1982)
12. Hutton, *Reminiscences*, pp. 55–6
13. Topham, *Letters*, p. 94
14. *Old Edinburgh Club*, vol. 19 (1933), p. 50, pp. 75–9
15. Gaskell, *Cranford*, p. 178
16. *Old Edinburgh Club*, vol. 9, (1916), p. 218
17. i.e. The Revd A.W.C. Hallen (ed.), *Account Book of Sir John Foulis of Ravelston*, (Edinburgh, T. & A. Constable, 1894), p. 40; p. 44; p. 49; p. 407
18. H. Arnot, *History of Edinburgh*, (Edinburgh, W. Creech, 1779), p. 383
19. Topham, *Letters*, pp. 133–5
20. Gaskell, *Cranford*, p. 217; p. 112
21. Hutton, *Reminiscences*, pp. 29–30
22. *Purefroy Letters*, vol. 2, pp. 214–38
23. Marshall, *Duchess Anne*, pp. 92–3

Chapter Fifteen

1. Tusser, *Pointes*, p. 123
2. It is interesting to compare the dinner menus suggested by Mrs Beeton in *Household Management* (n.d., 140th thousand), pp. 909–60 with those given in Mrs Beeton's, *Family Cookery* (Ward Lock & Co., 1923), pp. 831–6
3. Markham, *English House-wife*, p. 4
4. Ibid., p. 2
5. Hutton, *Reminiscences*, p. 57
6. By a lady, *Domestic Cookery*, p. xxvi
7. *Cassell's*, vol. 4, p. 220

8. Dorothea Jordan, née Bland (1762–1816), for many years mistress of the Duke of Clarence (William IV) and mother of numerous children; she continued to appear on stage throughout her pregnancies
   Sarah Siddons, née Kemble (1755–1831), of whom it was said 'the regularity of her [stage] appearances was disturbed by the birth of her children'
9. E. Blackwell, *A Curious Herbal*, 2 vols (Samuel Harding, 1737–9)
10. J.G. Nichols (ed.), *Autobiography of Anne, Lady Halkett*, printed for the Camden Society, 1875
11. For further information see S. Jex Blake, *Medical Women*, 2nd edn, (Oliphant, Anderson & Ferrier, 1886)
12. B. Makin, *An Essay to Revive the Ancient Education of Gentlewomen*, (California, The Augustan Reprint Society no. 202, 1980)
13. For further thoughts on the subject see V. Woolf, *A Room of One's Own*, (12th impression, The Hogarth Press, 1954)
14. Cockburn, *Memorials*, p. 268
15. S. Raven & A. Weir, *Women in History*, (Weidenfeld & Nicolson, 1981), p. 116
16. R. Bradley, *English Housewife*, p. 39
17. Margaret Cavendish, Duchess of Newcastle, *Poems and Fancies*, 1653 (Menston, Yorkshire, facsimile reprint by Scholar Press, 1972)

Further Reading

S. & S. Adams, *The Complete Servant*, (reprint), Southover Press, 1989

A. Adburgham, *Shopping in Style*, Thames & Hudson, 1979

S. Brooke, *Hearth & Home*, Mills & Boon, 1973

E.F. Catford, *Edinburgh, The Story of a City*, Hutchinson & Co., 1975

C. Davidson, *A Woman's Work is never done*, Chatto & Windus, 1982

D. Davis, *A History of Shopping*, Book Club Associates, n.d.

E. Drury, *The Butler's Pantry Book*, A. & C. Black, 1981

R. Feild, *Irons in the Fire*, Crowood Press, 1984

T. Fitzgerald, *A Taste of Scotland*, J.M. Dent, 1970; *A Taste of Wales*, 1971

A. Fraser, *The Weaker Vessel*, Weidenfeld & Nicolson, 1984

M. Girouard, *Life in the English Country House*, Yale University Press, 1978

D. de Haan, *Antique Household Gadgets & Appliances, 1860–1930*, Dorset, Blandford Press, 1977

F.E. Huggett, *Life Below Stairs*, Book Club Associates, 1977

R. Marshall, *The Days of Duchess Anne*, Collins, 1973

C. Morris (ed.), *The Illustrated Journeys of Celia Fiennes*, Macdonald & Co., with Webb & Bower, 1982

P.A. Sambrook & P. Brears (eds), *The Country House Kitchen 1650–1900*, Alan Sutton Publishing with The National Trust, 1996

D.C. Stuart, *The Kitchen Garden*, Robert Hale, 1984

C.A. Wilson, *Food and Drink in Britain*, Constable, 1973

L. Wright, *Clean and Decent*, Routledge & Keegan Paul Ltd, 1960

D. Yarwood, *The British Kitchen*, Batsford, 1981

Index

Index